SERVING THE TUDORS

JAMES TAFFE

Copyright © James Taffe

All rights reserved. No part of this publication may be reproduced, stored in a retrieval system, or transmitted, in any form or by any means, electronic, mechanical, photocopying, recording or otherwise, without the prior permission of the author, except as permitted by the UK Copyright, Designs and Patents Act 1988.

ISBN: 9798324393168

List of Illustrations:

Front Cover
A servant of King Henry VIII by Hans Holbein the Younger, 1534, from Wikimedia Commons
The wife of a servant of King Henry VIII by Hans Holbein the Younger, 1534, from Wikimedia Commons

Back Cover
Portrait of A Man in a Red Cap by Hans Holbein the Younger, c. 1532-35, from Wikimedia Commons

ACKNOWLEDGEMENTS

I must begin by acknowledging the pioneering research of R. C. Braddock, Nikki Clark, Elizabeth Ann Culling, Susan Doran, Steven Gunn, Barbara J. Harris, Maria Hayward, Dale Hoak, Catherine Louise Howey, Fiona Kisby, Suzannah Lipscomb, David Loades, J. L. McIntosh, Natalie Mears, Charlotte Isabelle Merton, John Murphy, Glenn Richardson, Gareth Russell, Neil Samman, Narasingha Prosad Sil, David Starkey, Simon Thurley, Alison Weir and Anna Whitelock, without which this book would not have been possible.

I am particularly grateful to Paul John, Jane King, Ceri Law, Jonathan Willis and Natalie Mears, for their support, training and advice throughout my studies.

I would like to thank everyone who purchased a copy of my first book, Courting Scandal: The Rise and Fall of Jane Boleyn: Lady Rochford. I never thought anyone would read it, and had all but retired in my mind from researching and writing history, but I was so overwhelmed by the response. I am especially grateful to those who took the time to leave a review, or host me on their podcasts. Natalie Grueninger, Rebecca Larson, Owen Emmerson, Carol Ann Lloyd, Julia Dietz, Adam Pennington, Daniella Ana Novaković and Jessica Faulker have been so generous with their platforms and have helped my research to find a readership. I would also like to express my gratitude to Owen Emmerson in particular for reading an advance copy of the book.

I would like to acknowledge the help of all the staff in the Department of History and Bill Bryson Library at Durham University, The Library of Birmingham, The National Archives in Kew, The British Library in London, and at all other institutions, libraries and archives that I have visited to undertake research.

This book is dedicated to my dear friends and colleagues, in particular Nikki Clark, Thomas Clifton, Lakshana Palat, Daniel Ramos-Smith, and to everyone I have met in the online Tudor history community, who have always been so encouraging.

CONTENTS

1. 'The accustomed good order':   1
   Offices and Ordinances

2. 'The nearer I were to you the gladder I would be':   18
   Appointments and Composition

3. 'I was made of the pliable willow, not of the stubborn oak':   33
   Oaths, Loyalty and Allegiance

4. 'If you serve us heartily, you shall not be forgotten':   45
   Wages, Perquisites and Advancement

5. 'Apparelled according to their degrees':   62
   Livery, Majesty and Magnificence

6. 'I care not to be groom of the scullery':   71
   Access, Interaction and Intimacy

7. 'Now here comes in the cogging of this place':   88
   Government, Politics and Patronage

8. 'I pray you pray for me your loving master':   105
   Religion, Faith and Reform

9. 'Honest and moderate play':   121
   Court Culture and Pastime

10. 'Expert in outward parts':   135
    War, Security and Diplomacy

11. 'It is hard trusting this wily world':   149
    Conspiracy, Intrigue and Treason

12. 'Natural passions of grief':   169
    Death, Mourning and Memory

Bibliography   183

Notes   189

1

'The accustomed good order'
OFFICES AND ORDINANCES

The Tudor royal household comprised many departments and rested on a broad stratum of servants. The *domus regis magnificencie*, 'Chamber' or household 'above-stairs' was responsible for attending upon the royal master or mistress, performing menial duties on their behalf, such as making their bed, waiting on them at table, dressing or undressing them, or standing guard in their chambers. The *domus providencie*, 'Household' or household 'below-stairs' was concerned with the day-to-day administering of provisions, like food, drink, light and fuel, for warmth, security and shelter. Royal palaces were labyrinthine, often crowded, essentially public spaces. Reflecting Henry VII's increasing concern for privacy in the 1490s, the Tudor period saw the development of the 'Privy Chamber', which functioned by restricting access to the sovereign. We might further distinguish between the Tudor royal household and the wider court, which encompassed all individuals who, at any given time, occupied the physical space surrounding the sovereign, like courtiers, councillors, noblemen and women, and other visitors like petitioners, ambassadors and dignitaries.[1]

All royal households were rigidly constructed hierarchies. Servants held a fixed position, defined by their office. 'Office', the title, rank and position held by a servant, determined the specific duties, tasks and functions they performed. The Chamber was headed by a Lord Chamberlain and Vice-chamberlain who managed appointments, kept strict attendance records and arbitrated disputes.[2] Gentlemen Ushers prepared lodgings and supervised yeomen, grooms and pages, ensuring that they were 'ready to do all such service'.[3] Yeomen Ushers and Yeomen of the Chamber were stationed in the Presence and Guard chambers, 'and in case they shall perceive any person to be there, not meet nor convenient to be therein', they were to escort them out immediately.[4] Grooms of the Chamber were responsible for maintenance, taking 'good heed' that all chambers were kept 'in right perfect manner'. This meant seeing that the roofs, windows and floors were 'clean from dust, filth, and cobwebs', that the chambers were furnished with chairs and cushions, that the cloth of estate was properly hung, and that the fires were made up wherever their master or mistress was likely to repair.[5] The Groom Porter was in charge of delivering provisions required from 'below-stairs'.[6] Pages had to be 'ready at all times' to 'wait upon' the royal chambers,[7] and, like the Messenger, often conveyed letters and ran errands 'out of court'.[8]

Servants in the Privy Chamber were responsible for the more personal, intimate and everyday needs of the Tudors. Gentlemen of the Privy Chamber on the king's side of the court maintained the 'quiet, rest, comfort and preservation' of his health. Adjacent to the king's Privy chamber and the innermost of his privy lodgings was the bedchamber, where his gentlemen would 'lie on the pallet within', wake their royal master and draw the curtains come morning.[9] These men would wash, bathe and dress the king, with none other presuming to touch his body, while keeping a 'convenient distance', and without being 'too homely or bold advancing themselves thereunto, otherwise than to their rooms does appertain'.[10] Esquires of the Body were now effectively shut out of the Privy chamber, but they continued to serve in the Presence chamber 'to help occupy the court and accompany strangers'.[11] Grooms of the Privy Chamber were responsible for making the king's bed, cleaning and arranging his linens, wardrobe and lodgings, and maintaining his Privy chamber and bedchamber in a 'wholesome and meet' condition. One of them would perform additional duties as a Barber, 'having in readiness, his water, cloths, knives, combs, scissors, and such other stuff' for 'trimming and dressing' the king's head and beard.[12] The Groom of the Stool attended upon the king in his bedchamber and 'other privy places' when he used the lavatory or 'close stool'.[13] They were also responsible for keeping all chamber pots clean, discreet, and in suitably rich and luxurious condition.

Tudor royal servants were well-rehearsed of the duties they were expected to perform. In 1558, John Norris, Mary I's gentleman usher, wrote up a set of instructions for his successor, drawing on decades of experience serving at court to provide an insight into the day-to-day running of the household. Few were as fastidious as Norris in describing their role, though his account too is somewhat lacking, as he concentrated on 'what every *man* ought to do in his office', and how he, specifically, as a gentleman usher, 'should behave himself', with little to no mention of the women who served in the queen's Privy Chamber.[14] Although Norris had limited access to the queen's innermost chambers, he would not have been unaware, or altogether ignorant, of their role. In the late fifteenth century, it was observed that 'the queen's service' must 'be nigh like unto the king'.[15] From 1485 to 1547, when the sovereign was a man, and the queen was his consort, the queen's household was firmly integrated with the king's household, sharing in its innovations, like the Privy Chamber. Unlike the king's household, a queen's household was headed by a woman, meaning that many of her servants necessarily had to be women. Offices were created, developed and defined by men, and for men, but few adaptations were required to accommodate women. Even when Mary I or Elizabeth I were on the throne as queens regnant, no further distinction was made between the responsibilities of male servants who served kings before them, and their female counterparts, who served the queen. The role of these women may thus be ascertained by identifying which offices held by men in the king's Chamber and Privy Chamber are absent from those of his queens, namely the Gentlemen of the Privy Chamber, Grooms of the Privy Chamber, the Groom of the Stool, and the Esquires for the Body, who, it is no coincidence, were the most intimate of the king's servants.[16]

Ladies and Gentlewomen of the queen's Privy Chamber (and later, the Bedchamber) would undertake the same duties as the king's Gentlemen of the Privy Chamber, such as dressing and undressing the queen, washing and bathing her, styling her hair and applying her make up. It is likely that one of these women also fulfilled the role of the Groom of the Stool. Chamberers were the female equivalent of Grooms of the Privy Chamber, as they too were responsible for cleaning the queen's chambers, arranging her clothes, jewels and bed linen, and fetching all manner of service on her behalf.[17] Ladies in Presence, or 'Great Ladies', and Maids-of-Honour, attended upon the queen in her Presence chamber. Maids were 'to come into the Presence chamber before eleven of the clock, and to go to prayers, and after prayers attend until the Queen be set at dinner'.[18] Like the Esquires for the Body, maids-of-honour remained in the Presence chamber 'until supper', or 'for some reasonable time, especially when any ambassador has audience'.[19] They were supervised and chaperoned by a Mother of the Maids, who ensured that they behaved in a sober and virtuous manner. These women were thought to be fit companions for a queen, accompanying her whenever she left her chambers, with one or many of them carrying her train behind her.

Although women fulfilled much of the same duties as men at court, there was one notable exception. When a queen was heavily pregnant, some time between four and six weeks before the birth, she was to 'take her chamber', a highly ritualised ceremony by which she, conducted by her ladies and gentlewomen, withdrew from the court to her confinement. The protocol for royal childbirth was outlined in the ordinances of 1494, which observed that, when Elizabeth of York was to 'take her chamber', she was conveyed to her bedchamber, richly adorned with tapestries, pillows and carpets. All of the queen's men would 'take their leave', no longer admitted to be in her presence, while her women were 'made all manner of officers', to undertake all of their duties.[20] Even after giving birth, queens remained in seclusion, surrounded only by their female attendants, as it was customary to 'lie in' for up to forty days until her 'churching', or purification, after labour.

Rarely in the evidence do we see servants actually performing their duties, though there are occasional hints of domesticity in action. At a banquet for the coronation of Anne Boleyn in 1533, Elizabeth Browne, Countess of Worcester, stood beside her chair and was to hold 'a fine cloth before the Queen's face' whenever 'she list to spit or do otherwise at her pleasure'.[21] Nearly fifty years earlier, at Elizabeth of York's coronation, this same duty was performed by one of her ladies, while two of her gentlewomen 'went under the table, where they sat on either side of the queen's feet all the dinner time'.[22] Sir Thomas Heneage, groom of the stool, reported that one night in 1539, Henry VIII, suffering with constipation, had 'slept until two of the clock in the morning', when he sat up sharply in his bed and made haste towards his close-stool. He would have been shadowed by a drowsy Heneage, who remarked that, 'by working of the pills', the king 'had a very fair siege'![23] There could hardly have been a job more unpleasant, but the position was still sought after. In fact, no role had greater intimacy with the crown than the groom of the stool. This was the nature of royal service in the Tudor period: onerous, and laborious, sometimes degrading or demeaning, and yet always an honour and a privilege to perform.

Although servants were formally circumscribed by the office they held, their role could be rather more elaborate and complex. The Eltham ordinances of 1526 required them to 'have a vigilant and reverent respect and eye' for their royal master or mistress, so that, merely by their 'look or countenance' they 'may know what lacketh', and to act on their pleasure 'to be had or done'.[24] John Norris would recall that he had to remain sharp, providing what 'he shall think by his discretion needful'.[25] Nothing was outside of the scope of their activity. What mattered was not necessarily what they were doing, but their ability or capacity to do it, and to do it well, to achieve whatsoever the king, queen, prince or princess commanded or desired. Acting as a hired henchman sent abroad to assassinate an enemy of the crown was not strictly within a servant's job description;[26] nor was chasing pirates by boat through treacherous waters,[27] purchasing and importing goods from abroad,[28] fetching a parrot and transporting the feathered friend from palace to palace,[29] or facilitating a fairly indiscreet extramarital affair.[30] The multiplicity, and complexity, of their demands, was interminable, and varied greatly depending on their personalities, ambitions, and interactions with the household. Servants were inevitably drawn in to the personal and political lives of the Tudors, and could be employed in almost any capacity to meet the needs of the crown, sometimes engaging in matters more ad hoc or further afield, in the wider court and kingdom, whatsoever they may be. Indeed, there are many obscure and tantalising references in the evidence to 'business' and 'affairs' conducted by these servants, the nature of which remains their secret.[31]

Everything in and of the Tudor royal household 'above-stairs' was facilitated by the operation 'below-stairs'. The 'Household', or household 'below-stairs', was headed by a Lord Steward, Comptroller, Treasurer and Cofferer, and comprised such departments as the kitchen, the buttery, the larder, the bakehouse, the pantry, the pastry, the poultry, the slaughterhouse, boilinghouse, the saucery, the spicery, the wafery, the confectionery, the cellar, the bottles, the pitcherhouse, the brewhouse, the ewery, the acatry, the almonry, the jewel house, the chandlery, the scaldinghouse, the scullery, the laundry, the woodyard and the hall, all of which were generally staffed with sergeants, yeomen, grooms, pages and clerks as required.[32] There were other sub-departments of the Tudor royal household, like the Wardrobe, who were responsible for the caretaking and transporting of their clothes, jewels, bedding, books and other goods, the Chapel, who performed divine services and music wherever their master or mistress was residing, and the Stables, who maintained horses, bred replacements, and kept ready all the necessary riding equipment for the Tudors to move from palace to palace, or to go on the hunt. Unlike those serving in the Chamber and Privy Chamber, few members of the Household, Wardrobe, Chapel and Stables would have known their royal master or mistress personally. Nor would they necessarily have had the opportunity to be near them, or even to have met them at all, as virtually none of them would have been admitted to their chambers. For this reason, we concentrate on the 'above-stairs', though there were exceptions, and occasionally the evidence glimpses these hidden figures of the court operating 'below-stairs' and on the periphery.

Tudor royal households were governed by ordinances, a set of rules by which all servants were to abide. At the end of 1525, Cardinal Wolsey met privately with Henry VIII at Eltham with plans to reform the king's household. Late into the night, many hours passed as a demanding cardinal and an impatient king addressed concerns with security, cleanliness, cost and waste, incompetency, corruption, idleness, and riotous or unlawful behaviour. By the morning, Wolsey had drafted many new articles for the household which would later become known as the Eltham ordinances of 1526.[33] These ordinances were set in a book, signed by the hand of the sovereign, so that they may be consulted as and when it was felt necessary.[34] As the Tudor royal household developed and evolved over time, certain innovations, like the Privy Chamber, required successive ordinances. The Eltham ordinances, for instance, did not replace Henry VII's ordinances of 1494; they built upon them, and all prior ordinances, as a foundation.[35] If existing ordinances proved ineffective or outdated, they were revised and reissued to crack down on bad practice. Despite their efforts, both Sir Robert Rochester, Mary I's comptroller, and William Cecil, Lord Burghley, Elizabeth I's secretary, tasked with reforming the household, found that 'the accustomed good order' continued to be 'greatly hindered' through the rest of the Tudor period.

What is striking in these ordinances is that the mundane, menial duties, like dressing the Tudors, or making the royal bed, were highly ritualised. Servants truly *performed* their duties, often in elaborate ceremony. Each act or gesture, no matter how trivial it may seem, was intentional and had meaning. Every morning, once the Tudors had risen at their leisure, they were to be dressed by their attendants. Yeomen, Grooms and Pages of the Robes brought clothes, shoes and accessories to the entry of their Privy chamber 'without entering into the same'.[36] The Eltham ordinances reveal that, by 1526, it was the staff of the Privy Chamber who would receive these items and begin the process of 'arraying' and 'unarraying' their royal master or mistress. Henry VIII's gentlemen had to rise at seven o'clock at the latest, ensuring that they were 'ready and prompt' for when the king awoke and came forth so that they could 'dress his Highness, putting on such garments, in reverent, discreet, and sober manner, as shall be his Grace's pleasure to wear'.[37] Strictly no other attendants were to 'approach or presume (unless they be otherwise by his Grace commanded or admitted) to lay hands upon his royal person, or intermeddle with preparing or dressing of the same'.[38] Similarly the 1494 ordinances detail how Henry VII's attendants were to make his bed. The ritual began with Yeomen, Grooms and Pages of the Beds, who were responsible for the keeping, repairing and transport of mattresses, bed-linen and coverlets and pillows to the door of the Privy chamber 'safely and cleanly, that no stranger shall touch it'.[39] Gentlemen ushers and yeomen flanked each side of the bed, keeping the curtains drawn while all of the necessary materials were prepared at its foot. At this time it was the esquires of the body who would 'lay hands thereon' and, 'as it pleases the King best', elaborately set an assortment of sheets, ermines and pillows, all of which had to be beaten, smoothed, and tucked to ensure that the bed was 'straight', 'even', and 'without any wrinkles'. This ritual was concluded when they 'cast holy water on the bed'.[40] The queen's bed was 'to be made with Ladies and Gentlewomen, as the King's is with men'.[41] All of the Tudors employed a laundress, who maintained their clothes and other linens by washing, starching and scenting them with sweet powders and herbs.[42]

Serving the Tudors at dinner or supper was no less ceremonial. The Tudor court typically ate three meals a day.[43] Sir Richard Blount, Edward VI's gentleman usher, recorded that, once the king was awake, he would 'seek to know his pleasure what time he will go to breakfast', and 'what time he will go to dinner'. Between meals, the gentleman usher would also 'command all times of the day bread, wine, beer and ale, to the chambers as he shall think good by his discretion'.[44] The Tudors had their own Carvers, Cupbearers, Sewers and Gentlemen Waiters, who served them 'at hours and time of dinner and supper'. The sewer was to 'fetch the service' before they would 'set and direct' the meal, while the carver came forward to cut the meat and, 'with the accustomed reverences', would 'see the meat honourably served to the board'.[45] A cupbearer would take the cup and pour out a few drops to taste the drink for themselves to prevent their master or mistress being poisoned, before handing it to them. If they were entertaining guests, the Tudors took their meals in their Presence chamber. Lupold von Wedel, a German noble who visited Elizabeth I's court in 1584-85, observed how the queen's servants prepared her meals. Each course, from the meat which was carved to the cup which was held before the queen, was presented with the utmost reverence. Servants who approached her, as Wedel recorded, would 'have to bow down deeply, and when they have reached the middle of the room they must bow down a second time'.[46] When the queen had finished her meal, a silver gilt basin was brought forward for her to wash her hands. Elizabeth, like her sister Mary before her, often preferred to dine in her Privy chamber alone or with 'very few attendants', specifically her women. On such occasions, the table would still be 'honourably' set in her Presence chamber with 'as much awe as if the queen had been present', before the meal was conveyed into the Privy chamber by her ladies so that their mistress could make her choice of the food that had been prepared.[47]

Strict regulations on hygiene and cleanliness were meant to maintain high domestic standards and protect the Tudors from infection and disease. The instructions for the household of Prince Edward in 1537 reveal that, 'to avoid all infection and danger of pestilence and contagious diseases that might chance or happen', the health and cleanliness of all his attendants was closely scrutinised. Their clothes and linens had to be 'washed, clean dried, kept, brushed, and reserved cleanly by the officers and persons appointed'.[48] Earlier the Eltham ordinances of 1526 dictated that, 'at his uprising', Henry VIII should find his chambers 'pure, clean, wholesome, and meet without any displeasant air or thing, as the health, commodity, and pleasure of his most noble person, do require'.[49] Men serving at court were to 'take special regard to the pure and clean keeping of his own person and apparel', without 'resorting to the company of vile persons, or of misguided women, in avoiding such dangers and annoyance as by that means he might do unto the King's most royal person'.[50] Certainly Henry was something of a hypochondriac. This may be why, in 1528, the king probed and perhaps embarrassed his treasurer, Sir Brian Tuke, suffering with an unknown disease which left him in 'marvellous pain'. As Tuke recalled, Henry 'began to tell me a medicine *pro tumore testiculorum*', though his master had been misinformed, as the treasurer's affliction was not in the testicles, but the bladder, and so the king proceeded to counsel him 'as any most cunning physician in England could do'.[51] Henry's fears also had drastic consequences for the size of his household and its itinerary. In 1517, and again in 1528, the king discharged most of the court, moving frequently to evade the threat of the sweat. 'The King shuts himself up quite alone', the French ambassador Jean du Bellay reported in 1528, observing that 'all but one' in his household had 'been or are attacked'. It must have been unsettling for Henry that more than a few servants who attended upon him personally, like Sir Francis Poyntz, esquire for the body, Sir William Carey, sewer, and Sir William Compton, groom of the stool, had perished of the sweat.[52] Edward VI would record in his diary the loss of Sir Thomas Speke and an unnamed groom, who 'fell sick and died' in 1551, having succumbed to the sweating sickness.[53] Later, in 1572, Elizabeth I was in her Privy chamber talking to her ladies when the mother of the maids 'suddenly became ill and died there and then'. Understandably, the queen 'took fright', and 'within an hour left Greenwich with a very small company'.[54] Panic ensued again when a page serving Philadelphia, Lady Scrope, died of a disease in 1593, leading to 'great alteration' at court, on account of the fact that Scrope herself was 'so near to her Majesty's person as of her Bedchamber'.[55]

Some royal palaces were so crowded and cramped it proved inevitable that illnesses would spread. For servants this became something of an occupational hazard. Mary, Lady Sidney, took care of Elizabeth I when she was afflicted with smallpox in 1562. Unfortunately, as was probable, Mary too caught the disease, which left her face noticeably disfigured. Her husband later remarked, rather charmingly, that he had 'left her a full fair lady, in mine eye at least the fairest, and when I returned I found her as foul a lady as the small pox could make her, which she did take by continual attendance of Her Majesty's most precious person sick of the same disease'.[56] The Tudors had at least one Physician, and an Apothecary, who counselled them on their physical and mental health, prescribing medicines and monitoring their diets, though they were chiefly in attendance when they fell ill, or, for queens, if they were pregnant.[57] Henry VIII had a book of recipes for plasters, balms, lotions and more, formulated by his physicians, notably Dr William Butts and Dr John Chamber, to remedy his various ailments through the 1540s. Some of these treatments, like the ointment 'to take away inflammations, and to cease pain, and heal ulcers', were actually 'devised by the King's Majesty' himself.[58] Catherine of Aragon commended her physician, Dr. Ferdinand de Victoria, and her apothecary, John Sotha, for having 'taken much pains' in the 'many years' they had served her, as she was 'often times sickly and diseased'.[59] A 1564 bill from John Hemingway, Elizabeth I's apothecary, reveals that he conveyed all manner of medicines, tonics, pills, lotions, scents and herbs to the queen's ladies and gentlewomen, who would administer them to their mistress and her chambers as and when it was deemed necessary.[60] Whenever Elizabeth was unwell, her gentlewomen were known to have 'tended to her in her bed'.[61]

The most intimate servants had charge of money, sometimes acting as keepers of the 'privy purse'.[62] For Henry VII, this role was largely undertaken by Hugh Denys, groom of the stool. If the king ever wanted to make a spontaneous purchase, or needed to settle an outstanding debt, he would turn to Denys. The accounts reveal that, out of the privy purse, Denys would oversee the king's expenditure in handing out rewards, distributing alms, repaying gambling debts, buying jewels and fine materials, building and furnishing palaces, and for costs incurred either at war or in state affairs. Across the hall, on the queen's side of the court, Elizabeth of York's gentlewomen, and Eleanor Jones in particular, dealt with the expenses of their mistress. Elizabeth often had to reimburse her own attendants for money they had 'lent to the queen', presumably when she was not carrying petty cash. It remains unclear how often these debts went unpaid or were forgiven by those lacking an opportunity, or the nerve, to remind their mistress of the money that she owed them.[63] Other servants were entrusted with clothing, jewels, plate and other personal possessions. The ladies and gentlewomen of Elizabeth I's Privy Chamber took responsibility for the delivery, care and maintenance of the queen's clothing. In 1587, for instance, 'a book of such jewels and other parcels' was drawn up to transfer custody of such items from Blanche Parry to Mary Radcliffe, when the former's eyesight began to fail her.[64] During Elizabeth's reign, more than a hundred items went missing, the details of which were carefully recorded, be it a precious jewel, a single glove or even some loose trimmings of cloth. One such entry from 1565, derived from statements and bearing the signatures of Elizabeth's ladies and gentlewomen, reads that 'her Majesty wore a gown of black velvet embroidered and set with certain buttons of gold with diamonds', and one of these diamonds 'fell from the button and was lost off from her Highness' back'.[65] Perhaps when items were 'lost off her Majesty's back', the queen had mislaid them, though evidently, it was tempting to suspect those who had charge of these items. Certainly in 1582, when a casket belonging to the queen containing 'two fine rings' and a diamond cross worth £20,000 went missing, it was reported that 'a suspicion exists that they have been pilfered by some of the principal ladies'.[66] Later, in 1600, Elizabeth's gentlewomen were once again called upon to take account of the plate and jewels in their custody 'as are unserviceable, from decay, imperfection, or being out of fashion', so that they might not be 'hereafter unduly charged concerning them'.[67]

Petty thievery and pilfering was apparently 'daily seen' in royal palaces, and servants were not exempt from suspicion.[68] For servants who had custody of any portion of the royal bounty, large or small, it must have been something of a burden, knowing they would be held responsible if anything went missing. In 1558, shortly after Mary I's death, one of her ladies, Jane Dormer, Countess of Feria, was forced to explain a 'deficiency of the jewels' which had been in her charge until she was prompted to deliver them to Elizabeth I's women.[69] Dormer was questioned on each of the missing items in turn, and for many of them her response was merely 'I confess the lack', or, in other words, she plead ignorance. Had she sold them off, or were there so many of the crown's jewels to keep account of that she lost track? Peter Osborne,

Edward VI's clerk of the Privy Chamber, kept large amounts of the king's money stashed in the Privy closet at Westminster Palace. On one occasion in 1553, £600 'remaining in our chamber there where we most accustomably do hear the sermons', was stolen.[70] The account books kept by Osborne were closely examined, and he was soon pardoned and discharged of the £600, no doubt to his great relief, as it was acknowledged that 'to require it of Osborne would be to his utter undoing'.[71] As servants themselves were lodged at court, their possessions too were vulnerable. Katherine, Lady Paget, had stolen 'out of her chamber' in 1587 plate worth around £50, 'after which' a 'great enquiry' was made, though it is unlikely that it was ever recovered.[72]

The Tudor court could be quite energetic and lively, if not chaotic. When the Tudors retired to their bedchamber for the night, their servants had to 'keep silence', and were warned sternly not to be too raucous. Elizabeth I in particular demanded that there was no noise 'of any office' near her bedchamber.[73] Frequently burdened by visitors and hordes of hangers-on, unwelcome and unwanted 'strangers' in the court crowded spaces, strained resources, and threatened the security of the monarch. The Eltham ordinances of 1526 meant to limit 'sickly, impotent, unable, and unmeet persons, as of rascals and vagabonds', the presence of which had led to 'great confusion, annoyance, infection, trouble, and dishonour'.[74] It was the responsibility of porters to ensure that they did not 'enter in at the gate at any time', while yeomen made 'due search' throughout the palace routinely throughout the day to find and put out any who had managed to slip by.[75] Periodically, attempts were made to identify by name all those had a right to attend at court. By 1540, the use of 'check rolls', registers on parchment for keeping attendance, would be drawn up, but these were insufficient, and the problem of hangers-on remained.[76] Burghley's reforms of 1576 noted that there were still men and women 'haunting in and about the court', and recommended again that 'a book may be made of the whole number of servants that shall be needful for her majesty's service in every office within her house'.[77]

Some distinction was made between those who held their office 'in ordinary', and 'in extraordinary', or rather, those who served daily, and those who served quarterly, for weeks at a time.[78] Henry VIII complained in 1521 that he had 'very few to give attendance upon his person in his Privy chamber', as Sir William Tyler had fallen sick, and Sir William Kingston had been granted licence to 'repair into his country'.[79] He requested that Wolsey send home Sir Henry Guildford and Sir Francis Bryan so that he might be properly served. Later, in 1528, Thomas Heneage bemoaned that he could not leave court, as his fellows William Carey and Anthony Browne were absent, and with the exception of Henry Norris, there was no other man 'to give attendance upon the king's highness when he goes to make water in his bedchamber, nor any other to keep the pallet but only I'.[80] By 1532, the king ordered that there be always at least six gentlemen and a lord, who would serve, in turn, for six weeks at a time. If any of these gentlemen were due to be absent 'during his term of service, from sickness or other reasonable excuse', he had to ensure one of his fellows could 'supply his place'.[81] This order became impracticable and was not upheld. As the king's Privy Chamber servants were frequently sent on local errands and diplomatic missions, a shortage of staff remained a consistent problem, as is evident in Edward VI's diary from 1550, in which he stressed that 'three of the outer Privy Chamber gentlemen should always be here, and two lie in the pallet and fill the room of one of the four knights; that the esquires should be diligent in their office, and five grooms should always be present, of which one to watch in the bedchamber'.[82] Servants would apparently 'give themselves many times to idleness, evil rule and conversation',[83] and many of them had lesser servants of their own perform their duties instead, even though this was explicitly forbidden. The Eltham ordinances of 1526 warned that 'no manner of servants shall do any service within the King's house in any room or office, by any substitute or other servants under them', yet in 1540, the Privy council had to summon the grooms of the king's Privy Chamber and remind them 'to do their office', or essentially, to do their job, 'and not suffer the pages or others to intermeddle except in case of necessity'.[84]

Servants could be reprimanded if they did not perform their roles as diligently as required. It was reported at the presentation of the Lord Mayor in 1582 that a few 'bold' men overstepped 'upon the carpet of the cloth of state, and did almost lean upon the cushions', leading Elizabeth I to scold her lord chamberlain, vice-chamberlain and gentlemen ushers 'for suffering such disorders'.[85] In the 1510s, George, Earl of Shrewsbury, serving as Henry VIII's lord steward, was frequently away from court on personal errands. His faithful agent Thomas Alen informed Wolsey in 1516 that his master was suffering with an illness. Alen assured the Earl that Wolsey was made aware this was 'no feigned matter', and that the cardinal had advised him to 'counsel my lord to get him into clean air and divide his household in sundry places, and if the danger of sickness be past by the next term then to be at London'.[86] A few days later, Alen wrote again to his master, urging that the king wished him to be in attendance to greet his sister, Margaret, queen of Scotland, 'for that you were the great officer of the King's household',[87] though ultimately, he was excused, as his agent reported that a 'contagious plague' was still rife among the Earl's servants.[88] The cardinal would inquire again the following month as to the Earl's absence, and the trusty Alen stalled for him, claiming he was 'very ill troubled, and full unmeet to come up'. Alen did not know how much longer he could excuse the Earl's absence, however, as there were 'so many things out of order' at court, and the Earl, as lord steward, was expected to 'be nigh the king daily'. 'I fear me some there be would take a thorn out of their own foot and put it in yours', Alen wrote, suspecting that the servants whom Shrewsbury had charge of might look to blame him for their misconduct.[89] The following year, when Wolsey threatened to discharge Henry Jerningham from his position as esquire of the body for non-attendance, Jerningham wrote in haste to challenge him:

> I understand that for the perfect establishment and determined order of the king's most honourable household... that such as have any rooms within the same shall give their attendance upon his person for more honour and surety of his Highness according to the rooms that they be put into. And forasmuch as I am one of the esquires for the body in the room of a daily attendant and that by reason of my being at Tournay I cannot exercise nor perform the office myself, his grace therefore is minded to have the said room furnished by such as a meet person as may exercise the same... I trust his grace will be so good and gracious lord unto me that for the service I have done and intend to do will not take from me that thing which stands me so dear and that I most set by. And if the necessity be such that the room must needs be furnished I beseech your grace that I may have licence to furnish it myself, for I had rather be in the king's presence... your grace shall know that I came not so lightly to it when I was first admitted to the same. I and my friends paid 200 marks to Sir William Parr and not without the consent of the king's highness, and at that time his grace gave it me during my life, and so I have it as strong as his laws may make it to me. Wherefore I beseech your grace that I have no further trouble in the same.[90]

Through the 1590s, Anthony Bacon's 'hard handling gout', among other ailments, prevented him from attending upon Elizabeth I personally. Dorothy, Lady Stafford, of the queen's Privy Chamber, sent him word that 'her Majesty marvelled you came not to see her being now so long a time'. On an earlier occasion, however, Bacon was reassured by his aunt, Elizabeth, Lady Russell, that the queen defended him to her company, 'protesting with others that', as he wrote, 'if I had but half as much health as honesty and other sufficiency, she know not throughout her realm where to find a better servant and more to her liking'.[91]

Absences had to be authorised. Servants were not permitted to 'depart from the court, unless they be licensed'.[92] William Latymer, Anne Boleyn's chaplain, recalled how, in 1533, when one of the queen's servants fell 'grievously sick', he, 'feeling his malady to increase, sent for his wife to come unto him'. His wife, Anne Joscelyn, the queen's chamberer, had been 'denied licence to visit her weak husband', and thus 'moved one of her chaplains to solicit her cause to the queen's majesty'. Upon hearing the request, the queen 'not only granted her licence to depart, to the comfort of her weak and sick husband, but also most bountifully commanded to be prepared for her sufficient furniture of horse and other necessaries for her journey, and ten pounds in money toward the charge of her travel'.[93] Licences for leave could be granted by the Tudors upon request, but they were by no means guaranteed. In 1568, a 'disquieted' Sir Francis Knollys, who had been sent to Bolton Castle by Elizabeth I as a custodian of Mary, queen of Scots, learned that, back at court, his wife, Katherine, Lady Knollys, was in ill health. He wrote to his 'very loving wife' begrudging 'her majesty's ungrateful denial of my coming to the court'. A frustrated Francis resented the queen for not granting him leave, so much so that he drafted a letter to her with a bitter remark: 'among all my griefs of mind, it is not the least to understand that my wife is ready to die in discomfort and in miserable state towards her children even in Your Majesty's court'. He did not send it, learning that his wife was 'well amended',[94] but unfortunately, her amendment was not to last, and Lady Knollys died just over two weeks later without seeing her husband.

All servants were to abstain from 'vicious living', 'blasphemy' and 'swearing'. Nor were they to fight, brawl or be 'pickers of quarrels nor sowers of discord and sedition'.[95] Inevitably, these rules were broken. A rather proud Sir Thomas Cheyney, of Henry VIII's Privy Chamber, fell out of favour with the king in 1528 when he used 'full opprobrious words, and endeavoured to dishonour those who were most glad to serve him'. Although Henry was petitioned to have Cheyney reinstated, the king maintained that 'he shall never come into the Chamber until he has confessed his fault', as 'he will have no grudge amongst his gentlemen'.[96] In Edward VI's Presence chamber at Westminster in 1552, Henry, Lord Bergavenny, of the king's Privy Chamber, 'struck a certain nobleman a blow with his right hand which drew blood'. His punishment by law was 'to suffer the loss of his right hand and imprisonment during the king's pleasure', though he was pardoned at the intervention of his friends, and 'in consideration of his frail youth'.[97] John Evans, Mary I's sergeant-at-arms, was not so lucky, as in 1554 he was committed to the Marshalsea prison for 'picking a quarrel' with another servant in the queen's Presence chamber, 'offering to fight with him'.[98] In 1591, when Robert, Earl of Essex, and Henry, Earl of Kildare, exchanged 'unfit words' in Elizabeth I's chambers, the queen's Privy Council intervened, threatening them both with a substantial fine if they dared to 'challenge, provoke or assault the other to the violating of her Majesty's peace'.[99] It was regarded as an affront on 'the honour of her Majesty' that they would dare to fight 'so near to her royal person'.

How far any one servant's life was actually governed, or restricted, by these ordinances, is difficult to discern. Such ordinances reveal how it was understood that servants ought to behave, but not necessarily how they did. For instance, servants were to expected to perform their duties 'without grudge, contradiction or disdain'.[100] Yet it was reported in 1597 that Elizabeth I was greatly upset by the behaviour of some of her attendants, and in particular spoke 'vehemently and with great wrath' of Mary, Lady Howard. Mary had refused to bear the queen's mantle when she desired to walk in the garden, failed to carry the queen's cup when she was served dinner in her Privy chamber, and neglected to attend upon her when she went to prayer. Her insolence did 'so disquiet her Highness, that she swore she would no more show her any countenance, but out with all such ungracious flouting wenches'. On one occasion, Mary even dared to speak back to the queen, which 'did breed much colour in her mistress'![101] Furious, Elizabeth would remark, 'I have made her my servant, and she will now make herself my mistress... she shall not'. What led to this breakdown in authority is unclear, but it does show how servants might neglect their duties, lack respect or any real fear for the consequences of their misconduct, and even, in exceptional circumstances, defy the orders of their royal master or mistress. All servants would have been made aware of the expectations set upon them. When they were sworn in, each ordinance was, in turn, read aloud to them by the lord chamberlain so that none of them could excuse themselves later 'by ignorance or for lack of knowledge'.[102] When Bridget Manners became Elizabeth I's maid-of-honour in 1589, her uncle was bound by 'love and honour' to see that her behaviour was 'to her Majesty's best liking'. Echoing the ordinances of the household, her uncle urged her to be 'diligent' in her attendance, 'reverent' to her officers, 'civil and courteous' to her fellows, and show 'favour and gentleness' to her inferiors, to 'be no meddler in the causes of others', and to 'use much silences, for that becomes maids, especially of your calling'.[103]

Some ordinances could be broken without fear of sanction. Other rule breaks would not go unpunished. Infrequent inspections were carried out to ensure adherence. The lord and vice-chamberlains were meant 'to search and oversee' the royal chambers and punish servants 'for any offence or outrage'.[104] In 1540, Henry VIII's Privy Council issued orders to Robert Tyrwhitt, the king's vice-chamberlain, Sir Edward Baynton, the queen's vice-chamberlain, and some sixteen of the king and queen's servants. They were instructed to keep 'sober and temperate order', and had to be reminded how they should properly interact with courtiers, councillors and their fellows 'of every degree'.[105] A few weeks later, the king's council had to send for them again, this time to warn that 'they should from henceforth in no wise molest his person with any manner or suit'.[106] All ordinances were meant to be duly 'observed, obeyed, and executed',[107] yet servants had to be constantly reminded of rules which had long been established, leaving the impression of a certain laxity in their enforcement. William Cecil, Lord Burghley, acknowledged in 1576 that Elizabeth I's servants had to believe that they acted 'upon pain of such punishment... or else all our labours shall be in vain'.[108] Punishments for not adhering to the ordinances varied from the docking of wages to being formally summoned and reprimanded. When Charles Smith, Elizabeth's groom of the pantry, departed from her lodgings in 1554 without a licence, Mary I's council ordered that he be given 'a round check and a good admonition' before he could be reinstated to his former position.[109] In 1574, when Elizabeth learned that her maid Mary Shelton had secretly married another of her attendants, John Scudamore, the queen 'dealt liberal both with blows and evil words and has not yet granted her consent'.[110] One account even claimed that Elizabeth was so enraged that she broke Mary's finger when she attacked her with a hair brush.[111] The use of corporal punishment in the Tudor royal household, however, lacks contemporary evidence. It is unlikely that Barnaby Fitzpatrick, gentleman of Edward VI's Privy Chamber, was actually his 'whipping boy', taking the prince's punishments by proxy whenever he misbehaved.[112] If servants were given an order, very few would have disobeyed it, and none would have done so lightly, or without the threat of dismissal. Indeed, the most grievous punishment facing servants was to be 'expelled out of their rooms' and discharged from their office, or worse still, exile, or banishment from court.[113] When Sir Edward Rogers had briefly fallen out of favour with Edward VI in 1550, he was not only discharged from his office but warned 'not to return into the Privy Chamber', and 'to not approach into the Chamber without licence'.[114]

2

'The nearer I were to you the gladder I would be'
APPOINTMENTS AND COMPOSITION

Households were first established for the Tudors shortly after they were born. Within a few months of the birth of Princess Elizabeth in 1533, the Imperial ambassador Eustace Chapuys reported that 'the King has already appointed a household for his newly born daughter'.[1] Resembling a nursery, the households of baby princes and princesses were headed by a governess. In 1538, Prince Edward's governess, Margaret, Lady Bryan, promised Thomas Cromwell that she would take great care in administering the boy's household: 'I shall order all things for my lord's honour the best I can', Bryan wrote, 'so as I trust the king's grace shall be contented with all'. She assured him that Edward was 'in good health' and 'merry', and in one report that he had 'four teeth, three full out, and the fourth appears'.[2] Bryan did not betray even a hint of fatigue, though she did have some help in minding the teething toddler. Royal children were to be 'nourished' by women employed by the crown, like a wet-nurse, who 'give the child suck', and chamberers, known as 'rockers', whose namesake came from their duty taking turns to lull the baby to sleep by rocking their cradle.[3] These households were expanded and restructured when the prince or princess came of age. Prince Edward may have been brought up 'among the women', but by 1544, the female staff of his household were discharged, and in their place a number of gentlemen and 'young lords' were appointed, alongside a tutor 'for the better instruction of the Prince, and the diligent teaching of such children as be appointed to attend upon him'.[4]

The household of the sovereign was established, or re-established, upon their accession to the throne. After Henry VII died in 1509, and his body had been laid to rest, the household of his son and successor, Henry VIII, became the new court. By the time he was crowned two months later, the king's entourage had grown considerably, befitting his new rank and status.[5] The households of consorts were formed shortly before or after they married the sovereign. Within a few days of marrying Henry in 1536, Jane Seymour was being attended 'by her own servants'.[6] The chronicler Charles Wriothesley recorded that, when Jane was proclaimed queen at Greenwich, she 'began her household that day', and went in procession 'with a great train of ladies following after her'.[7] On the other hand, the household of Anne of Cleves was prepared in 1539, weeks before she made the journey from Düsseldorf to Dover, where her servants would be gathered and waiting anxiously to receive their new queen.[8]

Positions in the Tudor royal household were highly coveted. In 1555, Edward, Earl of Devon, was thrilled to hear that his mother, Gertrude, Marchioness of Exeter, had been chosen to attend upon Mary I. 'I rejoice much Madam', the Earl wrote, 'to perceive (as you have written) that the Queen's Majesty has called you again into her Privy Chamber in such honourable wise, as it appears her highness does greatly favour you'.[9] Competition for places at court was intense. When a new household was established, or when an office became vacant, there was an urgent rush and scramble for preferment. Many went to extraordinary lengths to secure their place. From the view of the English nobility and gentry, royal service was an opportunity to be near to the crown, ensuring that their interests were represented at court. At the end of Mary I's reign, many sought an appointment to the household of her sister, Elizabeth, in anticipation of her succession. As the Venetian ambassador Giovanni Michiel remarked in 1557, 'there is not a lord or gentleman in the kingdom who has failed, and continues endeavouring, to enter her service himself or to place one of his sons or brothers in it, such being the love and affection borne her'.[10] Some forty years later, in 1597, upon the death of Elizabeth I's lord chamberlain Sir William Brooke, the court was 'full of who shall have this and that office', and the queen was 'troubled with motions for them by most that speak unto her'.[11]

What recommended men and women for royal service? As a prerequisite, all servants were expected to be sincere, truthful, respectable, with good manners, morals and behaviour, a pleasing temperament, upright in mind, conduct, character and appearance, as opposed to sly, deceitful, or explicitly seeking their own advancement.[12] Elizabeth I was felt to have good measure of character where it concerned who would be fit 'for her service'. As one man judged, 'she was proficient in reading of men as well as books'.[13] Shortly after Bridget Manners was appointed to serve Elizabeth as her maid-of-honour in 1592, Sir Thomas Heneage, the queen's vice-chamberlain, wrote to inform the young girl's mother of her 'modest and honourable behaviour'. 'Her careful and diligent attendance of Her Majesty', Heneage had observed, 'is so contenting to her Highness and so commendable in this place where she lives, where vices will hardly receive visards and virtues will most shine'.[14]

Few formal qualifications were required for serving in the Tudor royal household. Most offices did not need prior training or knowledge. Almost anyone could have ably undertaken the comparatively menial role as one of the grooms, pages, or chamberers, who were all unskilled and their duties straightforward. On the other hand, the duties of the lord chamberlain and vice-chamberlain were both manifold and diverse, and as such, educated and conscientious men might have been sought after. Yeomen surely had to be fit, and stout, and possessing certain 'wisdom and discretion' if they were to guard the innermost chambers and properly discern who should and should not be granted access.[15] Serving in the household 'below-stairs' generally required more expertise. Christopher Pays leveraged his knowledge for the position of sergeant of the poultry to Elizabeth I. He wrote a lengthy statement on why 'she shall be better served' by him, promising to save her £300 a year.[16] In 1548, before Elizabeth was queen, Sir Thomas Parry, her cofferer, came under investigation by Edward VI's council. They examined his account books and found them 'so indiscreetly made, that its does well appear, he had little understanding to execute his office'.[17] Others were passed over for an appointment if they were thought to be unfit for the position. In 1598, Sir Robert Sidney's agent Rowland White had heard murmurs that his master was to be appointed as the queen's vice-chamberlain, 'yet', White informed him, 'they say you are too young and too amorous to be conversant with and amongst the ladies'.[18] One man dared not accept an appointment as Princess Mary's physician 'considering his little experience and practice'.[19] Certainly beauty was something of a prerequisite for women who aspired to serve at court. Henry VII stressed that ladies 'should be of gentle birth and beautiful, or at least that none of them should be ugly',[20] while Henry VIII thought that the queen's maids-of-honour in particular 'should be fair' and 'meet for the room'.[21] Some servants, like Elizabeth Blount, maid-of-honour to Catherine of Aragon, excelled at 'goodly pastimes'.[22] An anonymous poet in Mary I's reign regarded not only the 'beauties' but the virtues of the ladies and gentlewomen of the queen's Privy Chamber. He observed one attendant whose 'talk' was 'nothing coy', another who 'sets all her care' in 'books' and 'learning', and a young maid who possessed a 'matrons wit', even in her 'tender years'. 'These eight now serve one noble Queen', the poet remarked, 'but if power were in me for beauties praise and virtues sake each one a Queen should be'.[23] Particularly skilful attendants, like Mary Seaton, who was regarded by her mistress, Mary, queen of Scots, as 'the finest dresser of a woman's head', could be assured of their place.[24] Social status was important too, as the Tudors had to be served by men and women of suitable pedigree, and those English noble and gentry families had to be honoured with appointments near to the crown. In 1500, before Catherine of Aragon's arrival in England, Don Pedro de Ayala, the residing Spanish ambassador, advised that the attendants sent over to serve the princess 'should belong to good families, for the English attach great importance to good connections'.[25]

It must be considered not only what, but *who* recommended an individual for royal service. No doubt the men serving as lord chamberlain and vice-chamberlain wielded significant influence over appointments. 'Look how strong he is in the king's court of his household servants', one man remarked in 1503 of Sir Giles Daubeney, Henry VII's lord chamberlain, 'for the more part of his guard be of those that were my lord chamberlain's servants before'.[26] The Eltham ordinances of 1526 stated that the lord chamberlain and vice-chamberlain were to 'name, prefer, and present' men and women they deemed fit to serve.[27] They were 'to make search and report thereof', and 'to put apart all favour, affection, hate, and partiality', so that only individuals 'of good towardness, likelihood, behaviour, demeanour, and conversation' were appointed.[28] If there were many individuals who were all qualified and contending for the same position, who held the power, or had the authority, to grant office? And how was their choice determined? The evidence, such as it is, is varied, and inconsistent. As a result, it can be difficult to trace the process by which these appointments were made, or to know more precisely who made them.

Petitions, for preferment, are thus crucial. The most important prerequisite to securing an appointment in the Tudor royal household was a patron. Would-be servants vying for office would often solicit the king or queen directly. These petitions, like that of Ralph Hodgeson to Henry VIII in 1527, typically emphasised their own hardship, acknowledged any prior service they had done for the crown, and pledged that, if they were appointed, they would be a loyal and faithful servant.[29] In 1540, Katherine Howard received a letter from Joan Bulmer, an old acquaintance with whom she had served in the household of Agnes Tilney, Dowager Duchess of Norfolk. Anticipating that Katherine would soon become queen, and finding herself, as she wrote, living a 'most wretched life', Joan urged her to remember 'the unfeigned love' she had always borne her, before entreating her more directly for preferment to her household: 'I beseech you to stay some room for me what you shall think best yourself, for the nearer I were to you the gladder I would be'.[30] After her coronation in 1558, Elizabeth I was solicited by Sir Nicholas Throckmorton, her ambassador in France, to appoint Henry Middlemore as a groom of her Privy Chamber. 'I trust your grace will be pleased with his service', Throckmorton wrote, promising that his 'poor kinsman' was 'fit', 'meet', and 'indued with good qualities'.[31] This was not enough to convince the queen, however, and over the next ten years, Throckmorton, having been 'put in some pretty hope' of success, would, time and again, renew his 'sad suit' for Middlemore's preferment.[32] He employed his cousin to bear dispatches from Paris to London so that Elizabeth might, on occasion, 'grant him access and audience'.[33] By 1562, the queen recalled Throckmorton from his post as ambassador and, finally, responded to his suit: she retained Middlemore, not, as her groom, but as her agent, to remain in Paris with Throckmorton's successor![34] Throckmorton's efforts eventually bore fruit. Middlemore would be admitted to the Privy Chamber, but not until 1569, and without pay, replacing the late John Tamworth in his office.[35]

Others appealed to those at court who they could trust were able to advance their suit. Shortly before Mary Zouche was appointed as a maid-of-honour, she solicited her cousin John Arundell, to have pity on his 'poor kinswoman' and ask Cardinal Wolsey to 'speak to the king and to the queen' that she 'may do her grace service'.[36] In 1538, Sir William Parr petitioned Thomas Cromwell on behalf of his nephew 'to move his Highness to admit him as one of his grace's Privy Chamber, which if by your lordship's goodness he attain unto whose wisdom he and I submit this poor suit'.[37] As the king's secretary and lord privy seal, Cromwell, like Wolsey before him, had a heavy hand in appointments, and intended to promote many of his own servants to offices in the royal household, drawing up an extensive list in around 1538 of those 'meet to be preferred unto the King's Majesty's service'.[38] One Sybil Penne surely owed her appointment as Prince Edward's dry nurse in that same year to her brother-in-law Sir William Sidney, Edward's lord chamberlain, who wrote to Cromwell on her behalf. Sidney recommended Penne's 'good ability', 'wisdom', 'honest demeanour, and faithfulness', and 'no lack of good will, truth, and diligence towards the good administration of that which unto her office and duty shall appertain'.[39] When Arthur, Lord Lisle, petitioned Cromwell in 1539 to be appointed as lord chamberlain to the queen, he was informed by his agent Husee that 'no suit will profit in that behalf', as Cromwell himself admitted that, regrettably, it 'lay in the King's disposition and not in his'.[40] Evidently the office of lord chamberlain was rather too important and lay outside even Cromwell's jurisdiction. Sir William Cornwallis, desiring that his cousin Thomas would be appointed as Elizabeth I's groom porter in 1597, feared that the position would be conferred upon another man, and thus, appealing to Robert Cecil, the queen's secretary, urged that it would be to his cousin's 'utter undoing and disgrace' if 'another of less time standing in Court, and no title to the place, should prevail'.[41] Women at court too were known to influence household personnel. Christopher Pays acknowledged in a letter to William Cecil, Lord Burghley, that he had been 'a long suitor unto her Majesty', Elizabeth I, to be appointed as one of her servants, and that his 'only mean unto her... from time to time was and is by the right honourable the Countess of Warwick'.[42] The Countess was Anne Russell, who clearly had the queen's ear. 'She intended to prefer me to be of the Privy Chamber,' her niece Anne Clifford later wrote in her diary, 'for at that time there was much hope and expectation of me as of any other young Lady whatsoever'.[43]

Of course, petitions were no guarantee of placement. In around 1531, John Creke found himself 'at point of preferment' to Catherine of Aragon's household after soliciting her servants to speak with their mistress on his behalf. 'My fall was so low, that, without help of friends,' Creke wrote, 'I cannot rise'. 'By the labour of' the queen's lord chamberlain, William Mountjoy, her almoner, Sir Robert Dymock, and her receiver-general, Griffith Richards, Creke expected that he would 'enter into service with the Queen at 7*d.* a day' as her gentleman usher.[44] It was unfortunate that Catherine, at the time of his suit, was exiled and ostracised by the king, as the queen ultimately had to inform Creke that she could 'take no servants till such time as she may be more in quietness than now she is'.[45] Other petitions required more work to ensure their success. Shortly after Jane Seymour became queen, Honor, Lady Lisle, began aggressively courting her gentlewomen servants to find preferment for her daughters, Anne and Katharine Basset. Lisle sent various gifts and tokens, and kept regular correspondence with the queen's servants through her agent in London, John Husee, who eventually informed her in the summer of 1537 that, at the suit of Eleanor, Countess of Rutland, and Mary, Countess of Sussex, both of the Privy Chamber, the queen had promised to take one of her daughters as her maid-of-honour. 'The matter is thus arranged that you shall send them both over', reported Husee, 'that her Grace may see them herself, and take which she pleases'.[46] Some were more imaginative in their attempts to secure an appointment. In place of a petition, Sir Humphrey Radcliffe approached Elizabeth I on New Year's Day in 1561, and, in jest, presented his daughter, Mary, as his gift. The queen accepted in good humour and retained her as one of her maids-of-honour.[47]

All appointments to Tudor royal households were subject to the consent of the sovereign. While the king was at war in 1544, Katherine Parr wrote to her husband directly to ask 'his pleasure as to accepting certain ladies into her chamber in lieu of some that are sick'. Henry VIII was quite clear in that he felt the women his wife had chosen to replace them were themselves too weak and not 'meet to serve'. 'You may take them into your chamber to pass time… with you at play', the king conceded, leaving it to her 'own choice'.[48] Some servants were reluctant to advance suits without the sovereign's knowledge or approval. In 1540, shortly after the king married Anne of Cleves, Lady Lisle once again solicited the Countess of Rutland to recommend her daughter, Katharine, 'to be one of the Queen's maids', but the Countess refused, as she was aware that the king preferred 'that no more maids shall be taken in'.[49] Knowing that Henry could appoint servants at will, petitioners would solicit him directly. When Anne Basset approached the king on behalf of her sister, she found that many others had already 'spoken to his Grace for their friends'. 'He would not grant me nor them as yet', Anne informed her mother.[50] Most men and women who aspired to serve at court were left disappointed. Lord Lisle, Katharine's father, was told that the queen's household had been appointed before her arrival, and although his agent 'begged that an exception be made in her favour', regrettably, it was 'of no avail'.[51]

Tudor royal households were complex networks of overlapping social, geographical, political, religious, even factional affiliations and obligations. The accession of a new sovereign, or their marriage to a consort, often led to the sudden and conspicuous promotion at court of attendants with pre-existing ties to the king or queen, be it family, friends, companions, clientele, or men and women who had served them or someone they knew previously. Few appointments would have been made unconsciously. From the view of the Tudors, appointments to their households had the potential to establish their own networks throughout the wider court and kingdom. They surrounded themselves as far as possible with men and women whom they knew well, liked and cared for, could trust and confide in, and whom they felt would serve them loyally and faithfully. Following their reconciliation in 1536, Princess Mary pledged to accept 'what men or women soever the King's Highness shall appoint' to wait on her 'without exception'. Yet, like all of the Tudors, she did have a preference, and could not resist naming but a few servants: 'albeit to express my mind to you, whom I think worthy to be accepted for their faithful service, done to the King's Majesty and to me, since they came into my company, I promise you on my faith, Margery Baynton and Susan Clarencius have in every condition used themselves as faithfully, painfully and diligently, as ever did women in such a case… one other there is, that was sometime my maid, whom for her virtue I love, and could be glad to have in my company, that is Mary Brown'.[52] On the other hand, it is probable that, on occasion, not even the sovereign could appoint whomsoever they truly wished to serve them, as their choice was somewhat constrained by the many obligations which had been accrued by the crown. Families of English nobility and gentry, with long traditions of royal service, were honoured with successive appointments, providing a marked sense of continuity and stability between reigns. Whereas some appointments were made in response to pressure by petition, others gave way to pressure unspoken, as more than a few servants felt they had rightful a claim to office.

Upon being sworn in, for how long did men and women serve? Servants usually left the royal household if they grew too old or became unwell. The Eltham ordinances of 1526 stated that those who were 'found impotent, sickly, unable or unmeet persons' had to be discharged, though not to be 'left without some competent living'.[53] Sir William Bulmer wished to excuse himself in 1528 from an appointment he was due to take up as lord steward to Henry, Duke of Richmond, in consideration of his old age and the 'diseases' which plagued him in the performance of his duties. Bulmer stressed that he could not even mount or dismount his horse without help.[54] In 1536, Thomas Bedyll reported to Cromwell that the king's 'old fool', Sexton, 'as good as might be… by reason of age is not like to continue', and further to that, Bedyll had already 'espied a young fool' who he deemed 'very fit for the court, and will afford the King much pastime'.[55] When one Cornwallis, Princess Elizabeth's gentleman usher, had in 1554 'fallen in to an old disease of an unclean leg', he was unable to serve his mistress more than two days a week. Sir Henry Bedingfield urged the Privy Council to send an 'honest man' to 'serve in his place'. The council recommended Richard Smith, but Bedingfield had heard that Smith too had 'been long sick and not so recovered as he is able to serve as yet, whereupon I retain Cornwallis still'. Another man by the name of Hill was chosen to replace Cornwallis, and when Bedingfield summoned him, he asked if he came 'of good will', and Hill replied, 'with all my heart, but I never served in that place, and I have one great impediment, that letteth me much in service, which is my hearing, but at this present, I thank God, I am very well of it'. Bedingfield was satisfied, and appointed Hill. Later, walking with Elizabeth in the gardens, the princess disclosed to Bedingfield that, although she regarded Hill as a 'very honest' man whom she did 'favour well', she knew him to suffer 'a great sickness', of which he had not been so forthcoming. 'The conceit of the man I fear is grounded upon that he knows himself to be vexed with a pitiful disease which I will not name', a frustrated Bedingfield wrote to the council. Upon further investigation, he found that Hill was 'unmeet' and 'unfit to serve', while Smith, Bedingfield was informed, 'continues in his ague'. Poor Cornwallis probably already had his one good leg out the door when they forced him to remain with Elizabeth until a suitable replacement could be found.[56]

All individuals appointed to the Tudor royal household had to be in good health to meet the often strenuous demands of service. Before Bridget Manners could be appointed as one of Elizabeth I's maids-of-honour in 1589, her mother was advised that 'the late watchings and sittings up' would be 'tedious', and that serving at court could be 'greatly chargeable to her' and potentially 'more painful than any would judge'.[57] 'God knows how lively a sense I have of her Majesty's bodily troubles', one man remarked shortly before the queen's death in 1603, 'which must affect all her good servants, and how continually I pray that divine mercy may grant her and all men relief'.[58] Few servants retired throughout Elizabeth's long reign, but by 1601, 'most of them being grown old and weary', there was apparently 'much jostling and suing for places in the Privy Chamber'.[59]

Most, but not all women, left service when they married. In 1537, John Husee informed Lady Lisle that Margery Horsman, one of the queen's maids, 'shall be married, but as far as I can learn she shall keep her old room still'.[60] Indeed after marrying Sir Michael Lister, Margery continued to serve Jane Seymour as one of her gentlewomen. That same year, another maid, Jane Ashley, was to marry Sir Peter Mewtas, of the king's Privy Chamber, and Husee reported to Lady Lisle that if one of her daughters 'had been now here she might have chanced to have furnished her room, but she must first be seen or known if she be taken into the Queen's service'.[61] Women left court temporarily when they were heavily pregnant, though often returned to fulfil the duties of their office quite soon after giving birth, with their children left in the care of a wet nurse. In 1560, Thomas, Duke of Norfolk requested that his pregnant wife, Margaret Audley, be excused from her duties in the queen's household 'being so pulling as she is unmeet to follow the court'.[62]

Servants could be discharged for breaking ordinances, or for incurring the displeasure of their royal master or mistress. Thomas Scaveby, Henry VIII's groom of the Chamber, was dismissed in 1541 for making a false complaint against the Archbishop of York, who he accused of having 'forcibly intruded upon the King's hospital of Kynwoldegraves, Yorkshire'. Evidently making such a claim rather too hastily backfired, as the Privy Council determined that the 'irreverent' and 'seditious' Scaveby could 'show no proof', and 'had imagined the matter to vex the Archbishop'.[63] In 1550, Henry, Earl of Arundel, Edward VI's lord chamberlain, was discharged and fined £12,000 for the somewhat frivolous crimes of 'plucking down of bolts and locks at Westminster' and, as the young king recalled, 'giving of my stuff away'.[64] The Earl was accused of distributing 'garments and furs no longer required by the king for his use, and of having appropriated certain pieces of plate'.[65] The sovereign could, and often did, exercise their royal prerogative to punish and discharge servants at will. In 1510, when Elizabeth Stafford was caught 'about the palace, insidiously spying out every unwatched moment, in order to tell the Queen', an enraged Henry intervened and, for her 'suspected tale-bearing', Elizabeth was discharged, which left Catherine 'vexed'.[66] The king's interference in the queen's household often led to conflict between them. In 1525, Henry discharged three of her Spanish ladies, known to be her 'chief counsellors', suspecting them of encouraging the queen to protest the elevation of Henry Fitzroy, the king's bastard child, as Duke of Richmond. 'A strong measure', wrote Lorenzo Orio, the Venetian ambassador, 'but the Queen was obliged to submit and to have patience'.[67]

Although consorts, princes and princesses shared in the custody of appointments to their households, they did not have as much control as they perhaps would have liked. When Henry, Duke of Richmond, discharged his cofferer, Sir George Lawson, in 1534, the Duke's father, Henry VIII, urged his son to have Lawson reinstated, or at least, to continue to pay his fee of £20 a year. 'We cannot a little marvel,' the king remarked of the Duke's decision to dismiss Lawson, 'considering the good and faithful service which our said servant daily does unto us'. He warned his son that he 'shall minister unto us at all times', or, in other words, that he was to consult the sovereign in matters concerning his household.[68] While Princess Elizabeth was kept under house arrest in 1554, appointments to her household were closely scrutinised. In one instance, Bedingfield, Elizabeth's custodian, informed Mary I's council that the princess wished to have Dorothy Broadbelt or Elizabeth Norwich to replace one of her gentlewomen who had been discharged against her will. Yet the queen, 'for diverse good considerations', refused her sister's request, and designated Elizabeth Marbery as the replacement, while the council charged Bedingfield with 'persuading the lady Elizabeth to be contented with this her Majesty's pleasure and determination'.[69] In 1556, Jasper Brockhouse, Lady Anne of Cleves' cofferer, made himself unpopular with her attendants for constraining her expenses. What is more, Brockhouse's wife, Gertrude, had apparently driven Anne mad 'by her marvellous impostures and incantations'. Anne's brother William sent orders to have them both discharged from her household, but she refused. 'Every exertion' was taken 'to have them removed from her service, but in vain'.[70] The queen, Mary I, intervened, and the servants in question were summoned before her council. Brockhouse was warned to 'depart from the house', never to return, 'nor to intermeddle or busy himself in the administration of the government of her household or other of her affairs as her servant or officer', and both he and his wife were instructed to 'clearly avoid and depart the realm', to return only 'at their uttermost perils'.[71]

Reshuffles in personnel were often fiscally motivated. In 1527, the household of Henry, Duke of Richmond was judged by the clerk of the Green Cloth to be costing the king 'not more than £25 a week', but upon closer inspection by Thomas Magnus, it was found to be more than £50. Unfortunately, the clerk became anxious and fretted so much that he died prematurely. 'What with watch, taking of cold, and thought for this matter,' Magnus reported, 'is all our opinions here, it was the cause of his death'.[72] Magnus inherited the unenviable task of putting the Duke's household in order. To 'lessen the charge', it was determined that some of his servants would have their wages reduced, a few would be banished 'for their offences', and others discharged 'for that their rooms were superfluous and not necessary to be had in household'. The council in charge of the Duke's household, however, were 'perplexed', when several of these attendants were reappointed by the king himself 'with greater wages than they had before'.[73] Those responsible for devising reforms of the household were accused of manipulating the staff of the household to their own advantage. Sir Thomas Boleyn wrote to Cardinal Wolsey in 1519 when he had heard that 'the king's grace had put out of his court divers that were his minions and of his Chamber', among them Sir Francis Bryan, Sir Nicholas Carew and Sir Henry Guildford. 'Their appetite governed the king the which was nothing honourable wherefore and for other their misbehaviours', it was reported, 'the king's pleasure was that they should no more come in the court nor in presence to sue to the king by no means to return there again'.[74] Their banishment from court 'grieved sore the hearts of these young men'.[75] Had Wolsey masterminded the expulsion of these 'minions', Henry's boon companions, whose presence threatened his own dominance at court?[76] Certainly Wolsey appears to have ousted men in the king's confidence, and replaced them with his own agents, or 'creatures', as they were known, like Sir Richard Wingfield, Sir Richard Jerningham, Sir John Wellesborne.[77] On the other hand, the men who were discharged were also judged to be immoral, frequently misbehaving in public, supposedly to the detriment of the king's honour, and so his council necessarily intervened.[78]

The most intimate courtiers and councillors could exercise influence over appointments, and thus servants had to be careful of who they made an enemy out of. Some feared in 1553 that, if Mary I married Edward Courtenay, Earl of Devon, he would move to 'dismiss and change all the Queen's councillors, servants and officers', probably starting with those who favoured a Spanish match for Mary over his own.[79] Later, in 1559, it was by the hand of Robert Dudley, Earl of Leicester, Elizabeth I's master of the horse, that Drue Drury, her gentleman usher, was temporarily discharged from service. Drury was imprisoned for 'conspiring' against the Earl, 'for that it was suspected lest he would have slain the Lord Robert, whom he thought to be uncomely to be so great with the queen'. 'From the miserable Fleet', Drury begged for 'clemency' from the queen, 'without the which', he wrote, 'I wish not to live one hour'. Drury was released in 1561, and soon reinstated to the queen's household.[80] In 1540, Katherine Howard was so 'offended' by the lack of respect shown towards her by Princess Mary that she threatened to intervene and have two of her maids discharged. Mary initially reported to Chapuys that she had 'found the means to conciliate her, and thinks her maids will remain',[81] but the following year, the ambassador had heard that the princess was 'distressed at the death of one of her maids, who died of grief at being removed, by the King, from her service'.[82]

Few were punished so severely as to be permanently discharged or banished from court. Royal service was characterised by stability in office and a relatively low turnover of staff. Many servants enjoyed a sustained, lasting career, retiring their offices when their royal master or mistress died, and the entire household was routinely dismissed. It is often unclear what happened to them when they were discharged, as they usually disappear from the record. Some would have retired to their estates, whereas others struggled to find work. Those who were discharged from

Mary Tudor, queen of France's household in 1513, for instance, 'had served her long in hope of preferment, and some that had honest ways left them to serve her, and now they were without service, which caused them to take thought in so much some died by the way returning, and some fell mad, but, there was no remedy'.[83] In 1526, those of Henry VIII's attendants 'far stricken in age' were forced to retire and were 'put to live in their countries'. 'Alas what sorrow, and what lamentation was made', the chronicler Hall recorded, as some of them were utterly 'undone', and even resorted to stealing.[84] When Princess Mary's household in the Welsh marches was discharged in 1528, her servants were ordered 'to depart to their dwelling houses or other places to their friends at their pleasure'. Mary's councillors wrote to Wolsey concerned that some of them were 'destitute of such houses or friends at this time to resort unto'. Intriguingly, it was even suggested that Mary's former attendants would now be overqualified to serve in a noble or genteel household, remarking that 'few or none will now accept their service considering whose estate they have served'.[85] 'To stay them from troubling your grace in suits about and for their comfort', the council solicited Wolsey and the king, firstly, to write to various abbots across the country to take them in, and secondly, to pay their wages 'until they may be stayed'.[86] Evidently, the same solution was proposed in 1532, when Henry, Duke of Richmond, was to travel to France, and, as the Duke was informed, 'such of my servants as do abide behind me in the realm of England shall be and is established in religious places, there to have meat and drink for themselves, horse meat for their geldings and chambers for their lodgings'.[87] The sudden death of the Duke in the summer of 1536 saw Sir Richard Cotton, his comptroller, and George Cotton, his governor, anxious to know 'what order shall be taken with all his servants at their departure', and whether the king 'will take them to his service or other wise bestowed at his pleasure'.[88]

Some servants relied on patrons in their time of need. Elizabeth, Duchess of Norfolk wrote to Thomas Cromwell in 1536 on behalf of a 'poor' man named Arnold, who had served the late Duke of Richmond as his brewer. 'It is so I hear say', the Duchess began, 'you have been good lord to all my lord of Richmond's servants and have taken many of them to your service'. She felt it necessary to remind Cromwell of Arnold 'to help to get him a living as his wife showed me that you promised', assuring him 'I know well he is a very honest man for I have known him many years'.[89] The following year, the Duchess wrote again for Arnold, who was 'now in his old days' after many years of 'true service'.[90] Some of the late Duke's servants were rewarded or subsidised. Although his attendants received a share of

£528. 17*d*.,[91] this may not have been sufficient, as in 1539, Thomas Eynus begged Cromwell to appoint him to serve Prince Edward in 'consideration of the great costs and charges' he had sustained since the death of the Duke, which left him 'more than half undone'.[92] Hugh Jones, the Duke's page, faired better than his fellow, as he was reappointed to Henry VIII's household, and in 1537 was granted a lease of the manors of Manorbier and Penally in Pembrokeshire, Wales, 'in consideration of his services to Henry late duke of Richmond'.[93]

Although their fortunes, and misfortunes, were closely aligned, the careers of these servants were not inextricably caught up with their royal master or mistress. Henry VIII's marital instability from 1527 to 1547 saw the queen's household discharged and its servants disbanded on no less than five occasions. When Anne Boleyn was arrested on suspicion of committing adultery in 1536, the king's councillors 'discharged all her servants of their offices clearly'.[94] On the day of her execution, it was reported that 'most of the late queen's servants are set at liberty to seek service elsewhere',[95] whereas a poem written shortly after described her servants as 'sheep without a shepherd'.[96] Few of the Boleyn kinsmen and women survived the scandal, though one exception was George Taylor, Anne's receiver-general, who, it was observed, was 'merry', for he had clearly been given some assurance of his place. 'I trust the King's Highness will be good and gracious lord unto me', he remarked, shortly after being discharged, 'and so I have a special trust in his Grace.'[97] And he was not the only one. Husee had heard that 'the King's Highness of his goodness hath retained, as is said, some of them'.[98] When the household was reshuffled between queens, a patron, or lack thereof, could be decisive in determining who kept their office, and who did not. John Croft, who served his cousin, Jane Seymour, struggled to find a foothold at court for many years after her death in 1537. Sir Wymond Carew, the late queen's receiver-general, wrote on Croft's behalf to Anthony Denny and John Gates, of the king's Privy Chamber, so that he might be appointed as a gentleman waiter to Prince Edward, Jane's son, 'even without wages'. 'I am bound to do for this gentleman, Mr. Croft, all I can', Carew began, before reminding them that Croft had served Jane 'honestly', and the queen 'did favour him well'.[99] When their mistress was divorced, beheaded, or if she died in the midst of their service, many such servants lost their claim to office. Yet the households of Henry's queens ran almost consecutively. This meant that there was an opportunity for the queen's servants to retain their offices and secure their position by transferring between households. Unlike Croft, Anne Basset was, by the king, 'promised she shall have her place whensoever the time shall come'.[100] 'I trust we shall have a mistress shortly', Anne wrote to her mother at the end of 1539, anticipating the arrival of Anne of Cleves, Henry's fourth wife.[101] Henry VIII's queens came and went, yet the king was a constant. The succession of a new queen did not necessarily require an overhaul in personnel, as many of them were kept in his favour.

3

'I was made of the pliable willow, not of the stubborn oak'
OATHS, LOYALTY AND ALLEGIANCE

Upon their appointment to the Tudor royal household, servants were obliged by the swearing of an oath. The oath administered to servants of Elizabeth I's Privy Chamber was dictated by her gentleman usher, Drue Drury, as follows:

> You shall truly serve the high and mighty Princess Elizabeth Queen of England, France and Ireland, defender of the faith, her Grace's Highness and lawful successors truly and faithfully, both in the office you be called unto, and in all things touching her honour and surety. You shall not do yourself, nor procure nor consent to be done by any others, any thing prejudicial to the surety of her royal person, state or honour. And if you shall hear or understand of any bodily hurt, dishonour, or prejudice, to be pretended by any whatsoever, you shall do as much as lies in you to let the same, and besides to disclose the same either to her own person, or such of her Grace's Privy Council attending near her person, as you may next come unto, and by all ways and means you may to procure the same to come to her Highness knowledge; you shall not know of any debate or strife... within the Privy Chamber, but you shall do the best to stay or utter it some of the Privy Council, so that it may be stayed: you shall not disclose any secret concerning her Majesty's person or state that you shall hear within the Chamber in all things concerning the service of her Majesty, and not to depart the distance of 12 miles from the court without licence... so help you God...[1]

Great sanctity was placed on the sworn word. The oath was a sacred and irrevocable act of faith which cited God to witness the truth, sincerity and integrity of their statement. It was meant to be treated with urgency, binding on their conscience, and not to have been taken lightly, passively, or too hastily.[2] Oaths were worded in such a way that might elicit powerful emotional responses from the servant. The affective language invoked positive virtues which could engender feeling, like a sense of duty to be 'loyal', 'faithful', 'good' and 'true'. Unfortunately, evidence for the actual 'taking' of an oath is scarce. When Anne Basset was appointed to the queen's household in 1537, John Husee reported briefly that she had been 'sworn the Queen's maid'.[3] Sir Henry Bedingfield, Mary I's vice-chamberlain, kept a diary in which he recorded administering the oath to new servants, as he did for Babington and Mackwilliam, esquires of the body, but on these occasions he noted only that this was done 'by the queen's majesty's commandment'.[4] In 1601, Audrey, Lady Walsingham was sworn 'of her Majesty's Privy Chamber in ordinary by the Queen's commandment', and Agnes Vavasour as one of Elizabeth I's chamberers, at which time Richard Coningsby, her gentleman usher, was sent to the countinghouse, presumably to have their names etched into the check-roll.[5]

Men and women who were sworn in by oath pledged their fidelity and allegiance to their royal master or mistress, to obey them in everything. 'I know my duty is to obey anything that her Majesty shall command', Elizabeth I's secretary, William Cecil, Lord Burghley, remarked in a letter to Sir Christopher Hatton. Cecil knew he was 'bound' to 'please' the queen. Likening himself to a gnat, and Elizabeth to a camel, Cecil acknowledged that, although he had his own wants, needs, mind and intentions, as her sworn servant, these would always be eclipsed by those of his royal mistress. He emphasised his devotion and dedication to the queen: 'I dare say, there is no servant, from her Porter's lodge to her Chamber door,' Cecil wrote, 'has more care in conscience and in deeds to serve her than I'.[6] One man compared the obligations of Mary Fitton, as a maid-of-honour to the queen, to those of Fitton's sister Anne, as a wife to her husband: 'Methinks it is pity that two bodies and one mind, so firmly united as your sister's and yours, should not endue so much distance of place, but that you are both bound – the one by her Majesty's service, the other by a commanding husband'.[7]

Traditionally, servants were retained by a master or a mistress, and their allegiance was sworn to them alone. In 1519, Sir William Bulmer, 'being the king's servant sworn', was summoned to the Star Chamber for 'diverse riots, misdemeanours and offences'.[8] Learning that Bulmer had 'refused the king's service' and was retained instead by Edward Stafford, Duke of Buckingham, Henry VIII, who presided over the trial in person, was enraged, exclaiming 'that he would none of his servants should hang on another man's sleeve'. The reason for this is obvious. To guard against multiple or conflicting allegiances, the oath sworn by the king's servants was explicit in that they must 'be retained to no manner a person but only to the king's highness'.[9] Bulmer fell on his knees 'crying the king mercy', having so far incurred his wrath that 'never a noble man there dared entreat for him'.[10] Arthur, Lord Lisle, would not make the same mistake. When Thomas Cromwell petitioned him in 1535 to retain a man named Clifford, Lord Lisle observed cautiously that Clifford was 'the king's sworn servant, and it becomes me not to take him to my service'.[11]

In the households of consorts, princes and princesses, servants were sworn to both their royal master or mistress, *and* to their sovereign. The oath sworn by Catherine of Aragon's servants does not survive, but in a 1533 report, Thomas Bedyll noted that 'those who appertain to the chamber were sworn to king Henry and queen Catherine'.[12] It is likely that this oath was similar, if not nearly identical, to that which was sworn by servants in the household of Katherine Parr, which bound them to the 'sovereign Lady the Queen', to 'withstand every and any person or persons of what condition state or degree they be of that will attempt or intend unto the contrary *except our sovereign Lord the King's most royal Majesty*'.[13] The phrasing of this oath suggests that careful attention was taken to protect against conflicting allegiances. The crown was sacrosanct. The king embodied order, commanded respect, and ought to be obeyed in all circumstances. Loyalty was due first to Henry VIII as the divinely appointed sovereign. He had royal prerogative, retaining ultimate authority, and the queen's servants, as his subjects, were obliged to obey and serve him first. Yet, the potential for conflicting allegiances remained. Shortly after Henry married Anne Boleyn in 1533, he ordered that his first wife must no longer use the title of 'Queen', and that her household must call for her only by the name of 'Princess Dowager'.[14] Catherine of Aragon, who was convinced that the Henry acted, not, 'by a scruple of conscience, but only by mere passion',[15] stubbornly refused, insisting that 'she would not damn her own soul on any consideration'.[16] And nor would her servants. As the king's councillors reported, they continued to call Catherine their queen 'for so she has commanded them'.[17] When a situation arose wherein the interests of their royal master or mistress no longer aligned with those of their sovereign, to whom were servants loyal, and why? It could be suggested that the oath alone was strictly an 'institutional', or contractual, obligation. Although Catherine's servants would invoke the power of the oath to legitimise their resistance,[18] they refused to swear a new oath, as it was observed, because their mistress 'herself protests against it, and her household regard less the King's commandment'.[19] Even though they were sworn to them both, Catherine's household held her authority in higher regard than that of their sovereign, having built and developed relationships with their mistress over time, some over two, nearly three decades, fostering familiarity, intimacy, and trust. Where the rhetoric of the oath found meaning was not merely in the pledging of the affective words but the actual feeling and experience of such emotions within the household.

Confronted with the question of their allegiance, servants could outright defy their sovereign and forfeit their careers out of obligation to their royal master or mistress. William Mountjoy, Catherine's lord chamberlain, refused the king's order to deliver the names of servants who he knew to be loyal to the queen. 'It shall not lie in me to accomplish the King's pleasure herein', Mountjoy informed Cromwell. He begged, 'without the King's displeasure', to be discharged, 'if it be thought by the King that any other can serve him in this room'.[20] Mountjoy felt that, though Catherine's servants 'never ceased to call her by the name of Queen', they did 'bear their true heart's service and allegiance to the King's grace'.[21] This was the conflict dealt with by many of the queen's servants who found themselves in an unenviable position. Mountjoy was anxious not to upset the king, but would not betray his mistress, and as such was forced to resign. Catherine's servants were so reluctant to take a new oath that the king's councillor, Charles, Duke of Suffolk, was 'in despair of having any one of them sworn'.[22] A frustrated Suffolk recommended at the end of 1533 that 'such as were about her' who had encouraged their mistress in her resistance 'should be put from her', and thus 'discharged a great sort of her household servants'.[23] Reflecting the king's control of the institution, servants who refused his orders were regarded as unfit to serve, and were dismissed. The following year, the household-in-exile kept up their resistance, and many of them were placed under house arrest.[24] The Imperial ambassador Eustace Chapuys noted that the king had 'sent messengers to her to make the ladies about her swear, with instructions in case of refusal to bring them away prisoners'. 'This the commissioners would have performed altogether', Chapuys observed, 'if it had not been for the difficulty of taking so many ladies away against their will'.[25]

Servants could be more outspoken in their loyalty, though they had to be cautious, as their actions sometimes put them at great risk. Elizabeth Stafford, Duchess of Norfolk, urged Catherine to be 'of good courage', promising to 'remain faithful to her',[26] and even smuggled to her mistress, secreted within an orange, letters from Gregory Casale, the English ambassador in Rome. She was discharged in 1531 'because she spoke too freely, and declared herself more than they liked for the

Queen'.[27] María de Salinas, Lady Willoughby, had served Catherine for more than thirty years before being discharged by the king. 'Even a Spanish lady who has remained with her all her life, and has served her at her own expense', Chapuys was informed, 'is forbidden to see her'.[28] María wrote to Cromwell at the end of 1535 asking that the king permit her to visit Catherine in her exile. 'I heard that my mistress is very sore sick again. I pray you remember me, for you promised to labour with the King to get me licence to go to her,' she wrote, 'before God send for her'.[29] Appealing to their 'goodness', María was careful in this letter not to address Catherine as queen, but only 'my mistress'.[30] She knew well that it was pragmatic to remain, if only outwardly, loyal to the crown, though neither Cromwell nor the king granted her petition, which was, perhaps, indicative of her fall from favour. A few days later, María arrived at Kimbolton, without a licence, forcing her way through to be with her mistress shortly before her death.[31]

Loyalty was a prerequisite for service. The Tudors could not be served by men and women who were untrustworthy, though it seems, in exceptional circumstances, they did not have a choice. The Duke of Suffolk acknowledged in his 1533 report that a few of Catherine's servants were eventually 'sworn to accomplish the King's pleasure'.[32] This made her furious, and she shut herself away in her Privy chamber. Those who had sworn to serve her as a Princess Dowager were 'utterly refused' by her. Catherine 'affirmed that she would not have any others', and 'by her wilfulness may feign herself sick, and keep her bed, or refuse to put on her clothes'.[33] 'She has refused to eat or drink anything that her new servants bring her', Chapuys wrote a month later, observing that 'the little food she takes in this time of tribulation is prepared by her maids-in-waiting within her own bedroom'.[34] 'She will not regard them as her servants', Catherine protested, 'but only her guards, as she is a prisoner'.[35] Catherine maintained that if her servants 'took any further oath than they has done to her she would never trust them again', and later remarked that she would be satisfied with having only a few attendants, but asked that they 'shall take no oath but to the King and to her, and none other woman'.[36] By the time Catherine had fallen ill, it was thought that 'those with the Queen are guards and spies, not servants, for they have sworn in favour of Anne, not to call her highness Queen, nor serve her with royal state'.[37] By complying with the king's orders, these 'guards and spies' proved their loyalty to their sovereign and remained in service.

Consorts, princes and princesses began as figureheads of their own households, and control of the institution remained firmly in the hands of the sovereign. But control, or more specifically, command, of the servants within that household, required loyalty, which could be won. Like her mother Catherine, Princess Mary resisted the king's efforts to make her, and her household, conform. A set of articles directed towards Mary's household in 1533 accused her of 'arrogance', declaring that she must no longer use the title of Princess.[38] On one occasion, however, Mary refused to move to a new residence until she was addressed as such. Anne, Lady Shelton, appointed by the king as Mary's governess, was exasperated by her protests. Henry suggested that Mary had been persuaded to remain stubborn: 'there must be some one near her who maintains her in her fanciful ideas by conveying news of her mother to her'.[39] The governess suspected one of her maids, who had been 'shut up in a room of the house' and 'compelled' to swear the oath, before she was discharged. This 'grieved' Mary, 'for she was the only maid whom the Princess could trust', and, as Chapuys reported, 'by her means she had letters from me and others'.[40] 'Finding herself nearly destitute', Mary was forced in 1534 to send one of her gentlemen to the king 'to take money or the clothes, but not to accept any writing in which she was not entitled princess'.[41] Anne, Lady Hussey, one of Princess Mary's gentlewomen 'who did her most service', and whom 'she most trusted' with 'all her secrets', was imprisoned in 1536 for calling her princess when summoning a lowly servant to bring her mistress a drink.[42] Hussey claimed that she did this inadvertently, and out of habit, having treated her with the utmost reverence for more than a decade. Yet it appears that, like her mother's servants, Mary's household were refusing to abide by the king's orders. Hussey would be interrogated at length on when and how often she visited Mary, who else in the household had called her a princess, and if she had received any messages or tokens from her mistress. For having 'offended the King's majesty', Lady Hussey suffered in the Tower, where she became 'very sick'. Sir Thomas Audley could not help but feel sympathy, and wrote to Cromwell asking that she be allowed to 'take the air', arguing that 'her offence was nought but you perceive how she abhors it, with that she never speak it but by event and not of will deliberate nor malice'.[43]

By retaining individuals in their service, the Tudors created and reinforced ties of obligation. This became crucial for Mary I upon her accession to the throne.[44] In the summer of 1553, days after the death of her brother Edward VI, Mary sent word to his Privy Council in London instructing them to proclaim her as queen. Her succession would not be so straightforward, however, as some of the late king's councillors had already declared their allegiance to Lady Jane Grey. An account of the succession crisis, Sir Robert Wingfield's *Vita Mariae Reginae* (1554) doubled as a 'household tract', providing an unprecedented insight into the role of servants and the importance of their allegiance to their mistress.[45] Wingfield observed that Mary summoned her household, declared herself the true successor to her brother, and expressed that 'she was most anxious to inaugurate her reign with the aid of her most faithful servants, as partners in her fortunes'. 'Roused by their mistress's words,' Wingfield continued, 'everyone, both the gently-born and the humbler servants, cheered her to the rafters and hailed and proclaimed their dearest princess Mary as queen of England'. Wingfield also noted that these attendants 'scarcely numbered more than sixty' and identified nearly thirty of them by name, distinguishing between the more senior officers of her household, like Robert Rochester, Henry Jerningham, Francis Englefield, Thomas Wharton, Richard Freston, Ralph Chamberlain and Robert Strelley, and those who, 'though considered inferior in rank, yielded nothing to their superiors in faithfulness, courage and perseverance'. It is remarkable, and uncharacteristic of accounts like the *Vita Mariae Reginae* in this period, that Wingfield identified so many of Mary's individual attendants by name. He makes his intention clear: 'I consider that it is unfitting to relegate to the obscurity of an unthankful silence the names of those to whom their country and their most gentle sovereign owe so much'. What is more, the author dedicated his account to Edward Waldegrave, one of Mary's most senior and loyal councillors, having served in her household for many years prior.[46]

The Tudors could command and draw upon the loyalty of those who were sworn to them. Rallying for support at Kenninghall, Mary 'passionately' exhorted her servants and followers 'to try the hazard of death if need be'. She urged that their commitment, which went so far as to put their own lives at risk, would prove vital in securing the succession. Wingfield praised those who 'did not hesitate to face an untimely death for their queen'. Mary's servants successfully mobilised her neighbours and clientele, and many of them had their own affinities to recruit and ready in her name. A few of her attendants were also dispatched as messengers to towns and villages bearing the proclamation of her accession. Some dared even to read it aloud in those areas where the local nobility and gentry had already declared Jane as queen, stressing that it was Mary who was the legitimate heir to the throne. They did this 'boldly', as Wingfield recalled, and no doubt, somewhat precariously. After proclaiming Mary as queen in Ipswich, one Thomas Poley 'hurriedly left the town, taking refuge in flight lest his men fall in with the gathering of the leading men supporting Jane'. Their efforts were not in vain. Conflicted in his loyalties, Sir Thomas Cornwallis, who 'had reached the crossroads', ultimately renounced Jane, 'since he saw clearly enough from the latest proclamation that everyone's sympathies manifestly lay with Mary'. He made haste to her and 'most humbly prostrated himself before her Highness'. Sir Thomas Wentworth too was convinced to declare for Mary when John Tyrrell and Edward Glemham, two of her attendants, were sent 'to apprise him of the queen's message that he should take a good care for himself and for his family not to forsake the queen's cause, which would be to the perpetual dishonour of his house'. Echoing the conflict experienced by Catherine's servants in the 1530s, Wentworth claims that, 'although he had pledged his fealty to Jane by the obligation of his oath, his inner conscience constantly proclaimed that Mary had a greater right to the throne, so that he would pay no more heed to that obligation but set it aside and join his true sovereign with all speed'.[47]

Servants who were utterly devoted put themselves at great risk in the name of loyalty to the Tudors. When Mary required one of her attendants to approach the late king's Privy Council demanding that they 'belatedly renounce Jane, falsely styled queen, and recognize and welcome herself as their undoubted liege lady', Thomas Hungate 'eagerly offered himself for this task, despite all its danger'. As the foolhardy Hungate later told Wingfield, he 'bravely delivered the queen's commands', and, inevitably, and unsurprisingly, was imprisoned in the Tower of London, but not before John, Duke of Northumberland remarked, rather brutally, 'Hungate, I am truly sorry that it was your lot to be so immature and thus rashly to throw yourself away in this embassy'. At least two others, Sir Anthony Browne and Sir Francis Englefield, 'had not only been imprisoned but had suffered many other indignities because of their unswerving loyalty to their queen'. They were later released from custody. Another dangerous mission from which Thomas Wharton, another of Mary's servants, was said to have 'only just escaped unharmed', was to intercede with Henry, Earl of Sussex, and discern where his loyalties did lie.[48] Mary's network of attendants ensured that she evaded capture, accommodating her as she moved between residences, from Hunsdon to Kenninghall, and on to Framlingham. Her household and affinity grew until it began to resemble an army. Sir Edward Hastings and Sir Edmund Peckham, two of Mary's servants, prepared for an armed uprising in Northamptonshire and Buckinghamshire, to force the Duke of Northumberland to split his garrison and intimidate the Privy Council into submission. Even with the support of much of the English nobility and gentry, Lady Jane Grey's challenge lasted only nine days, and their defeat can be attributed to popular support for Mary throughout the kingdom, her presence as a regional land magnate, and her Catholic sympathies. Perhaps most importantly, Mary commanded a much more personal allegiance from her household, which formed the core of her support as she established herself as the true successor. She was confident of their dedication to her and could depend on their compliance with her orders. On the other hand, some of the late Edward VI's servants, determined in 1553 to carry out his plans for the succession, refused to conform, forfeiting their careers, and many of them, their lives. Several gentlemen of the king's Privy Chamber were among those who declared Jane as their queen and marched against Mary. Some of these men were 'commanded to keep their houses', while others, like Sir John Gates, were taken as prisoners, conveyed from the Tower to Westminster to be arraigned, and were eventually sentenced 'to be drawn, hanged and quartered'. While his brother Henry Gates was eventually pardoned, John would be executed for his unfailing loyalty to his master.[49]

The Tudors often had to rely on their servants for political backing, to establish themselves securely and reaffirm their status. In times of crisis, they depended on their households to accomplish key objectives and undertake often perilous missions in the interests of the crown. Henry VIII's gentlemen, rallied in the north during the Pilgrimage of Grace in 1536, were instructed to apprehend at once the ringleaders and 'all suspicion persons' among the rebels to examine them.[50] The king entrusted Peter Mewtas, of the Privy Chamber, to quietly, but quickly, escort Robert Aske, leader of the rebellion, down to London to answer to his offences.[51] These missions did not always go as planned. Days before rebellion broke out, Sir Robert Tyrwhitt, squire for the body, was among a group of the king's men who had been sent on a commission for the subsidy in Lincolnshire.[52] The rebels 'rose against' them, and although it was reported that they had been 'taken against their wills',[53] Henry was sceptical. 'We cannot but marvel', the king wrote to them, 'that you, being our sworn servants, and warned of their assembly, should put yourselves in their hands, instead of assembling for the surety of your own persons and for their suppression'. Making little distinction between Tyrwhitt and the rebels, Henry was far from impressed that his squire had found himself in this most 'heinous' assembly, and warned him that he and the other commissioners must 'persuade them, for the safety as well of your lives as theirs to disperse'.[54] If this was not compromising enough, Tyrwhitt's party found the rebels 'in such fury at the reading of the king's letter' that, as they reported, 'we were in jeopardy of our lives'.[55] Soon enough they either escaped or were released to secure a pardon for the rebels.[56] Although they pledged their 'truth and fidelity' to 'accomplish the king's command', even 'offering to die against the rebels and do their best for the apprehension of the ringleaders', Henry remained suspicious. The king sent orders to his council to interrogate the captured rebels to determine how Tyrwhitt and his fellows 'really used themselves', and 'what gentlemen came to them of their own will'.[57] Some surviving depositions indicate that many were questioned about the commissioners' conduct, and most indicate that they were taken 'by force', and were even 'compelled to be their captains'.[58] Tyrwhitt might have been more than cooperative with the rebels,[59] but while swearing a new oath or signing a letter rallying support for the commons warranted suspicion, he likely acted under duress.[60] The rebels openly discussed potentially killing the men they had captured, suspecting that they intended 'to deceive them'.[61] Perhaps Tyrwhitt had witnessed first-hand their brutality when Thomas, Lord Burgh, had escaped, and the rebels, frustrated, lynched Burgh's servant, Nicholas, for having 'occasioned his Lord's escape', threatening that Burgh must return 'to be their captain' or else they would 'pull him out of his house' and burn it.[62]

In spite of the oath their servants had sworn, the Tudors sometimes came to doubt their allegiance. At the outset of the insurrection in 1536, some six thousand rebels intended to 'set fire' to Hull. Sir Ralph Ellerker, of the king's Privy Chamber, was sent to protect it. 'You have and do endeavour yourself with all your forces and power to defend our town', the king wrote to Ellerker, 'from the spoil of such rebels as being assembled'.[63] Henry acknowledged his servant's bravery, promised not to forget his loyalty, and assured him that reinforcements were on the way. Ellerker and his forces were 'famished', and would receive provisions of gunpowder 'and such other necessaries as they need to defend themselves unto such time as they shall have better succour'.[64] 'Taken with force', Ellerker was briefly captured, but shortly released to carry the rebel's demands and express their grievances to the king in London. Although Henry appears from his letter to have trusted Ellerker, Thomas, Duke of Norfolk, was hesitant to bring him 'in to the court', near to the king's person, as he had been 'with the rebels' and may have been compromised.[65] They heeded his advice and Ellerker was kept at a distance until the king was able to consult with his council.[66] After a brief visit to court, Ellerker was sent back to the rebels in Yorkshire, but only 'with general instructions of comfort'.[67] Thereafter Henry would accuse him of 'great slackness' in accomplishing his mission, and although his anger was rather more directed towards the rebels, the king seemed to have developed a distaste for Ellerker's rubbing shoulders with the enemy. He even suggests that Ellerker's reports were not entirely accurate, if not deliberately misleading, suspecting that there were many who 'willingly entered into this rebellion', as opposed to being 'taken against their wills', as Ellerker alleged.[68] The gentleman's subsequent actions may have somewhat quietened lingering doubts as to his allegiance. In defence of Hull in 1537, it was reported that, after 'a great conflict and many slain', Ellerker had captured many of the rebels.[69] The king wrote again, this time to thank him for his 'repression' of the 'traitorous attempters', and to assure him of the horses, guns, gunpowder, and other munitions he required 'with all possible diligence' to continue his defence of Hull 'if need shall so enforce'. Had his faith in his gentleman been restored? Betraying a hint of mistrust, Henry obliged Ellerker to explain 'the grounds and causes that moved' him in bailing out some of the captured rebels, and to 'advertise us plainly how any man that we put in trust touching that matter shall behave himself'.[70] Perhaps his paranoia was justified, if misdirected. Later, when Ellerker was sent to seize any letters left in the houses of the rebels, their contents made it apparent that there were spies among them.[71]

Loyalties were not always so steadfast, as servants adapted to the political and religious climate. Sir William Paulet, who served Henry VIII and all three of his heirs in office, was asked how his career had survived the tumultuous Tudor period. Paulet remarked, 'I was made of the pliable willow, not of the stubborn oak'. Metaphorically, Paulet meant that loyalty, his loyalty, could be and was necessarily realigned with whomever his master or mistress was, and that ultimately, he was loyal to the crown.[72] A career in royal service negotiated freedom with constraint, power with subservience, advancement with dependence. To comply, to conform, or to resist, in all measures, embodied a choice made by the servant. It is often impossible to provide a satisfying, and irrefutable, explanation as to why any one servant would act or align themselves in one way or another. Yet all servants had to reconcile their office, the professional ethos of serving their master or mistress, their duty, obligations and identity as a servant, with their own interests, convictions, political and religious, their networks and relationships, with their own families, friends, patrons and clientele. Some made their careers in professionalism, honour, obedience and loyalty, others in ambition, treachery, and opportunism. Evidently, the sworn oath alone could not reassure the Tudors of their allegiance. More compelling was the relationship forged between them, and it remains to examine these relationships to uncover how and why servants came to feel obliged, and likewise, how and why they came to be trusted, or distrusted.

4

'If you serve us heartily, you shall not be forgotten'
WAGES, PERQUISITES AND ADVANCEMENT

Servants in the Tudor royal household had to be paid and provided for. Most servants received wages, an annual salary which was paid monthly, quarterly or yearly, and these stipends were calibrated against their office. In 1540, Henry VIII's lord chamberlain was paid £100 a year, whereas his deputy, the vice-chamberlain, received £66. 13s. 4d. In that same year, maids-of-honour to the queen, Anne of Cleves, were paid £10, while her chamberers received £6. 13s. 14d.[1] Women serving at court were paid more when the sovereign too was a woman, but this was still comparatively less than the men who had previously performed the same duties: the gentlemen of Henry VIII's Privy chamber were in receipt of £50 each,[2] but throughout Elizabeth I's reign, her ladies and gentlewomen received only £33 6s. 8d.[3] Wages remained steady throughout the Tudor period, though one exception was Anne Harris, Henry VIII's laundress, who twice successfully petitioned for an increase in her salary, from £10 to £16 3s. 4d., and again to £20 a year, suggesting that her skills were worth retaining.[4] By 1583, Sir James Croft, comptroller of Elizabeth I's household, complained to William, Lord Burghley, that many of the queen's servants below-stairs had 'only the bare wages of ancient time allowed, wherewith no man in these days is able to live'. In their 'poverty', these 'honest' men were driven 'to make spoil of as much as they can embezzle'. Croft thought that these 'disorders' could not be redressed 'until man may have such wages and allowances as in reasonable sort they may live'.[5]

In addition to wages, some servants were given their own lodgings at court.[6] The most intimate attendants slept on pallets in the Privy chamber, which were 'every night prepared and made ready' by the lowlier and more humble servants.[7] Some lodgings would have been more spacious and accommodating than others, varying considerably depending on where the court was resident. Sir William Paget, Henry

VIII's secretary, wrote to Sir William Petre in 1545 to complain that the chamber he had been appointed 'will scant receive my bed, and a table to write at'. 'His Majesty's affairs be not to be written in every place, but where they may be secret,' Paget urged, 'and where I may resort to see the doing of the same.' Paget hoped that Petre would 'move' Sir Thomas Cawarden and Sir Anthony Denny, of the king's Privy Chamber, if not the king himself, to find him a more suitable lodging, 'not so much for my own self, as for His Majesty's service'.[8] Returning to court in 1574, having recovered from an illness, Mary, Lady Sidney, was more than a little upset to find that, in her absence, her lodgings had been assigned to someone else. She excused herself from serving the queen on the grounds of her ill health until the state of her lodgings was addressed. 'Her Majesty has commanded me to come to the court and my chamber is very cold and my own hangings very scant and nothing warm', Lady Sidney wrote to the lord chamberlain, who had charge of allocating rooms. She stressed that her 'great extremity of sickness' meant that she could not 'venture to lie in so cold a lodging without some further help'.[9] 'I dare say her Majesty would not wish me to be in it',[10] Sidney remarked angrily, and demanding 'the most convenient chamber for my repair to her Majesty', she argued that the lodgings she had been assigned were wholly unfit for her position, not to mention their 'coldness' and 'wideness' would only exacerbate her 'weakness and sickliness'.[11] A few years later, Sidney would again petition the lord chamberlain so that her husband might have his own lodging when he visited court. 'For the night time, one roof, with God's grace, shall serve us', she acknowledged, while 'for the day time the Queen will look to have my chamber always in a readiness for her Majesty's coming hither'.[12]

Royal palaces could be cramped, and privacy at court was virtually non-existent. In 1580, Elizabeth I's maids-of-honour complained about the lack of privacy at Windsor Castle, expressing that they wished 'to have their chamber ceiled, and the partition that is of boards there, to be made higher', as their own prying servants tended to 'look over'.[13] A new roof was indeed 'made unto the chamber where the maids-of-honour do lie'.[14] The following year, Sir Edmund Carey moaned that the chamber for the squires of the body was 'ruinous and cold', and requested that it be 'ceiled overhead and boarded under foot'.[15] Sir Robert Cecil grumbled of the state of his lodgings at Greenwich in 1594 to Henry Carey, Lord Hunsdon, who, as lord chamberlain, resisted the urge to make a scapegoat of Richard Coningsby, gentleman usher, who was responsible for preparing them: 'I am very sorry that you are so ill lodged, but it is the more excusable because I perceive it was long of yourself, if the usher had done it, I should have been very angry withal'.[16]

Servants were entitled to eat in royal palaces. The allocation of diets, meals or 'messes' varied according to their office. In 1554, Mary I's gentlemen of the Privy Chamber, for instance, received two messes each, whereas her grooms had just one.[17] Most servants took their meals in the Great Hall, though some, 'if there be room', were permitted to eat and drink in the Presence chamber, or in the Privy chamber, accompanying their royal master or mistress.[18] Others will occasionally have taken their meals in their own rooms, though ordinances forbade the practice of dining in dark corners and 'secret places' as this inevitably led to increased expenditure and saw the palace 'greatly impaired'.[19] Diets could be converted to 'board-wages', a cash payment which compensated those who did not have their meals. Some servants could also claim 'bouche of court', the right to retrieve food, drink, and other necessaries provided at the expense of the crown. The gentlewomen of Mary's Privy Chamber were entitled to one manchet loaf, a gallon of ale, a half pitcher of wine, candles and wood 'for their bouche'.[20] John Norris recorded that the queen's gentlemen ushers were to 'have always a chamber within the court allowed to them and their livery unto their chamber of bread, ale, wine, wax, white lights and fuel and carriage'.[21]

Servants could potentially claim back for expenses they had incurred. Robert Gascoigne, Elizabeth I's messenger, was given £11 in 1581 'for riding in post, hiring of horses and guides to and fro in the settling of posts laid for her Majesty's services'.[22] Some tried their luck and claimed for more than they should have. A few years later, Richard Ferrys, another messenger, was caught out when he 'set down in his bills' some 2,664 miles 'more than he rode', which at a rate of two pence per mile meant he had overcharged the crown £22 4s. for his services.[23] Not all servants received perquisites or had their expenses reimbursed. George Alysbury, who supplied Henry VIII with rosewater and other infusions complained to Thomas Cromwell in 1537 'for some living to do his Grace service', as he wrote, he 'had never penny allowed me for meat, drink, horse or boat hire for bringing such things as his Grace commanded, wheresoever he did lie'.[24]

If a servant retained their position until they retired from court life, they would have been a likely candidate for an annuity or pension. Many men and women served the Tudors in successive households, and over time deserved recognition for their commitment. Eleanor Verney was granted an annuity of 50 marks 'for life, in consideration of her services' to Henry VII, Elizabeth of York, Mary, queen of France and Margaret, queen of Scots.[25] Henry Neville, who served both Henry VIII and his son Edward VI as a gentleman of the Privy Chamber, was granted an annuity of £50.[26] Margaret Morton, who served as Katherine Howard's chamberer, and eventually testified against her, was granted £10 a year by Henry VIII. Later, as Mary I's gentlewoman, Morton's annuity was augmented to £20 a year for life.[27] Even after Blanche Twyford had disobeyed the king's orders by refusing to turn against her mistress, Catherine of Aragon, Henry, some years later, would acknowledge 'her long and painful service', and rewarded her with an annuity of £66 13s. 4d.[28] Annuities allowed the Tudors to show their gratitude to their attendants when they were no longer able to serve them, ensuring a quiet and comfortable retirement. In 1596, Lawrence Dutton, Elizabeth I's messenger, was granted a pension of 12d. a day 'for life, because he broke his leg in the service'.[29] A few years later, Henry Morry, the queen's yeoman, 'his lameness preventing the executing of his place', received a pension at the same rate.[30]

A royal master or mistress was felt to be responsible for maintaining the physical wellbeing of their servants, ensuring that they were kept in good health and properly cared for when they fell ill. When Henry VII's esquire of the body was suffering from 'great diseases' which prevented him from fulfilling his duties, the king insisted that he continue to be paid even in his absence, in recognition of 'his long continued service done unto us to our singular good pleasure'.[31] In 1502, Elizabeth of York covered the cost of boarding for eight weeks for her gentlewoman, Anne Say, 'being sick' at Woodstock, and later at Abingdon. On another occasion later in the year, Elizabeth laid out 26s. 8d. for Nicholas Matthew, yeoman of her Chamber, 'towards his charges when he was hurt by the servants of Sir William Sandes'.[32] In his account of the most idyllic mistress of the household, William Latymer, Anne Boleyn's chaplain, recalled 'the loving kindness of this gracious prince towards her trusty servants, whose necessities, sicknesses and other adversities she relieved so abundantly that they all protested themselves more bound to her highness for her gracious benevolence then they might be able in any kind of service to acquit'. He understood the obligations of his mistress to her servants as 'that principally she was bound to provide for such as were in her own household'.[33]

What is more, the Tudors could alleviate the financial hardship endured by their servants by lending them money. A book of debts which were still outstanding to Anne Boleyn when the queen died in 1536 show that Sir Edward Baynton, her vice-chamberlain, owed her £200, John Ashley, her sewer, owed her £100, Sir James Boleyn, her uncle and chancellor, owed her £50, George Taylor, her receiver-general, owed her £30, and Elizabeth Browne, Countess of Worcester, of the queen's Privy Chamber, owed her the sum of £100.[34] 'As touching the sum of one hundred pounds which I did borrow off queen Anne', the Countess wrote to Thomas Cromwell some time after, 'I doubt it not but she would have been good to me'.[35] The late queen Anne, the Countess felt, was unlikely to have called in the debt of £100, and that this was an informal loan between friends is indicated by the fact that she had borrowed it in confidence: even her husband, Henry, Earl of Worcester, was 'utterly ignorant both of the borrowing and using of the said hundred pounds'. 'And if he should now have knowledge thereof', the countess feared, 'I am in doubt how he would take it'.[36] Of course, a loan was just a loan. In 1536, Sir Brian Tuke, Henry VIII's treasurer, was compelled to write to Arthur, Lord Lisle, begrudgingly calling in the 'great' debts he owed to the king, which had 'hanged a long time':

> Seven years and more that I have been treasurer of the king's Chamber... and in all that time have not received one penny. If I shall neither receive it nor have discharge nor sue for it nor tell the king, what will your lordship think I should do, or how much would your lordship esteem or trust a servant that would serve you so?[37]

It was understood that men and women should be sufficiently endowed to ensure they served the crown with appropriate dignity. As Katherine Champernowne remarked to Thomas Cromwell in 1536, when she was appointed to serve as a gentlewoman to Princess Elizabeth, 'as much as it has pleased the king's majesty by your means to call me to that room which I am not able to maintain to his honour unless his grace appoint me some yearly stipend towards my living'.[38] A few years later, Anthony Denny too wrote to Cromwell, informing him that the king intended for one Susan Gilmyn to serve the new queen, Anne of Cleves. 'The poverty of the woman willed me to give you knowledge of his pleasure,' Denny noted, 'that he thought it meet to set her forth as appertains to such a one'.[39] Thomas Neville, Henry VII's sewer, had to petition the king for an advance on his annuity, due to be paid at Easter, so that he might 'the better apparel him to serve us at the same feast as it appertains'.[40]

Wages alone were rarely sufficient for servants to cover the costs incurred by their attendance at court. When Henry VIII's yeomen of the Guard learned that their wages would no longer be paid quarterly, but half-yearly, they complained to Cardinal Wolsey that, because they already laid out what little they had 'for meat and drink, and other things necessary', many of them had 'not a penny left to convey himself for the three months to come'. Through the cardinal, the yeomen petitioned the king to reconsider the change to their salary, and urged him 'not to take displeasure' with 'their rude writing unto your Grace' as 'poverty and necessity constrains them to write'.[41] In 1535, Anne Owen, wrote to Henry for the money, jewels and plate left by her husband Sir David Owen, claiming that she had spent as much as £113 19s. 8d. on their son Henry, now deceased, for his attire while he was in the king's service.[42] When Anne Basset was appointed to the household of Jane Seymour in 1537, John Husee, her mother's agent in London warned that 'the Queen will be at no more cost with her but wages and livery'. Months later, Husee reiterated with a telling remark that 'the Queen will give her *but* £10 a year'.[43] The accounts of Mary, Lady Sidney, who served for many years in Elizabeth I's Privy Chamber without receiving wages, provide a view of her expenses, varying from apparel, gifts, horses for riding to and from court, and other unspecified charges incurred 'when the Queen was with her', totalling £252 3s. 6d. in 1575 alone.[44]

If wages were modest, if not meagre, there were many nonmonetary perquisites accrued from royal service that supplemented their income. Gifts and rewards to servants, often miscellaneous, occur frequently in the account books of the Tudors, and could vary from money, food, drink, clothes, jewels, plate or tokens, affirming their ties of obligation and loyalty. Mary, Lady Scudamore, who served in Elizabeth I's bedchamber, was in 1594 granted £300 'as the Queen's free gift'.[45] Catherine Carey, maid-of-honour to Anne of Cleves, received from the queen in 1540 the sum of £15, worth more to Carey than a whole year's wages.[46] What warranted such bounty is unclear, but royal largesse functioned to strengthen and reaffirm the bonds between mistress and servant. Inventories too demonstrate the overwhelming generosity of the Tudors towards their servants. Books for the queen's jewels taken for Jane Seymour in 1537 and Katherine Howard in 1541 show that both queens gave an entire catalogue of precious jewels, beads, brooches, chains and girdles to their ladies and gentlewomen attendants.[47]

The Tudors became quite invested in the personal lives of their servants. Much of the evidence alludes to the fact that servants must have made their interests known, be it in person or by petition. How else did Elizabeth of York know to hand out 40s. to William Paston, her page, 'towards the buying of his wedding clothing', to Bridget

Crowmer, her gentlewoman, 40s. 'at her departing from the court', and Nicholas Grey, her clerk, 60s. 'towards such losses as he sustained at the burning of his house'?[48] How did Anne of Cleves know to give John Wallys, her groom, a 10s. advance on his wages 'towards the finding of his poor daughter', and £7. 10s. to one of her footmen 'towards his marriage'?[49] Surely some conversation had to have taken place between mistress and servant before Mary, queen of France solicited Wolsey in 1514 to be a 'good lord' to John Palsgrave 'and provide for him living that he may continue at school'. 'If he had been retained in my service I would have done for him gladly myself', Mary wrote, but, regrettably, he was 'put out' like many of her attendants shortly after she married Louis XII.[50]

The Tudors often arranged and even financed the marriages of their servants. In 1517, at the request of William Symonds, his sewer, Henry VIII wrote to a widowed Mrs. Coward, enclosing a token and recommending him to her in marriage.[51] 'For the true, diligent and faithful service which he has heretofore done unto us, as well within this our realm, as also in our wars', the king also wrote on behalf of Nicholas Harvey in 1519 to an unknown widow, who had shown herself disinclined towards the prospective match. In this letter, Henry expressed his disappointment that Harvey had been rejected by the widow despite having, as the king informed her, 'set his heart and mind upon you, to honour you by way of marriage'. He emphasised Harvey's 'notable qualities and singular virtues', assuring her that she would not find 'a more honest gentleman'. If this was not persuasive enough, the king then reminded her, quite unsubtly, that if she did not comply, she would be subject to fines levied upon her as a widow.[52] In 1525, Catherine of Aragon wrote to Wolsey soliciting him to obtain consent and confirm the jointure of Elizabeth Dannet, one of her maids, for her marriage: 'the goodness of my woman causes me to make all this haste, trusting that she shall have a good husband and a sure living'.[53] The king urged Thomas Broke, his yeoman usher, 'not to marry without his advice, as he is intended for one of the Queen's maidens'.[54] Some servants appear to have held out for royal favour before marrying. In 1537, the marriage between Jane Ashley, Jane Seymour's maid-of-honour, and Peter Mewtas, of the king's Privy Chamber, was reportedly 'as yet uncertain', as 'it depends on the King's goodness to look towards their living'.[55] In 1556, in consideration of the service of George Bredyman, Mary I's groom of the Privy Chamber, and 'his intended marriage with the queen's consent to' Edith Brockwess, her maid, they were both given the reversions of lands in Milton, Bedford.[56]

What made serving the Tudors a viable, if not attractive and lucrative career, was the potential for advancement. The service they performed, exalted, humble or menial, could prove to be rewarding, and quite profitable. Some found promotion from within the household. Roger Beck, for instance, served Henry VIII as a yeoman of the Chamber from his accession in 1509, and by 1514, he had been made a yeoman usher. He was appointed to be one of the king's sergeants-at-arms in 1523.[57] Robert Cotton, who initially served in Mary I's Wardrobe, was so favoured by the queen that he was promoted to her Privy Chamber, though he returned to the Wardrobe when Elizabeth I acceded the throne.[58] There does not appear to have been any set pattern or trajectory for a career in the Tudor royal household, and the opportunity to rise through the ranks was by no means guaranteed. In 1546, William Reskymer, a page who had been serving Henry VIII for more than sixteen years, now eyed a promotion to the position of gentleman usher. An impatient Reskymer approached Edmund Harman, the king's barber, to move the suit, and, as a result, he was assured of the appointment 'upon the next vacation of any such room'.[59] It would appear, however, that Reskymer's efforts were in vain, and that the promise of his promotion had been forgotten, as he remained a lowly page until his death. Upon their marriage, women could progress from their positions as maids-of-honour, or as chamberers, to serve their mistress as ladies and gentlewomen of the Privy Chamber. Frances Newton began her career as Elizabeth I's chamberer, and gradually rose through the ranks from this most menial position to the most senior as lady of the Bedchamber by the time of her death in 1592. This progression was in part accelerated by her marriage in 1560 to William, Lord Cobham, which elevated her status from gentry to nobility.[60]

Many men and women were granted land and properties for their service to the crown. By 1555, Susan Clarencius, lady of the Privy Chamber, 'in consideration of her service' to Mary I over three decades had accumulated lands and lordships in Essex, among them the manors of Loverdown, Thamberley Hall, Runwell and Riverhall.[61] Sir Thomas Cawarden, gentleman of the Privy Chamber, was so far in Edward VI's favour in 1547 that he was able so wrest into his possession the palace of Bletchingley from Lady Anne of Cleves. The palace had been promised to Anne for life as part of the annulment of her marriage to Henry VIII, though Cawarden was granted the reversion of Bletchingley in 1546.[62] Henry had not intended for Cawarden to have the property until Anne's death, yet within months of Edward's accession, Cawarden was able to convince his new master to force Anne to surrender the title and her interest in the manor.[63]

The Tudors would often appoint their servants as stewards, bailiffs, receivers, keepers and constables, entrusting them to administer their lands, exercise local authority and arbitrate disputes on her behalf. In 1485 alone, Henry VII appointed, among others, James Parker, his gentleman usher, as constable, porter and gaoler of the castle of Gloucester; Edmond Edy, his groom, as keeper of the park of Hillesdon; David Philip, gentleman usher, as steward of the manors and gardens of Coliweston, and Thomas Hurd, groom, as bailiff of Ilston.[64] The following year, Christopher Sandes, servant 'to the king's most dear mother' Lady Margaret Beaufort, was appointed 'in consideration of good and true service' as porter of the town of Carlisle.[65] Certainly these offices could be financially profitable. Sir Thomas Heneage, Henry VIII's groom of the stool, accrued a substantial income from lands which he either owned outright or held office in. Heneage served as steward and bailiff of the manor of Hampton Court at £6 13s. 4d. a year, and steward of Caster at 66s. 8d.[66] When Sir Roger Salisbury died, his office as steward of Denbighland, worth £40 a year in fees, was granted to Roger Radclif, of the king's Privy Chamber. Salisbury's brother, John, bargained for the office with Radclif, who, 'by his goodness', sold it to him for 400 marks. Shortly after, Salisbury was understandably 'crazed' to learn that Denbighland was to be made a shire, meaning that new officers would have to be appointed, and the stewardship, he feared, would be diminished in authority and gain. One wonders if Radclif knew of the forthcoming change before he sold the office.[67]

Upon the disgrace or death of Tudor royal servants, most grants were redistributed by the crown. To avoid confusion, leaving no doubt as to who was now the rightful beneficiary, successive warrants typically rehearsed the legacy of the grant. When James Braybrooke, Henry VII's page, died in 1509, his office 'lately held' as ranger of Groveley forest in Wiltshire, and the corrodies in the monasteries of Hyde and Chichester, were granted to William Tyler, Henry VIII's groom of the Chamber,[68] while another groom, John Sharp, received the manor of Brockdish, in Norfolk, which Braybrooke 'had of the gift of the late King Henry VII'.[69] In that same year, Ralph Egerton, Henry VIII's gentleman usher, was made steward and receiver of the lordship of all lands 'lately belonging to' Sir William Stanley, who was Henry VII's lord chamberlain before he was executed for treason in 1495.[70] Vacant positions attracted many suitors, and there was often something of an indecent, albeit necessary rush to secure them. Reports in 1534 that Sir William Sandes, Henry VIII's lord chamberlain, was 'very sore sick and likely to die', were quite enough for one ghoulish petitioner to write to Cromwell and urge 'whether my lord chamberlain die or not, that you will get my bill signed' to secure the poor man's offices as his own.[71] Throughout his career as Henry VIII's groom of the stool, Sir William Compton was spoiled by the king. Immediately upon Compton's death in 1528, as Heneage reported to Wolsey, there were many at court who made 'suits to the king for his offices'.[72] John, Bishop of Exeter for one petitioned on behalf of Princess Mary's household 'for their preferment to some of those offices now being void by Master Compton'.[73] Henry, Duke of Richmond too wrote directly to his father 'for the preferment' of his servants Sir Giles Strangewish and Sir Edward Seymour 'to such rooms and offices as by your most gracious favour... late void by the death of Sir William Compton'.[74] The offices which had been granted to Compton by the queen, Catherine of Aragon, were to be redistributed at her discretion. For 'such offices as Compton had of her', Catherine was to 'bestow them at her pleasure, to her own servants', with the exception of the keepership of Odyam park, which Henry wanted for Richard Hill, his sergeant of the cellar.[75] Consorts, princes and princesses shared in the custody of royal patronage. As the Duke of Richmond understood it,

> when any like offices or benefices appertaining to my gift, should chance to be void, that I, by the advice of my Council should dispose and give the same, at my liberty. Whereupon considering the great number of servants that I have, and that none of them in any wise have been rewarded with any thing since their coming unto me.

And so, he did. The Duke granted Sir William Parr and Sir George Cotton the stewardships of his lands in Dorset and Somerset, with their respective fees of 100s. and £6. 13s. 4d. 'in like manner as had the said Sir William Compton'.[76]

Licences too were granted to men and women in recognition of their service. These varied from permission for Roland Hunt, Henry VIII's groom of the Privy Chamber, to marry Alice Moore, a widow,[77] to the yeoman John Allen, who was allowed to bait bears in Southwark.[78] Warner van Gymnych, cupbearer to Anne of Cleves, was permitted to export 800 tonnes of beer.[79] Sir Brian Tuke, Henry VIII's treasurer, was granted a licence to enclose and make 200 acres of land, meadow and pasture into a park,[80] while John Heron, the king's sewer, was allowed use his crossbow and hand-gun in forests.[81] Thomas Tothoth, Henry VII's gentleman usher, was given permission to hold a weekly market and a fair in his local town of Burgh,

Lincoln.[82] Sir Francis Barmade, Henry VIII's servant, was granted a licence to import and sell 'all manner of kind of goods, jewels, pearls, precious stones, as well set in gold as embroidered in garments as unset or otherwise', with the stipulation that the king 'has first choice of all'.[83] Sir Christopher Morris, master of the ordnance, and Sir Anthony Knyvett and Sir Peter Mewtas, of the king's Privy Chamber, were authorised to start a guild or fraternity dedicated to the 'science of artillery'.[84] John Lumkyn, Mary I's yeoman, was permitted 'to travel and labour at his own charges' for the recovery of the wreck of *The Mary Rose* 'drowned in the sea beside Portsmouth', and was even promised any goods that could be reclaimed.[85] Henry Middlemore, Elizabeth I's groom of the Privy Chamber, was granted a licence 'to transport a quantity of beans', overriding the general limits in place,[86] while Barbara Rice, her gentlewoman, was given six months of protection 'freely to pass to and from in and about London, without any arrest of impeachment'.[87] James Morice, Lady Margaret Beaufort's servant, was licenced to be the 'weigher of wool' at Boston port,[88] while William Bowman, Henry VIII's page, was appointed to be the king's 'fisherman of the Thames'.[89] Wardships, the charge of a minor, usually from a noble or genteel family, were valuable, and many of them were granted to servants, like Thomas Denys, Henry VIII's esquire of the body, who was granted the wardship of Anthony, the son and heir of Humphrey Monke of Richmond,[90] or Margaret ap Owen, who, having served Catherine of Aragon as one of her gentlewomen for many years, was assured of the wardship of Rees, son and heir of Thomas Ap Owen, her late husband.[91]

The Tudors intervened to enforce these grants and protect the interests of their servants. Edward Darcy, Elizabeth I's groom of the Privy Chamber, had been given an exclusive patent to sell playing cards. In 1601, Darcy's interests were represented by the queen's Privy Council when he complained that merchants were 'secretly' importing playing cards, undercutting the groom's profits. Worse still, they were 'defrauding the patentee to whom her Majesty's grant is made of the benefit thereof and deceiving her Majesty of her ordinary custom'.[92] The council ordered that their premises be searched, and that the cards be seized and delivered to Darcy. Prohibiting the sale of any cards 'but those with the seal of' the queen's servant, the council also summoned these 'delinquents' before them to make them 'enter into sufficient bonds for refraining from the same in future'.[93] The following year, Darcy complained again, as his patent for the 'sole licence' of selling playing cards continued to be 'infringed', with some claiming that a new proclamation against monopolies made

Darcy's patent void by law. An exasperated council once again intervened, determining that the proclamation 'carries no such meaning', and reasserted that 'no persons are to sell, transport, or make playing cards without his licence, except on bond to satisfy him'. The more 'obstinate' offenders were to be summoned before the council 'for their contempt', and now faced prison.[94] All this must have reached the ears of Darcy's royal mistress, as when a suit was taken to the Court of Common Pleas questioning the validity of Darcy's patent, the council wrote directly to the judges to inform them that 'the Queen wishes you to understand that her prerogative royal may not be called in question', and ordered them thus 'to stay the suit till informed of her further pleasure.'[95] Darcy would be permitted to take legal action against those who continued to sell playing cards without his licence, and could invoke 'the prerogative royal' of his mistress, as he did against Thomas Allen of London in 1602.[96] Eventually, the council tired of Darcy's grievances, and so that 'neither her Majesty nor their Lordships may be hereafter troubled with any more complaint or examination', they set up a commission headed by William Knollys, her comptroller, to deal with them.[97] Knollys too would excuse himself of Darcy's incessant moaning by delegating the responsibility to another body, remarking that 'our leisures do not serve us to attend so many complaints as are made of daily abuses and contempts against the said patent and grant and her Majesty's patentee'.[98]

The Tudors cooperated as patrons for the preferment of their servants. Consorts, princes and princesses often petitioned the sovereign to secure grants which were in the custody of the crown. Mary, queen of France, wrote to her brother Henry VIII in 1515 for her almoner, Denton, who had been assured of the prebend of St. Stephens but had been 'supplanted' by one of Wolsey's chaplains.[99] Henry, Duke of Richmond wrote to Cromwell in 1535 for his gentleman waiter, John Travers, 'that he may peaceably and quietly hold, occupy and enjoy the farm of the fishing' in the River Bann, anticipating a resumption of all grants in Ireland to the king's hands.[100] 'It has not been my chance as yet hitherto to prefer any one of my servants to any manner of promotion', the Duke protested to his father, urging him to recognise the 'true and diligent service daily done' by his yeoman usher, Robert Markham, and grant him the office of bailiff and keeper of the town and park of Torpell, Northamptonshire. 'In time coming', the Duke was confident that Markham would 'be much more able to do good service unto me, like as full well and diligently at all times he has done'.[101] He wrote again for his chaplain, William Swallow, whose 'poor living' meant he was most in need of the king's 'most gracious favour',[102] and Richard

Tempest, who he emphasised 'at all times is ready to do unto me all the pleasure he can not only in giving his attendance upon me at sundry times, but also otherwise'.[103] In 1544, Katherine Parr wrote directly to the king on behalf of one of her gentleman ushers, Henry Webbe, for the house and demesnes of the nunnery of Holywell. 'We shall heartily desire, and pray you, to be so favourable to him,' wrote the queen on Webbe's behalf, 'at this our earnest request, as that he may for his money have the purchase at your hands'.[104]

Patronage sustained and strengthened bonds of obligation and goodwill between the Tudors and their households. By maintaining, rewarding and advancing their servants, they gave recognition to, and in turn, encouraged 'good' service. Thus the matter of advancing their own servants was treated urgently. Henry VIII was incredulous in having to remind his servant, Sir William Bulmer, who had been retained by Edward Stafford, 'that he was as well able to maintain him as the duke of Buckingham': 'if you serve us heartily, you shall not be forgotten'.[105] All of the Tudors had to be conscientious in providing for their households. Henry, Duke of Richmond's council complained that offices and fees 'in his gift' were by the king granted elsewhere 'to the great grudge and discomfort of all his servants, they be almost despaired to obtain or get any promotions by his service'. His 'poor' chaplains, the council continued, were unpaid, and 'be at the point to depart from him', to seek refuge elsewhere. 'For the better encouraging of his said servants and chaplains to take pain in his service', the council urged Wolsey to ensure that such offices and benefices may be distributed amongst them 'henceforth as they shall fall and happen to be void'.[106] Catherine of Aragon was particularly anxious to provide for those who, as she felt, in her own words, were 'good, and take labour doing me service'.[107] Anne Boleyn, according to her chaplain William Latymer, 'would assuredly prefer her own servants first', and was 'resolved that of duty her painful and ancient servants should first enjoy such benefits as were in her majesty to employ, for they are true servants to yield me their service, take pain to death'. 'Since I enjoy their service', Anne remarked, 'they may have some portion of my living'.[108] Anne's daughter Elizabeth I too ensured she kept up 'her old wont, which is, always to hold both ears and eyes open for her good servants'.[109] When Sir Thomas Shirley was accused in 1595 of relying too far on the Earl of Essex for his good fortune, he refuted the charge, stating that he did 'not depend upon him nor any other, but only upon the Queen'. Shirley regarded it as 'base for her servant and officer' to 'depend upon any man living'.[110]

Servants could make some claim to royal patronage, but it had to be earned over time. When Sir William Compton died in 1528, Thomas Heneage, of the king's Privy Chamber, reassured Wolsey that he would not petition for his offices. 'I assure your grace I have not nor will speak for any of the said offices for myself', the humble Heneage wrote, 'for if I should I think his highness will think much presumptuousness in me considering the little time that I have been in his service.'[111] On the other hand, William Mucklow, cofferer to the Duke of Richmond, wrote to Wolsey after Compton's death 'for one of his offices or rooms which your grace shall think most expedient, whereby I may be the more able to do such service'. Mucklow wisely drew attention to the fact he had been a loyal servant to the crown for seventeen years and 'nothing hitherto had', this being, as he stated, 'the first petition on my behalf'.[112] A few years later, upon the death of Dr William Clayton, who, like Compton, had enjoyed the king's patronage, Thomas Bedyll wrote to Thomas Cromwell, 'I am so new a man in the king's grace's service that I will not desire neither look for any of these promotions'.[113] Both Heneage and Bedyll recognised that those who had been in service for longer than them were perhaps more deserving, and could expect to be rewarded. Certainly Nicholas Jakson, Henry VIII's yeoman usher, having served the king since he succeeded to the throne in 1509,[114] felt by 1533 that he was entitled to some reward for his long service, and that Cromwell should secure it for him: 'You promised me the farm of Canne Hall, for which several persons are making labour with the king. Make what haste you can, and let the lease endure for 60 or 80 years. As I am the king's servant I should have it as well as another'.[115] In 1585, the husband of Anne, Countess of Warwick complained to Francis Walsingham, Elizabeth I's secretary, that, in one particular suit, the queen failed to recognise his wife's service 'considering she has spent the chief part of her years both painfully, faithfully, and serviceably, yea after such sort as without any dishonour to her majesty any kind of wage nor yet any blemish to her poor self'.[116]

Servants sometimes endured long periods without pay. In 1520, Margaret, queen of Scots was unable to afford the expenses of her household and found herself 'on the point of pawning her jewels'.[117] She claimed to have discharged all of her servants for, as Margaret said, 'I have nought to give them', and would have been 'shamed' to live like 'a poor gentlewoman', if not for Robin Barton, her comptroller, who laid out £500 from 'his own purse'.[118] Catherine of Aragon's attendants were often left without wages while she was a princess. She wrote to her father Ferdinand of Spain in 1507, remarking 'I let my servants walk about in rags, and they live in such misery that it is shameful to think of it'; 'they have always served me in the hope that things would be mended'. 'I am at a loss what to say to them', Catherine sighed, begging her father 'not to forsake her servants, and especially her women'.[119] It would appear, however, that very few, if any of them, grumbled: 'they have not complained to her, and have attended on her as willingly and as respectfully as though they had been always punctually paid'.[120] Catherine's pleas were eventually heard by the king, Henry VII, who pledged 'to pay anew as much money as she wants for her person and servants, so that she may not only not suffer from indigence, but be able to live honourably', though not before bitterly blaming her household for their own destitution.[121]

The Tudors could be accused at times of being far too generous, and at others, not generous enough. 'I have nothing for all the long service that I have done', Sir John Rainsford remarked in 1538. Bemused that he had enjoyed so little favour, his friends apparently cried out, 'Why does not he ask as well as others? Is he not the King's servant? Has not his service been acceptable? Is he not a true man?'[122] Later, in 1553, the Imperial ambassador reported that 'discontent' was 'rife' among 'those who stood by the Queen in the days of her adversity and trouble, who feel that they have not been rewarded as they deserve'.[123] The following year, Sir William Paget, one of Mary I's councillors, observed that 'whereas the country was formerly so well off as to be able to supply its friends and neighbours, it is now sorely embarrassed itself, and the Queen unable to find money for her household expenses or her officers' pay'.[124] Another of Mary's servants, William Harrys, was examined by the queen's Privy Council for 'certain lewd words that he was accused to have spoken' at an alehouse in Deptford, which he confessed to, amounting to some grumbling about unpaid wages: 'The Queen has given this day a great alms, and given that away that should have paid us our wages; she has undone us and has undone this realm too, for she loves another realm better than this'.[125] By the time Elizabeth I acceded the throne in 1558, the crown was indebted to many of her predecessors' servants. The yeomen of the Guard, for instance, were still owed arrears for service to Edward VI some six years earlier.[126] At the end of Elizabeth's reign, the crown was so financially constrained that, when the Lord Deputy of Ireland recommended her groom, Daniel Savage, for reward in recognition of his 'good service', the Privy Council, albeit acknowledging that 'he is her Majesty's servant', and they 'would be willing to do him that good', concluded 'it is no time (as you can judge) to move her Highness in these kind of suits'.[127]

Some servants felt they were not appreciated or adequately rewarded. In 1547, on his deathbed, Henry VIII dictated what he wished to bestow upon his loyal attendants. Sir William Paget advised, however, that it was 'too little, and stood much with him therein, and then', as Paget recalled, 'he bid me speak with them, and know their dispositions and he would after tell me more, wherewith I satisfied myself.' Unsurprisingly, when Paget spoke with those Henry intended to advance, he 'found them not well satisfied, some labouring to remain in their old degrees, and the others thinking the land too little for their maintenance which was appointed to them'. Paget returned to the king and urged him to grant them more than he had initially intended.[128] Mary, Lady Sidney, who had retired from court in 1579, felt that Elizabeth I had not shown her gratitude for her devotion. She asked Sir William Cecil for help in raising her allowance from the queen, moaning 'I have worn down my friends at Court' with the suit, and still her mistress was 'no more careful of' her, and would 'stick at so small a trifle' as £22 a year for her twelve years of service.[129] In 1596, Elizabeth lost her patience with another of her attendants, remarking scornfully that he 'never came to attend her' unless it served his own interests. The queen resented that he 'had been in hand with her for a suit' ever since arriving at court, 'and was never without something'. Although the queen had warned him not to trouble her further, the man dared to write, at length, to her secretary: 'I have deserved something, having been her servant ten years,' he argued, 'and attended Court like a gentleman'.[130]

Occasionally, the Tudors needed to be reminded of their obligations to their servants. In 1600, a distressed Margaret, Lady Denny, recently widowed after the death of Sir Edward Denny, who has served Elizabeth I, wrote an extraordinary begging letter to Sir Robert Cecil, believing that the queen would not 'be void of compassion for the children of her dead servants, now ready to starve'. It would appear that Lady Denny's sick husband had been promised the fees of his office to cover his outstanding debts and to relieve the financial difficulties of his family. Yet the queen, perhaps by mistake, had granted the same office to another of her servants, who, as Lady Denny resented, 'had little need to suck this small portion of her Majesty's favour from the hungry mouths of my children'. The widow suggested that the matter touched Elizabeth's honour, as 'the world would think the Queen deals hardly with a servant who served seventeen years in her chamber, spent all that he had, and ended his life by the sickness he took in her service'. What is more, Lady Denny suggests that her husband was at risk of going 'to his grave in so obscure manner as never any of his place did', and even claims that she was not able to buy herself a mourning gown. She was quick to remind Elizabeth that she too had attended upon her for many years, and 'to furnish and maintain' her 'in the Queen's service', her father had apparently laid out an astonishing £1300.[131] All this must have been quite enough to sufficiently shame Elizabeth into action, as the queen commanded that £200 a year 'shall go to the relief, bringing up and bestowing of the children, who, if the office shall be otherwise bestowed, are like all to beg at her Majesty's Court gates for relief'.[132]

5

'Appareled according to their degrees'
LIVERY, MAJESTY AND MAGNIFICENCE

Livery was the clothing worn by men and women to mark them publicly as servants of the Tudor royal household. All servants had to be 'apparelled according to their degrees'.[1] When Anne Basset was first appointed to serve Jane Seymour as her maid-of-honour in 1537, John Husee, her mother's agent in London, urged that Anne 'must have such apparel' as 'a bonnet or two, with frontlets and an edge of pearl, and a gown of black satin, and another of velvet'.[2] Later Husee advised that Anne 'must have cloth for smocks and sleeves, for there is fault found that their smocks are too coarse',[3] and again, on another occasion, 'she must have against the Queen's churching a new satin gown, and against Christmas a new gown of lion tawny velvet'.[4] Although Jane died prematurely, Anne, anticipating that the king would soon remarry, wrote to her mother the following year asking that she send her 'an edge of pearl'.[5] Within a few weeks, Anne would insist that she 'must needs have her pearl, as shortly as is possible'.[6] She wrote again, just over a week later, 'if you would send me an edge of pearl... I shall be much bound to you'.[7] The pearls were soon conveyed to Anne, yet she grumbled still, as 'six score are not enough'. 'Indeed they are not to be worn in the Queen's service', she complained, 'unless they can be set full'.[8] A day later, Anne's mother would hear that 'the six score pearls' sent to her daughter 'be all rags, and too few to serve'.[9] The urgency with which Anne requested the pearls indicates the importance of proper attire for servants attending upon royalty.

Livery was issued *en masse* for coronations and funerals. Liveries of scarlet silk, for instance, were made in 1533 for the ladies and gentlewomen who attended upon Anne Boleyn in her coronation procession.[10] Henry VIII wrote a letter of summons to Anne, Lady Cobham, having appointed her to attend the coronation 'as to her estate and dignity'. 'Trusting that for the liveries and ordering of your said women as well in their apparel as in their horses', the king wrote, 'you will in such wise provide for them as unto your honour and that solemnity appertain'.[11] The new queen would be attended by her ladies 'following in robes of scarlet furred with ermines and round cornettes of gold on their heads', and after these ladies in her train the queen's maids-of-honour would follow 'in gowns of scarlet edged with white lettice fur'.[12]

Upon the death of a Tudor king, queen, prince or princess, new livery had to be distributed to their servants. Preparations for Catherine of Aragon's funeral in 1536 specified that, 'after her estate and degree', black cloth had to be provided for thirty ladies and gentlewomen, as well as ten gentlemen, to make up their mourning gowns, and to furnish their own servants, horses and chariots. Henry issued yards of black cloth sufficient to attire one Grace, Lady Bedingfield and her attendants, 'all which apparel', the king informed her, 'you must cause to be made up'.[13] These garments could take some time to produce. The mourning livery for Catherine's ladies was completed nearly three weeks after the death of their mistress.[14] All those in attendance at court wore plain clothes until their mourning garments were ready. In the days prior to Elizabeth of York's funeral in 1503, it was observed that her attendants were dressed 'in such most sad and simplest clothing that they had' until their livery could be made.[15] At the funeral procession for Jane Seymour in 1537, 'all the ladies and gentlewomen did put off their sumptuous apparel and took on them the habit of mourning, leaving off their bonnets richly apparelled and took white kerchiefs to apparel their heads'.[16] Following the chariot which held Jane's coffin were 'lords and gentlemen riding all in black gowns and coats'.[17] For how long they wore their mourning livery is unclear. Husee reported to Lady Lisle that her daughter Anne, having served briefly in the late queen's household, 'shall need nothing till her mourning gear be cast off',[18] and although 'it was uncertain how long the King's pleasure should be that they should wear black', he anticipated that Anne would eventually need to wear traditional livery colours again and suggested a new tawny satin gown be made for her out of hand.[19]

The Tudors provided their servants with livery as and when it was required. A book kept by Richard Justice, groom of the robes to Catherine of Aragon, itemised entries for livery to be distributed to the queen's servants from 1515 to 1517, such as 'a gown of tawny velvet' for Maria de Salinas, Catherine's maid-of-honour, three yards of black velvet 'for a night gown' for Isabel de Vargas, her chamberer, and a further seven yards for Roger Radclif, her gentleman usher.[20] In 1532, William, Lord Sandes, Henry VIII's lord chamberlain, complained to Thomas Cromwell that 'no warrant has yet been signed' for the yeomen, grooms and pages under his charge to 'have their liveries in doublets, hose, and bonnet'.[21] Providing livery for one's household not only meant purchasing silks, satins, damask, velvet, linen, cloth of gold, but covering the costs for the making, and mending, of their gowns, kirtles, petticoats, coats, doublets and more. A warrant drawn up in 1542 for livery to be issued to John Gates and his fellows in Henry VIII's Privy Chamber listed the costs incurred for the materials, like damask, fustian and velvet, and for the trimming and lining of their gowns, coats and doublets, totalling £27 15 s.[22] Elizabeth of York laid out 12 d. for the making of a kirtle for Bridget Crowmer, her gentlewoman, a further 3 d. 'for hemming of a kirtle of the same', 12 d. 'for lining of a gown' for a Mistress Zouche, 8 d. 'for mending of two gowns' for Jane Popingcourt, maid-of-honour, and 3 s. 4 d. 'for making of two doublets for the queen's footmen of crimson velvet'.[23]

Each of the Tudors had their own distinct livery colours by which their servants could be identified. For instance, one chronicler identified Henry VII's servants by the king's livery of white and green, and Elizabeth of York's attendants by the queen's livery of blue and murrey or purple.[24] Livery was often embroidered with the heraldic badge or motto of their royal master or mistress. Hans Holbein the Younger painted a miniature, dated to 1534, of an unnamed gentleman servant in the household of Henry VIII wearing, over a black doublet, his red livery coat, which had embroidered on the chest the letters 'HR', for *Henricus Rex*.[25] Spanish emblems of pomegranates and sheaves of arrows were sewn into Catherine of Aragon's livery. John Glynne, Catherine's yeoman, was given a green velvet gown with sleeves lined with cloth of gold 'of the Spanish fashion', and Agnes, Duchess of Norfolk, received a gown of crimson velvet with Spanish sleeves lined with 'green cloth of gold of damask'.[26] In 1557, Mary I's Privy Council granted her messenger, Barbour, enough money 'as will buy him a coat and pay for the embroidering of the letters after the accustomed manner of the Queen's servants coats'.[27] Warrants were drawn up in 1594 for the payment of Elizabeth I's embroiderers, who embellished the red coats worn by her grooms and pages 'with E. R. set in Venice gold', and those worn by her yeomen 'with roses and crowns imperial'.[28]

A servant's livery could even be fashioned to make pointed, politically charged statements. Anne Boleyn apparently had her livery embroidered with the motto, 'Ainsi sera, groigne qui groigne' ('What will be, will be, grumble who may'), in reaction to murmurs at court against the king's 'Great Matter'. Shortly after the king married Anne in 1533, Catherine of Aragon provocatively had her servants 'arrayed entirely in new apparel', embroidered with the letters 'H' for Henry VIII and 'K' for Katherine.[29] Knowing the power of livery to accentuate status, Henry ordered that servants of their daughter, Princess Mary, who had also fallen out of favour, were no longer permitted to wear her badge on their coat-of-arms.[30] Throughout the court, and wherever else they went, servants wearing livery were a physical extension of the crown's presence and authority. Their bodies were, quite literally, appropriated in its construction. One groom of Henry VIII's Privy Chamber, tasked in 1540 with making an arrest in the king's name, was said to have worn the 'excellence and estate of monarchy like a tangible and terrible cloak'.[31]

Typically, only servants wore livery, strengthening their identification and creating social cohesion within the Tudor royal household. In 1547, the French ambassador reported an incident wherein two merchants had 'made themselves servants of the King and wear the livery coats of his household'. The ambassador felt their wearing of the coats was suspicious, as he did not think they had been sworn in to serve the king, nor were they in receipt of wages.[32] When the officers of the Works petitioned to wear Mary I's livery, their request was initially refused, as they were not considered strictly to be 'household' servants. They appealed the decision and were ultimately granted the right to wear the queen's livery.[33] Upon being discharged from the royal household, a disgraced Thomas Wyriot, who had previously served as Elizabeth I's yeoman, was commanded by the vice-chamberlain 'to forbear to wear her Highness's coat, which nevertheless he contemptuously did in the country'. For this and other 'misdemeanours', Wyriot was committed to the Marshalsea prison, though he was released in 1580, on the condition that 'he should not wear his coat until such time as he should be otherwise licensed by her Majesty'.[34]

Livery was a visual, symbolic representation of their identity as servants and a mark of the protection they were assured. This is probably why, in 1535, Thomas Cromwell wanted to wear the livery worn by the gentlemen of the king's Privy Chamber, though attaining it was not so straightforward. Cromwell's agent wrote to inform him that 'the patron of the coats for the Privy Chamber is not yet come'.[35] Certainly those who wore livery were glad of the privilege, as reflected in a letter from Anthony St Leger, Henry VIII's servant stationed in Ireland, written to his master back at court: 'Most humbly rendering mine obedient thanks to Your Majesty for the apparel Your Majesty sent me for myself, and for my livery coat of your Chamber, which was more welcome to me, than so much gold'.[36] One man who wore the king's livery in public at around the time of the Pilgrimage of Grace in 1536 caught the attention of another disgruntled man who remarked, 'thy master is a thief, for he pulls down all our churches in the country'.[37] Others were perhaps a little too hasty to lose their material association with the crown. Matthew Justice, Thomas Nodding and John Singwell, three of Elizabeth I's servants, were apprehended as they attempted to flee for Spain 'to seek their livings'. 'Their conduct seeming very suspicious', the men were searched, and it was found they had 'neither passport nor licence to pass', and their 'livery coats' had been 'thrust into a fardell'. Perhaps they thought it too risky to bolt it out of the country still wearing the queen's livery. Renouncing their oath to serve her, they had shorn themselves of the physical representation of their ties to their royal mistress.[38]

Some tried to use the power of livery to their advantage. When Anthony Babington's plot was first uncovered in 1586, he urged John Savage to make haste to Elizabeth I and assassinate the queen immediately, yet Savage replied, 'I cannot go tomorrow for my apparel is not ready and, in this apparel, shall I never come near the queen'. In other words, Savage felt he would have been far too conspicuous in the court if he was not properly attired, and seems to suggest that servants wearing livery walked in royal chambers freely and without suspicion.[39] In 1535, the trial of suspected murderers, arrested and held in the castle of Holt, was 'respited and delayed' at the intervention of Henry, Duke of Richmond. Rowland, Bishop of Coventry advised Cromwell to ensure 'some persons that be about my lord of Richmond's grace be not so quick to move his grace to write in such causes'. When the Bishop remarked that it was 'not for his honour to see his badge and livery... worn upon strong thieves backs', it is unclear if he meant that those imprisoned were actually wearing the prince's livery, or if he was using the livery as a metaphor for the protection which cloaked the murderers by their association with him.[40]

It is not difficult to conceive of how, upon being sworn in to the household, servants, like the Tudors, will have urgently besought their silkwomen to ensure that they were properly attired. A book of debts owed by Anne Boleyn at the time of her death in the spring of 1536 indicate that she owed three silkwomen, Curtis, Kelling and Phillips, £5. 19*s*. 4*d*., £1. 2*s*. 10*d*. and 10*s*. 8*d*. respectively, for silk and other materials 'to the use of the said late queen as appears by her bills'.[41] Margery Vaughan also served as a silkwoman to Anne Boleyn. Her husband, Stephen Vaughan, a merchant, had heard that the new queen was in need of a silkwoman to 'prepare, furnish and trim her grace with such things as her grace shall accustom to use and wear', and recommended his wife for the position in a letter to Cromwell: 'You know what she can do. I suppose no woman can better trim her grace'.[42] Margery even 'devised certain works for the Queen her grace, which although she did bring unto her grace to be seen was neither seen nor her good will and humble service known'. Her husband wrote again to Cromwell in the summer of 1533: 'Your pleasure may be to have her in remembrance with her grace, who in her faculty I dare well say can serve her better then any woman in the Realm'.[43] Eventually Margery was appointed as the queen's silkwoman, likely at Cromwell's suit, or perhaps her 'works' were eventually brought to Anne's attention and impressed her. At her death, the queen owed Margery a substantial sum of £68. 4s. 1½d. for 'gold fringe silk and other stuff' provided by her for the queen's Wardrobe.[44] Margery served as a silkwoman to Katherine Parr too, and the cost of her work amounted to £336. 10s. 3d. before her own death in 1544.[45] Her husband complained in 1546 that the queen owed him 'more money than he can well forbear' for 'labour and stuff of his wife's, wherein she spent her life, and has owed it since'.[46] 'I pray you help my reasonable desires', Vaughan wrote to Sir William Paget, the king's secretary, 'that, whilst my wife died and lost her life with painful serving, I be not altogether forgotten'.[47]

Livery worn by servants contributed to the visual and material majesty of the crown. If their households were 'attired unseemly', the royal master or mistress could be judged to be 'of such a mind as the servants are, or at least, too remiss and careless of their government'.[48] Royal magnificence had an intangible, almost spiritual quality. As Sir John Hayward wrote of Elizabeth I at her coronation, she was wise to be

> most royally furnished, both for her person and for her train, knowing right well that in pompous ceremonies a secret government doth much consist, for that the people are naturally both taken and held with exterior shows... the rich attire, the ornaments, the beauty of the Ladies, did add particular graces to the solemnity, and held the eyes and hearts of men dazzled between contentment and admiration.[49]

The Tudors had to be seen, and thus the royal household moved frequently with their master or mistress, chiefly between Whitehall, Greenwich, Hampton Court, Richmond and Nonsuch. Its size often fluctuated with the seasons of the liturgical calendar. Through the autumn, winter and spring, the household was in its full, 'itinerant' form, and in the summer, it could be reduced to a smaller retinue of around one half or less for its 'progress' form, with a 'riding' or 'travelling' group of servants.[50]

On royal progress, the Tudors visited the homes of chief noblemen and women, and sometimes even their own servants, who had the enormous responsibility of entertaining them. When Henry VIII stayed at the Benedictine abbey of Reading in 1518, Richard Pace informed Wolsey that the abbot had made 'good cheer' to the king and 'all his servants' too.[51] On another occasion, Pace informed Wolsey that Henry intended to stay with him at Greenwich 'with a small number of his chamber' and 'without any such persons as should make any provision for him'. 'His pleasure', Pace advised, 'is also that your grace should command such of his Wardrobe as be in London to prepare the house for him, with such his grace's stuff'.[52] In 1552, Edward VI wrote to his servant and friend Barnaby Fitzpatrick in France to inform him of the summer progress in Hampshire, during which he stayed often in the homes of his gentlemen:

> being now almost in the middle of our journey which we have undertaken this summer... to Guildford, from there to Petworth, and so to Cowdray, a goodly house of Sir Anthony Browne's, where we were marvellously, yes rather excessively, banquetted. From there we went to Halnaker, a pretty house besides Chichester. From there we went to Warblington, a fair house of Sir Richard Cotton's, and so to Waltham, a fair great old house, in times past the bishop of Winchester's, and now my lord treasurer's house. In all their places we had both good hunting and good cheer.[53]

News of a forthcoming visit from the sovereign was a cause for much panic in noble households. As Elizabeth I intended in 1567 to visit William More in Guildford, Surrey, it was the responsibility of Anthony Wingfield, the queen's gentleman usher, to ensure that More could host his mistress. Finding More's house 'unmeet', and with but a 'few small rooms', Wingfield advised that the queen stay elsewhere, but as he wrote to More, the queen was 'determined to come unto your house, and for that it shall be a great trouble and a hindrance unto you'. Wingfield urged More to declare this to the Earl of Leicester so 'that her Majesty might not come unto your house'.[54] It was not only the Tudors but all their attendants too who had to be accommodated. 'Here is as much as I have any ways able to do in this house', Simon Bowyer, Elizabeth I's gentleman usher, wrote from Croydon Palace in 1574, having identified rooms for all of queen's household except for her gentleman waiters: 'I cannot as yet find convenient room to place them in, but I will do the best that I can to place them elsewhere'. Evidently there was much to consider in designating lodgings, as, in this instance, Bowyer raised his concerns that the grooms of the Privy Chamber 'have no other way to their chambers but to pass through that way again that my Lady of Oxford should come'.[55]

Whenever the Tudors went further afield, they were accompanied by their servants. In the months prior to the Field of Cloth of Gold, a diplomatic summit which took place in 1520 between England and France, Sir Richard Wingfield, the English ambassador at the court of Francis I, reported that 'great search is made to bring to the meeting the fairest ladies that may be found' to accompany the French queen, remarking that Catherine of Aragon must 'bring such in her band that the visage of England, which hath always had the prize'.[56] Henry VIII 'wrote letters of summons to all such lords, ladies, gentlemen and gentlewomen as he felt should give their attendance on him and the queen'.[57] Dressing the Tudors and their attendants for such occasions required the utmost attention to detail. It was observed that the king's household had to be 'warned to prepare themselves in their best mans apparelled, according to their estates and degrees, to attend upon his grace at this meeting'.[58] The accounts of Elis Hilton, Catherine's yeoman of the robes, reveal that she laid out vast sums on clothes – as much as £710, 3s. 1½d. from April to May 1520 alone – indicating that the queen took care in outfitting her household appropriately, concerning herself with the detail of their attire.[59] Servants were to overawe and impress visitors and other onlookers through extravagance. Catherine's ladies and gentlewomen had approximately two or three months to 'put themselves in a readiness after the most costliest fashion' for the summit, and they did not disappoint. As the chronicler Edward Hall remarked, 'to tell you the apparel of the ladies, their rich attires, their sumptuous jewels, their diversities of beauties... I assure you ten mens' wits can scarce declare it'.[60] Extensive reports by ambassadors in attendance too concentrated on their physical appearance, but these accounts, distorted by their own prejudices or tastes, did not hesitate in their scrutiny. Soardino, the Mantuan ambassador to France, was unlikely to be neutral in observing that Catherine's ladies 'were ornamented in the English fashion, but were not richly clad'. Claude, on the other hand, was 'accompanied by forty ladies of high rank, richly dressed and with jewels'.[61] Whereas the English ladies were described as 'well-dressed but ugly', at a later masque, the French ladies were 'richly attired', all 'dressed in the Italian fashion with velvet caps, round which were feathers'.[62] This contrast is reiterated by an anonymous report, which described Catherine's women as 'handsome and well arrayed', though again, compared them unfavourably with the French ladies, 'all dressed in crimson velvet, their sleeves lined with cloth of gold, a beautiful fashion, which the English is not'.[63] Not all of the attendees were altogether impressed with the attire of the French ladies, Polydore Vergil felt it was 'singularly unfit for the chaste', and regretted that many of the English ladies in attendance had taken up the fashion, 'abandoning for the most part the far more modest costume of their forebears'.[64] It was inevitable that England and France would be measured against one another. Mirroring the rivalry of the kings Henry and Francis, as the ambassador Wingfield had predicted, there was much comparison, even competition, between the queens and their women, with one report stating that they were 'all vying with each other in beauty and ornamented apparel'.[65]

6

'I care not to be groom of the scullery'
ACCESS, INTERACTION AND INTIMACY

All royal residences had a king's side and a queen's side. Their households were established separately, but accommodated in close quarters and occupied physical space, quite literally, under the same roof. In many royal palaces, there was a large passage between the king and the queen's chambers, and if they met, dined or slept together in their respective lodgings, a few of their own attendants would accompany them there.[1] Henry VIII regularly treated his queens' chambers as an extension of his own. Unlike the king's side, however, wherein Henry often transacted affairs of state, the queen's side of the court was a place for him to relax and take solace. John Norris, Henry's gentleman usher, drew up a set of instructions outlining how 'the king and the queen's lodgings shall be made'. Queens consort were to 'have as many chambers as the king has',[2] and 'where the king and the queen be in one house, the king's pleasure is that the queen shall have the fairest and the largest rooms, for the king', Norris observed, 'will always resort unto the queen's chamber for his comfort, pastime, solace and disport'.[3]

It is not difficult to conceive of when or where servants might have had the opportunity to interact with the Tudors. All of the staff of the *domus regis magnificencie*, the household 'above-stairs', had some measure of access, corresponding with the office they held. A useful distinction can be made between the 'outward' chambers, like the Presence and Guard chambers, and the 'inward' chambers, the space 'from the door of the Privy chamber onwards', which constituted the Privy chamber and bedchamber, and any additional rooms, lodgings or galleries built on this side of the palace, where the Tudors retreated and relaxed in private. This distinction is reflected in the architectural layout of many royal palaces. The 'outward' chambers were more often a stage for ceremonial occasions, while the 'inward' chambers were less permeable, with greater seclusion. Virtually all servants 'above-stairs' moved without restriction in the 'outward' chambers, but access to the 'inward' chambers was, at least formally, restricted to servants of the Privy Chamber.[4] Henry VII's ordinances of 1494 stated that the groom of the stool, with a page 'or such as the king will command', was to 'wait in the king's secret chamber specially and no one else'. The Privy Chamber was distinct from the Chamber and staffed with humbler men like Hugh Denys, Richard Weston, James Braybrooke, Piers Barbour, Francis Marzen and William Smith. By 1519, it became more fully developed, and was attended by Henry VIII's 'boon companions', like Sir Francis Bryan, Sir Henry Guildford and Sir Nicholas Carew.[5] In 1538, Thomas Cranmer wrote to Thomas Cromwell on behalf of a man named John Culpeper, for whom he was seeking an appointment to the king's Privy Chamber. Henry, probably reluctant to admit someone he did not know personally so close to him, appointed Culpeper to the Chamber, to serve in the 'outward' chambers as a gentleman waiter, and assured Cranmer that he would 'see for him upon convenient opportunity'. Cranmer asked that, when 'any alteration shall be made within the king's grace's Privy Chamber', Cromwell might push for Culpeper's advancement, promising that he would do the king 'true and faithful service' and be at Cromwell's 'commandment during his life'.[6] The physical proximity of Henry's closest attendants to their sovereign lent itself to a colourful remark made by the ambassador Charles de Marillac in 1541. Upon learning that Katherine Howard was suspected of committing adultery with another Culpeper, Marillac noted that the gentleman 'had been from childhood brought up in the King's chamber, and ordinarily shared his bed, and apparently wished to share the Queen's too'.[7]

Access was carefully controlled, and some attendants had the responsibility of ensuring that no one could approach their royal master or mistress. John Norris would recall that, for Mary I's household, it was ordered 'that no man or woman, of what estate or degree whatsoever they be, shall presume to come into the Privy chamber other than be appointed' or 'called in by her commandment'.[8] When Philip Gerrard, yeoman of the Guard, attempted to present Edward VI with a tract on 'the cruelty of the rich sort', he was intercepted by John Gates, of the king's Privy Chamber.[9] Simon Bowyer, Elizabeth I's gentleman usher, was 'charged by her express command to look precisely to all admissions into the Privy Chamber', to be certain that all those who were let inside had right of *entrée*. He was quite diligent in this duty, so much so that he angered Robert Dudley, Earl of Leicester, when he refused entry to one of his hangers-on who 'was neither well known, nor a sworn servant to the Queen'. Anticipating the Earl's complaint to the queen, the 'bold' but 'well-beloved' Bowyer went to his mistress first and 'fell at her Majesty's feet'. Elizabeth ultimately sided with Bowyer, protecting her servant and ensuring that the regulations of her household were properly enforced. As she warned the Earl, 'my favour is not so locked up for you, that others shall not partake thereof, for I have many servants, unto whom I have, and will at my pleasure bequeath my favour'.[10]

Establishing the measure of access to which servants in office could claim by right is straightforward. More difficult is determining how these servants interacted with their royal master or mistress. All servants had to know their place, acting always with deference. The Eltham ordinances of 1526 declared that servants had to be of 'good towardness, likelihood, behaviour, demeanour', and 'humbly reverent, sober, discreet, and serviceable, in all their doings'.[11] Ordinances for the household of Princess Mary in 1525 instructed the women 'being about her person' to 'use themselves sadly, honourably, virtuously and discreetly in words, countenance, gesture, behaviour and deed with humility, reverence, lowliness, due and requisite, so as of them proceed no manner of example of evil or unfitting manners or conditions, but rather all good and godly behaviour'.[12] Giles Duwes, Mary's tutor, wrote an account of her household in the 1520s in which he imagines her servants adhering strictly to these ordinances, treating her with the utmost reverence. As might be expected, Mary's attendants addressed the princess invariably as 'my lady and mistress', 'right excellent' or 'most sovereign', and, acknowledging her authority, one declared 'there is nothing in my power that I never did for the honour of you'.[13] Such interactions were ritualised, and potentially constrained, by custom and protocol which dictated how far and in what manner, physically, or emotionally, servants could behave.

The Tudors ruled and presided over their own households, commanding their obedience and conformity. If ordinances laid out the rules by which servants were to abide, it remained for the royal master or mistress to uphold and enforce them day-to-day. Lady Margaret Beaufort, grandmother of the Tudor dynasty, was praised by Bishop John Fisher for instituting 'reasonable statutes and ordinances' to govern her attendants and 'lovingly encourage' them to obey. If there was any 'strife', 'controversy', 'factions' or 'bends' within her household, Margaret, Fisher acknowledged, would personally 'bolt it out'.[14] Anne Boleyn's chaplain William Latymer recalled how the queen gave 'careful charge' to her officers, her lord chamberlain and vice-chamberlain, to supervise the rest of her servants and communicate her orders. Her officers 'reprehended divers and sundry persons' for 'their horrible swearing as for their inordinate and dissolute talk, together with their abominable incontinency'. Latymer observed that her lord chamberlain and vice-chamberlain reported to Anne herself: 'finding certain persons incorrigible', they 'denounced their unhonest demeanour to the queen's majesty, who either princely rebuked them or sharply punished, or else utterly exiled them her majesty's court for ever'.[15]

Authority had to be continually practised and constantly legitimated by the Tudors, sometimes through ritual and ceremony, but more often, socially, through their interaction with their servants. The 'good' master or mistress, in the view of Latymer, governed their servants by giving them moral guidance, 'to instruct them the way to virtue and grace, to charge them to abandon and eschew all manner of vice', to 'vigilantly to watch their doings', and to 'suffer no contention amongst them, admit no brawling altercations nor seditious quarrels'.[16] Anne Boleyn herself would, apparently, on occasion, 'call before her in the Privy chamber' her ladies and gentlewomen and 'would many times move them to modesty and chastity'. She 'would give them a long charge of their behaviours', warning them that they 'should not consume time in vain toys and poetical fancies'.[17] The queen gave her maids-of-honour 'a book of prayers' to hang from their girdles for each of them to use as 'a mirror or glass wherein she might learn to address her wandering thoughts'. When Anne learned that Mary Shelton had 'written certain idle poesies', she called her maid before her and 'rebuked her that would permit such wanton toys in her book of prayers'.[18] This view of Anne as the strict and matronly mistress of the household is corroborated by at least two more of the queen's servants. Joan Wilkinson, Anne's silkwoman, would tell John Foxe that 'in all her time she never saw better order amongst the ladies and gentlewomen of the Court, then was in this good Queen's days',[19] whereas Anne Gainsford, her maid, likely informed the account of George Wyatt, who wrote that the queen 'had in court drawn about her, to be attending on her, ladies of great honour, and yet of greater choice for reputation of virtue' whom the queen had 'trained upon with all commendations of well ordered government'.[20]

Ordinances for the Tudor royal household were prescriptive, not descriptive. They could not govern their every word or gesture. Although Giles Duwes recorded the more rigid, reverential culture of a young Princess Mary's household, he also imagined her engaging her attendants in much more casual conversation;[21] likewise

William Latymer concentrated on how Anne Boleyn ruled her attendants, but also alluded to relationships which had greater depth. Servants were not altogether restricted to 'monarch-worshipping' in fear and circumspection. Sometimes the evidence provides an extraordinary, if tantalising view, of how the Tudors might have interacted with their attendants more intimately. In the early years of Henry VIII's reign, his 'boon companions' were charged with 'not regarding his estate nor degree, were so familiar and homely with him, and played such light touches with him that they forgot themselves'.[22] The irreverent Sir Francis Bryan in particular was 'accustomed to speak familiarly to the King'. One man remarked that Bryan would 'dare boldly speak to the King's Grace the plainness of his mind and that his Grace doth well accept the same'.[23] In 1529, Bryan wrote a letter to his master expressing his frustration at being stuck in Rome: 'I could tell Your Grace more of my mind in an hours talking, than I can write in a week.'[24] When Anne Boleyn was served hippocras and other wines at her coronation, she had them 'sent down to her ladies' for them to enjoy, before Anne 'withdrew herself with a few ladies' to relax in her chambers.[25] Mary Woodhull, Katherine Parr's chamberer, shared the queen's bed during her pregnancy, and Mary, Katherine would later recall, 'being abed with me had laid her hand upon my belly to feel it stir'.[26] Likewise Dorothy Broadbelt, Elizabeth I's gentlewoman, was recognised by the Venetian ambassador to be 'so intimate with her Majesty that oftentimes she slept in the same bed with her'.[27]

The evidence, albeit anecdotal and fragmentary, would indicate that the Tudors often spoke candidly with their servants. In 1540, Henry VIII, for instance, muttered his distaste for Anne of Cleves to his nearest attendants. Sir Anthony Browne, master of the horse, recalled that the king confided, 'I see nothing in this woman as men report of her, and I marvel that wise men would make such report as they have done', which left Browne 'abashed'.[28] Sir Thomas Heneage, groom of the stool, heard the king say plainly that he felt he 'had been evil served of them that his Grace had put in trust', that 'he mistrusted her to be no maid, by reason of the looseness of her breasts, and other tokens', and that 'he could have none appetite with her to do as a man should do with his wife, for such displeasant airs as he felt with her'.[29] Henry told Sir Anthony Denny that 'he could not induce himself to have affection for her, for she was not as reported and had her breasts so slack and other parts of her body in such sort, that he suspected her virginity, and that he could never consummate the marriage'.[30] With so much as a word or gesture, the rigid, hierarchical relationship between master, or mistress, and servant, could be broken down or circumvented.

Anne Gainsford, Anne Boleyn's maid-of-honour, would recall that, before her royal mistress married the king, she came upon a book of 'old prophecies' in her chambers, and 'called to her maid': 'Come hither, Nan', 'see here a book of prophecy; this he says is the king, this the queen, mourning, weeping and wringing her hands, and this is myself with my head off.' 'I would not myself marry him', Gainsford said, before her mistress assured her, 'I am resolved to have him whatsoever might become of me.'[31] When Katherine Parr lay on her deathbed in 1548, she confided in her gentlewoman, Elizabeth Tyrwhitt, that 'she did fear such things in herself, that she was sure she could not live'. 'My Lady Tyrwhitt, I am not well handled,' Katherine insisted, 'for those that be about me care not for me, but stand laughing at my grief.' 'I perceived she spoke with good memory,' Tyrwhitt later revealed, 'and very sharply and earnestly, for her mind was unquieted'.[32] It would appear that Elizabeth I felt at ease to joke with her ladies. Katherine, Countess of Huntingdon's husband Henry complained when he had heard that, 'at my wife's last being at court to do her duty, as became her, it pleased her majesty to give her a privy nip [a mocking remark], especially concerning myself, whereby I perceive she has some jealous conceit of me'.[33] In a letter she wrote in 1497 to Thomas, Earl of Ormond, Elizabeth of York's lord chamberlain, Lady Margaret Beaufort betrayed her own sense of humour and the familiarity between them. The Earl had been in France on an embassy, having purchased some gloves for Margaret, who, upon finding them to be much too large to fit her own hands, remarked, 'I think the ladies in that parts be great ladies all, and according to their great estate they have great personages'.[34]

The Tudors inspired friendship and affection too from their attendants, who provided emotional comfort in difficult times. In 1515, Catherine of Aragon remembered that her maid, María de Salinas, whom she loved 'more than any other mortal',[35] had 'always comforted her in her hours of trial'.[36] At Blackfriars in 1529, in the midst of the king's 'Great Matter', Catherine, after making an impassioned speech knelt before the king, 'rose up' and, strikingly, 'took her way straight out of the house, leaning (as she was wont always to do) upon the arm of' Griffith Richards, her receiver-general.[37] When Anne Boleyn suffered a miscarriage in 1536, it was, surprisingly, the queen who 'consoled her maids who wept, telling them it was for the best, because she would be the sooner with child again'.[38] In 1540, when Anne of Cleves heard that her marriage to the king was to be annulled, Thomas, Earl of Rutland, the queen's lord chamberlain, commiserated with her: 'And for that I did see her to take the matter heavily, I desired her to be of good comfort'.[39] When the pressure of transacting state affairs became all too much for the Tudors, their attendants were always at hand. In dealing with the question of sovereignty in the Netherlands in 1575, Elizabeth I became so frustrated that

> she entered her chamber alone, slamming the door after her and crying out that they were ruining her over this business, and those who were there, her ladies-in-waiting and others, were much distressed, saying that if she did not open the door they would burst it open, as they could not bear her to be alone in such trouble.[40]

Similarly, the queen was so 'alarmed' by reports of a Franco-Spanish alliance in 1582 that 'she did not sleep all night', and 'constantly woke' Dorothy, Lady Stafford, 'who sleeps in the same room'. No doubt her gentlewoman attempted to console the queen, whose 'agitation was so terrible that in the morning she was in a high fever'.[41] On another occasion, Thomas, Earl of Sussex urgently recalled Mary, Lady Scudamore to court to attend upon the queen in her bedchamber: 'I fear until you come her Majesty shall not in the night have for the most part so good rest as she will take after your coming'.[42]

Relationships in the Tudor royal household could thus have emotional significance. This is perhaps most clear when these bonds were severed. Elizabeth I 'greatly grieved' the death of her gentlewomen, Kat Ashley, in 1565, and Blanche Parry, in 1590.[43] When Katherine, Lady Knollys, fled England for exile under Mary I, Elizabeth wrote to her with assurances of her devotion: 'Relieve your sorrow for your far journey with joy of your short return… the length of time and distance of place separates not the love of friends'.[44] Elizabeth signed the letter 'cor rotto', or 'broken hearted'. Upon her return, Lady Knollys was appointed to serve Elizabeth in her Privy Chamber. When Knollys fell ill, her husband Sir Francis Knollys became frustrated that the queen would not grant her leave, remarking that, 'for the outward love that her Majesty bears you, she makes you often weep for unkindness to the great danger of your health'.[45] It would seem that Elizabeth could not bear to be separated from her, as Nicholas White reported shortly after Knollys' death:

> From this she returned back again to talk of my Lady Knollys. And after many speeches past to and fro of that gentlewoman, I perceiving her to harp much upon her departure, said that the long absence of her husband… together with the fervency of her fever, did greatly further her end, wanting nothing else that either art of man's help could devise for her recovery, lying in a prince's court near her

person, where every hour her careful ear understood of her estate, and where also she was very often visited by her Majesty's own comfortable presence.[46]

Sir Christopher Hatton, Elizabeth I's vice-chamberlain, lamented the distance he kept from his mistress in 1580 while he was away from court: 'If I wrote how unpleasant and forward a countenance is grown in me through my absence from your most amiable and royal presence, but I dare not presume to trouble your Highness with my not estimable griefs... duty shall do me leave off to cumber your heavenlike eyes with my vain babblings'.[47] Their fondness for one another would not go unnoticed. One hostile observer remarked bitterly in 1571 that Hatton 'had more recourse unto her Majesty in her Privy chamber than reason would suffer if she were so virtuous and well-inclined as some noiseth her'.[48] It is telling that, in 1578, when Elizabeth's physicians were reluctant to advise that they had to extract her tooth to relieve the ache she suffered in it, Lord Burghley enlisted Hatton 'to her ease in this point':

> I heard of her Majesty's indisposition by some pain in her head; and then how can any of her poor members, having life by her as our head, be without pain? If my coming thither might either diminish her pain, or be thought convenient, I would not be absent; although in grief I am present, and do most heartily beseech God to deliver her from all grief, praying you to let me know of her Majesty's amendment: not doubting but you are careful by the physicians to provide the remedy, which is said to be only the withdrawing of some one tooth that is touched with some humorous cause, and, except that be removed, her Majesty's pain shall not quit.[49]

The surviving source material sometimes evokes a sense of closeness between a royal master or mistress and their households, revealing ties which were distinctive of service. Barnaby Fitzpatrick, for instance, was Edward VI's gentleman of the Privy Chamber and the young king's dear friend. Between 1551 and 1552, Fitzpatrick was dispatched to France 'to remain there for a season', and the two of them exchanged letters in his absence.[50] In such letters, master and servant kept each other informed of goings-on at their respective courts. Occasionally they reveal a genuine, affectionate and sometimes humorous tone you might expect to be shared between boyhood companions. The king even laid down a spirited challenge to Fitzpatrick: 'Now shortly we will prove how you have profited in the French tongue,' the king wrote, 'for within a while we will write to you in French.'[51] Fitzpatrick rose to it and began one of his letters in French, though only briefly, 'being loath to trouble your highness any more with my rude and unframed French, I thought good to certify to your highness of the occurrences that be here in English'.[52] Within a year of Fitzpatrick's departure, Edward came to miss his company, and, as he wrote, 'upon consideration of your long absence from us', the king 'thought good to call you home again', to 'repair to our presence with as much haste as conveniently you can make'. He advised Fitzpatrick to request Henry II of France grant him leave 'to visit your friends, declaring that for your part your will at any other time, when he shall have need, with leave of your master, serve him with all you can make'.[53]

Publicly, interactions between the Tudors and their servants necessarily met set expectations and conventions. Privately, they could interact in ways more relaxed, personal and intimate. The development of the Privy Chamber in the 1490s created an atmosphere which encouraged familiarity and the forming of close bonds. All Privy Chamber servants had to be circumspect and discreet. 'All such persons as be appointed of the Privy chamber' were explicitly sworn to 'keeping secret all such things as shall be done or said in the same, without disclosing any part thereof to any person not being for the time present in the said chamber'.[54] This meant that the Tudors could conduct their own affairs in private. Some time in around 1529, when Wolsey went to Bridewell to visit Catherine of Aragon, he, 'being in the chamber of presence', waited until the queen 'came out of her Privy chamber'. 'If it please you,' the cardinal advised Catherine, 'to go into your Privy chamber, we will show you the cause of our coming', to which the queen replied, 'my lord, if you have any thing to say, speak it openly'. The ensuing conversation was recorded in detail by George Cavendish, Wolsey's servant, until Catherine took the cardinal 'by the hand and led him into her Privy chamber', where they 'were in long communication', during which Cavendish remained 'in the other chamber'. There Cavendish and the rest of the court 'might sometime hear the queen speak very loud, but what it was we could not understand'.[55]

The staff of the Privy Chamber were responsible for maintaining the privacy of the Tudors. Yet, there were cracks, as these servants could later recall private interactions that they had with their royal master or mistress. John Fowler, groom of the Privy Chamber, remembered a conversation he had with Edward VI in 1548, instigated by Thomas, Lord Seymour, who wished to obtain the young king's consent to marry Katherine Parr, queen dowager. As Fowler later testified:

> That night, his highness being alone, I said to his majesty, "And please your grace, I marvel my lord admiral marries not." His highness saying nothing to it, I said again, "Could your grace be contented he should marry?" His grace said, Yes, very well. Then I asked his majesty whom his grace would he should marry? His highness said, My lady Anne of Cleves; and so, pausing a while, said after, Nay, nay, what you what? I would he married my sister Mary, to turn her opinions. His highness went his ways, and said no more that time.[56]

When Fowler related this to Thomas, he laughed, and asked, 'I pray you, Mr. Fowler, if I may soon, ask his grace if he could be contented I should marry the Queen'.[57] In 1540, Anne of Cleves would confide in Eleanor, Countess of Rutland, Jane, Lady Rochford, and Katherine, Lady Edgecombe, of her Privy Chamber, all of whom later journeyed from Richmond to Westminster and swore to a deposition relating their conversation with the queen. Anne's servants maintained that the queen herself admitted to them one night the truth of the king's contention that the royal marriage had not been consummated:

> First, all they being together, they wished her Grace with child. And she answered and said, She knew well she was not with child. My Lady Edgecombe said, How is it possible for your Grace to know that, and lie every night with the King? I know it well I am not, said she. Then said my Lady Edgecombe, I think your Grace is a maid still. With that she laughed. And then said my Lady Rochford, By our Lady, Madam, I think your Grace is a maid still, indeed. How can I be a maid, said she, and sleep every night with the King? There must be more than that, said my Lady Rochford, or else I had as leave the King lay further. Why, said she, when he comes to bed he kisses me, and takes me by the hand, and bids me, Good night, sweet heart: and in the morning kisses me, and bids me, Farewell, darling. Is not this enough? Then said my Lady Rutland, Madam, there must be more than this, or it will be long or we have a Duke of York, which all this realm most desires.[58]

This deposition, supporting the claim that Henry and Anne had not consummated the marriage, would secure for the king the annulment he desired. It is almost incredible that Anne would have spoken so openly with these ladies, having met them only six months prior. Perhaps she was pleading ignorance to avoid the intrusive nature of their questions, or she was caught off-guard in the supposed intimacy of the Privy chamber.

The more intimate servants of the Privy Chamber saw the Tudors at their most relaxed, and their most vulnerable. Throughout her reign, Elizabeth I became increasingly anxious, lonely and distant. As one man observed, she 'frowns on all her ladies', and 'constantly paced the Privy chamber, stamping her feet at bad news and thrusting her rusty sword at times into the arras in great rage'.[59] The queen must have been considerably more difficult to serve when her moods became quite unpredictable. In her later years, Elizabeth was 'more forward than commonly she used to bear herself toward her women', and her temperament could be so short 'as to make these fair maids often cry and bewail in piteous sort'.[60] Another report noted that the queen was 'ill-tempered' and 'rudely scolds all the ladies and others in the Chamber'.[61] Mary I's closest attendants were likely the source of stories which circulated in 1556 reporting that the queen, frustrated at Philip's long absences from court, began 'complaining to the picture of the king's image in her Privy chamber', before taking the portrait and kicking it out of sight.[62] Near-contemporary accounts which relate from memory entire conversations from their innermost chambers might be viewed with some suspicion. Nevertheless, they illustrate the manner in which the Tudors conceivably interacted with their attendants. During her 'phantom' pregnancy in early 1555, Mary withdrew, as was customary, with her female attendants. One account described them as 'parasites' for assuring Mary that she was with child, 'insomuch as the Queen was fully so persuaded herself being right desirous thereof'. One exception was Frideswide Knight Strelley, of the queen's Privy Chamber, who had fallen out of favour when she expressed her doubts as to Mary's pregnancy. The queen 'bid her take a towel that lay there by and warm it at the fire and lay it upon my belly', which Strelley, 'kneeling down', did, before her mistress asked her, 'how now feel you not the child stir?' 'And it shall your Grace', Strelley replied astutely, knowing she could only go so far to shatter the illusion without breaking the heart of her mistress. Strelley left court, but was soon recalled, and to her Mary sighed, 'Ah, Strelley, Strelley, I see they be all flatterers, and none true to me but thou'.[63]

Office-holding merely laid the foundation for a career in service. 'Nearness', and intimacy, was crucial for advancement. 'You see what it is to serve out of the King's Majesty's sight', Stephen Vaughan once moaned, having frequently been sent out of London on errands for Henry VIII.[64] 'When his Grace is disposed to give gifts and rewards to his true servants, as I suppose that he is now', one man advised in 1537, 'the presence and sight of a man in the sight of his prince that is in his Grace's favour is much worth'.[65] In that same year, Ralph Sadler sent word to the king that his own servant was 'not well at ease' and 'very sick' from an unknown disease. Much to Sadler's 'great regret and discomfort', Henry seemed to suspect that he was merely making excuses not to attend upon him, and Sadler thus urged Cromwell that, being 'compelled to be so long from the Court as I was lately, unless your lordship be good lord unto me it would much hinder me'.[66] Sadler feared that if he were kept from the king and his favour much longer he would 'never be able to recover it'.[67] In 1552, Roger Ascham recalled that, some years earlier, he was summoned to Prince Edward's chamber to teach the young boy how to write, 'at which times his Grace would oft most gently promise me one day to do me good, and I would say, 'Nay, your Majesty will soon forget me when I shall be absent from you', which thing he said he would never do'. 'I do not mistrust these words because their were spoken of a child', Ascham later remarked to Sir William Cecil, 'but rather I have laid up my sure hope in them because they were uttered by a King'.[68] In 1597, Sir William Cornwallis pursued an appointment as Elizabeth I's groom porter: 'She would not make me one of her Council, yet if she will one of her Court, by this means I may have a poor chamber in Court, and a fire, and a title to bring a pair of cards into the Privy chamber, at 10 o'clock at night'. It was over such a game of cards that master and servant became more familiar with each others lives and needs. Cornwallis' next remark is rather telling on the distinction of serving 'above-stairs', nearer to the queen, rather than 'below-stairs': 'So that I may be about Her Majesty, I care not to be groom of the scullery.'[69]

The title and position held by servants conferred status, measured authority, and denoted rank and precedence in the hierarchy of the Tudor royal household. But this order was inevitably circumvented by the Tudors themselves, and those to whom they did, or did not, grant access, and those in whom they did, or did not, trust. Undoubtedly, trust was the most important prerequisite to service. It is no coincidence that the most ubiquitous descriptor of servants in the Tudor period is 'trusty and well-beloved'. Upon Edward VI's succession in 1547, Sir Anthony Denny was judged to be 'the most confidential of any of the gentlemen of the chamber'.[70] Susan Clarencius, Mary I's gentlewoman, was distinguished in 1553 by visiting ambassadors as one of the attendants 'whom she trusts'.[71] The mother of Bridget Manners, maid-of-honour to Elizabeth I, was reassured in 1592 that her daughter was 'in very great favour with her Majesty and is employed with the nearest service about her, for she carves at all times and is no way at commandment but by her Majesty'.[72]

It would appear that Manners heeded the advice she received when she was first appointed in 1589, serving the queen 'with all meekness, love and obedience', and remaining 'secret and faithful' to her.[73]

Access could be measured both physically, in terms of proximity, and emotionally, or psychologically, in how far servants were privy to the innermost thoughts and feelings of their royal master or mistress. In this the Tudors had to exercise great caution. Margaret, queen of Scots, advised her brother Henry VIII in 1523 that he may write to her jms'secretly' by her 'trusty and true servant', Patrick Sinclair, 'but not with the other'.[74] She dared not to have written 'so plainly' if Sinclair had not been the bearer.[75] At this time, Margaret was quietly cooperating with her brother to see John, Duke of Albany, ousted as regent of Scotland. Fearing that her intentions had been uncovered, she begged Henry for leave to come to England. 'Let me come into that realm with my true servants, for I will come away and I should steal out of it', Margaret wrote to the Earl, stressing 'what you will do in to this in all haste with this bearer Patrick Sinclair, for I dare not trust to no other and he will make great diligence, praying you to be good lord to him for my sake, and to do for him when he desire you in his need'.[76] Clearly Margaret judged that she and others could confide in her servant. 'I pray you my lord to send me your mind with Patrick Sinclair', the queen wrote to Thomas, Earl of Surrey.[77] She wrote to Sinclair too, rather more candidly, urging him to be wise, as she felt they were both at risk.[78] In another letter, the queen thanked him for the 'great pain and travel that you take for my sake and the great danger that you put you in'.[79] The following year, however, Henry Stuart, Margaret's new treasurer and her future husband, came between Sinclair and his royal mistress. As the Earl, now Duke of Norfolk, wrote in 1524, after dispatching Sinclair with his most recent report,

> supposing that she had trusted the said Patrick as much as any man, for by him she advertised me at all times of her mind, but now since that time I have since heard that Henry Stuart and the said Patrick fell at variance, so that whatsoever the said Patrick does or says cannot content nor please... to please the said Henry she made a quarrel to the said Patrick that he brought her not a letter from which I wrote to her the same night after his departure, and sat till midnight for the same.[80]

Evidently, trust did not always endure. By 1525, Thomas Magnus, the English ambassador residing in Scotland, reported that some of Margaret's servants had been 'discharged from the presence of her grace, only upon suspicion that they should disclose unto me some part of her secrets'.[81] Magnus would also report that Patrick Sinclair was 'of good honesty having many friends and kinsfolk most specially have resorted unto me, and have kept me company continually', even at the risk of incurring the 'displeasure of the queen's grace in her time'.[82] Many years later, Margaret remained cautious. She wrote to her brother in 1536 asking that he send a 'secret servant to whom she may show her mind', and, acknowledging her request, he sent Thomas Holcroft, sewer of the Chamber, to hear her.[83]

Some servants were trusted more than others. Disrupting the institutional hierarchy of the household, the Tudors often cultivated their own 'inner circle'. Katherine Howard's affair in 1541 with Thomas Culpeper, gentleman of the king's Privy Chamber, reveals how the Tudors might judge and discern in their servants who they could, and who they could not, trust. When Culpeper was arrested and interrogated by the king's council, he recalled how the queen had initially sent for him by Henry Webbe, her gentleman usher, to the entry between her Presence and Privy chambers. Here Katherine 'gave him by her own hands a fair cap of velvet garnished with a brooch and three dozen pairs of aglets and a chain'. 'Put this under your cloak', Katherine warned him, '[and let] nobody see it!' 'Alas, Madam,' Culpeper sighed, 'why did not you this when you were a maid?'[84] She could not have been unaware of how her actions might be misconstrued by others: why else did she exhort him to conceal her gift under his cloak? Later when Culpeper had fallen ill, Katherine became anxious to see or hear from him,[85] but she could hardly visit him herself without arousing suspicion. She dispatched Morris, her page, with food to aid his recovery.[86] This may be the same 'poor fellow' who she sent thereafter with a letter to Culpeper: 'one of the griefs that I do feel,' the queen wrote, 'to depart from him for that I do know no one that I dare trust to send to you'. Clearly Katherine had considered which of her servants could be trusted to undertake this sensitive, if otherwise menial task. 'I pray you take him to be with you', the queen urged, 'that I may sometime hear from you', before advising Culpeper that he 'instruct my man to tarry here with me still, for he says whatsoever you bid him he will do it'.[87] In her letter to Culpeper, Katherine solicited him to 'come when my Lady Rochford is here, for then I shall be best at leisure to be at your commandment.' Jane, Lady Rochford, was retained by Katherine in her Privy Chamber 'to contrive meetings in the queen's stool chamber and other suspect places'.[88] The surviving depositions of the accused and of eyewitnesses illustrate the depths of trust that could be placed in a servant. It was Jane who 'moved her for him',[89] and it was Jane who sent word to and received Culpeper in the queen's chambers.[90] Jane chaperoned them on at least three occasions at Lincoln, one of them until 'three of the clock in the morning or thereabout',[91] and 'every night' at Pontefract, 'the queen being in her bedchamber having no other with her but my Lady Rochford'.[92] At York, Jane even accommodated them in her own bedchamber.[93] Jane 'would at every lodging search the back doors and tell her of them if there were any', and even had one of her own servants 'watch the door one night and the next to see if any of the watch or any other went in or out'. She carried and exchanged letters, gifts and tokens between them, and even advised the queen to 'give men leave to look for they will look upon you'.[94] Jane warned the queen that 'if you confess you undo both yourself and others', though it was she who later provided the king's council with their most incriminating evidence, in admitting that 'she thinks that Culpeper has known the Queen carnally, considering all things that she has heard and seen between them'.[95] Katherine even restricted access to her bedchamber to Jane, and explicitly forbade the attendance therein of the rest of her servants. Jane was not merely Katherine's confidante. In the words of one of her chamberers, 'my Lady Rochford was the principal occasion of the queen's folly'.[96]

All of the Tudors had their favourites, and this favouritism often created tensions within the household. In the midst of Katherine's affair with Culpeper, Lady Rochford was her confidante, but her ascendancy in the queen's affections provoked the jealousy of those less fortunate servants who did not share in her mind and favour. When Margaret Morton and Maude Lovekyn, the queen's chamberers, defied her orders not to come into her bedchamber unless they were called, Katherine angrily threatened to 'put them away' for their insolence. Morton grumbled that, if she and Lovekyn were, in fact, discharged from the queen's household, then Katherine would have 'taken other of my Lady Rochford's putting'.[97] So intimate and secure was Lady Rochford in Katherine's favour that, it was felt, at least by Morton, she exercised undue power over the queen, and her Privy Chamber, to her own advantage.

The Tudors could not advance all of their servants equally. Nor could their favour be distributed evenly or fairly. When Katherine appointed Francis Dereham, an old acquaintance, the queen 'had him in notable favour above others', and 'gave him divers gifts and sums of money'.[98] Inevitably, favour led to favouritism, leading to accusations of corruption. This was escalated by Dereham himself, who felt that 'men despised him because they perceived that the queen favoured him'.[99] An incident occurred one evening at supper in the queen's chambers. Dereham was sat at the table 'after all other were risen', the custom being that strictly the queen's council were to remain after supper. Henry Johns, Katherine's gentleman usher, sent a messenger to take Dereham away, who retorted, 'go to Mr. Johns and tell him I was of the queen's council before he knew her and shall be when she has forgotten him'.[100]

Rivalry, competition and conflict was rife, as patrons and clients alike vied for advantage. Serving in Edward VI's Privy Chamber, Nicholas Throckmorton boasted of the 'great favour' in which he was held by the boy king. So secure was Throckmorton that he regarded himself singularly as 'the King's familiar' and was thus 'devoid of care'. 'In childish cradle of security,' Throckmorton wrote, 'I rocked myself asleep'. He also recalled that the king 'would jest' with him 'most merrily'. The 'special grace' in which he was kept above all others apparently led to 'false reports' against him and resentment from within the household. He made an enemy of John, Duke of Northumberland, who, Throckmorton knew, 'much misliked our secret conference', and 'the privy whisperings that the King did use'.[101] Robert Rochester, Mary I's comptroller, lamented in 1553 that 'that the Queen did not speak to him of her affairs as familiarly as she once used'. He had apparently fallen out of favour, probably for being a little too overbearing in promoting a match for his mistress with Edward Courtenay, Earl of Devon, when she preferred a matrimonial alliance with Philip of Spain. To air his grievances, Rochester visited Simon Renard, the Imperial ambassador, 'twice in three days'. 'Speaking for himself', Rochester felt that 'he had served the Queen long and faithfully, and he could do more in her service in every way than those whom she now trusted'. As the ambassador observed, Rochester was now 'eager to prove his duty and devotion to the Queen', and was particularly anxious to know if his mistress had ever spoken of him. Above all, Rochester resented the influence of the 'energetic' and 'capable' Sir William Paget. He claimed that 'many regretted to see that Paget had the Queen's ear', though the ambassador paid little heed to this, disregarding Rochester as being merely 'jealous' of the councillor.[102]

Servants sometimes forged meaningful, lasting friendships while in office. In 1535, Thomas Broke, Henry VIII's yeoman usher, asked Thomas Cromwell to 'recommend' him to his 'fellows and friends of the Privy Chamber', and 'especially' to Henry Norris, Thomas Heneage, John Russell, Richard Long and Peter Mewtas, as well as Edward Baynton, William Coffin and John Uvedale on the queen's side of the court. 'I humbly desire you', Broke wrote, 'to thank them for the great kindness that they showed unto me'.[103] Later that same year Broke urged Cromwell again 'in most heartily saluting my friends and fellows of the Privy Chamber in my name'.[104] There does appear to have been a sense of fraternity in the king's Privy Chamber in particular. Each gentleman had 'his brethren',[105] and like Broke, during their absences from court wished to be remembered by their 'good friends and fellows of the Privy Chamber'.[106] Sir Thomas Darcy, for instance, addressed John Gates in one letter in 1545 as 'my very loving friend', and signed off 'desiring you to make my commendations' to Thomas Heneage and Anthony Denny 'with all the rest of my fellows'.[107]

Tudor royal households were not always so harmonious. The same John Gates, Henry VIII's groom, charged John Holland, yeoman usher, with the death of his brother in 1533. The accusation was not taken lightly, and the king commissioned his Privy Chamber to investigate and resolve the matter between them.[108] In 1536, Margaret Bryan, Princess Elizabeth's governess, complained to Cromwell that Sir John Shelton 'says he is master of this house'. 'What fashion that shall be, I cannot tell', Bryan sniped, 'for I have not seen it before'. As far as Bryan was concerned, she was to 'have the rule of' Elizabeth's household, but she anticipated that Shelton would 'not be content' to concede to her authority. Their infighting, Bryan claimed, was preventing the household from being 'honourably ordered', and thus she urged Cromwell to intervene.[109] Petty arguments and power struggles often gave rise to tensions between servants. Shortly before Philip II of Spain married Mary I in 1554, a new household was appointed for the consort staffed with a number of English noble and genteel men, leaving the Spanish attendants who came with him frustrated and 'confused'. One Spanish gentleman remarked, 'we all wander around like vagabonds being unneeded', while another observed that 'if any of us wants to lend a hand in something, they take it ill and do not wish to allow it'; another grumbled plainly that the English attendants 'did not wish to let us serve'.[110] Once the king had settled in, a reversal of fortunes occurred, as his Spanish attendants eventually came to serve in the Privy Chamber, while the English were effectively barred from accessing the king.[111] Sir Thomas Radcliffe for one moaned that his ability to speak Spanish was regressing, as he had so little interaction with his master.[112] These jealousies eventually erupted, and quite violently too, as it was briefly reported that there were 'daily stabbings in the palace between Englishmen and Spaniards', which resulted in a number of fatalities before a special commission was set up to investigate and punish such offences within the households of both the queen and her consort.[113]

7

'Now here comes in the cogging of this place'
GOVERNMENT, POLITICS AND PATRONAGE

Sovereign kings and queens often conducted affairs of government and high politics in their chambers, and their most intimate attendants became convenient agents, for instance, in obtaining their signature. They could carry and present documents to their royal master or mistress and, more importantly, knew *when* to submit them. Cardinal Wolsey would sometimes convey letters to Henry VIII through William Compton, groom of the stool, 'to get them signed of the King's grace'. On at least one occasion in 1528, he entrusted Henry Norris, Compton's successor, with a letter 'to have it to the King, then being set at supper'.[1] Thomas Cromwell was well-acquainted with Thomas Heneage for the same purpose. Heneage wrote to Cromwell in the autumn of 1539 to advise him that Henry had taken to his bed 'grugging' with a cold, but assured the secretary that, 'as for your bills, I shall as soon as his grace has signed them to see them conveyed to you'.[2] Clearly Henry was in no mood to be approached, and thus Heneage waited patiently.[3] A few days later, the king was 'in as good temper and prosperous health as ever his grace was', and Heneage reported to Cromwell that he had now 'procured his grace to sign your three bills'.[4] Elizabeth I's gentlewomen would fulfil the same role, if not necessarily by carrying the documents themselves (although they may have done so on occasion) then by advising courtiers and councillors when to broach their business with the queen. As Robert Beale, clerk of the Privy Council, urged in 1592: 'Learn, before your access, her majesty's disposition by some in the Privy chamber with whom you must keep credit, for that will stand you in much stead'.[5]

Servants worked in cooperation with councillors and ministers to gauge the moods of, raise certain topics and direct conversation with their royal master or mistress. Robert Beale's widow, Edith, later informed Sir William Cecil that she had one such patron at court in Mary, Lady Scudamore: 'I find all willingness to do me any good that she may... if it may please your honour that with your good liking she may remember me unto her majesty at some convenient time, when your honour shall be present'.[6] From 1547 to 1549, Thomas, Lord Seymour, regularly communicated with Edward VI through Sir Thomas Wroth and John Fowler, of the king's Privy Chamber, and John Cheke, Edward's tutor, to 'break with the King' on certain agendas, and put the king 'in remembrance of him'.[7] Servants were in a position to know when the Tudors were in good humour, and how and when they might be solicited for their favour. One of Elizabeth I's ladies, Elizabeth, Lady Clinton, for instance, advised her kinswoman, Mary, Countess of Southampton, to wait before approaching her mistress because of 'how unprepared the queen's Majesty' was 'as yet to receive suit'.[8]

Although it was the Privy Council who were responsible for transacting matters of state, it was not unheard of for kings and queens to take the counsel of their servants. In 1553, it was recognised that Mary I's attendants were able to influence the queen, particularly on the issue of her prospective marriage. Her gentlewomen, Susan Clarencius and Frideswide Knight-Strelley, favoured Philip of Spain as a fit suitor.[9] Philip knew well that these attendants were in the queen's ear, and arranged for 'sundry jewels' to be bestowed 'of the ladies in the Court to further the marriage'.[10] The Imperial ambassador Simon Renard advised the Emperor that 'something must be given to Clarencius, another lady-in-waiting and two women who have been faithful and discreet and have always been present when I have negotiated with the Queen'.[11] Others in Mary's household, like Sir Robert Rochester, Sir Edward Waldegrave and Sir Francis Englefield, sided with Stephen Gardiner, Bishop of Winchester, and recommended Edward Courtenay, Earl of Devon as her suitor. They advised the queen that a match with Courtenay 'would be most welcome to the people, for no foreigner had ever before been king of the country, and the very name of stranger was odious, whilst Courtenay was well-born, of good conduct and virtuous'. Mary received them well, and as Renard noted, 'she would do well to give some thought to their advice, which was dictated by whole-hearted affection and devotion to her service, for they had emboldened themselves to speak in the knowledge that they were her oldest servants'.[12] Renard himself judged Courtenay to be 'proud, poor obstinate, inexperienced and vindictive in the extreme', but acknowledged that it was wise for Mary to 'conciliate' Rochester 'and her other old servants, and give them some share in the negotiations'.[13] Mary Kempe-Finch, one of the queen's gentlewomen, also appears to have been opposed to a Spanish match. During a 'familiar talk', the queen asked her 'whether she thought in her conscience between them two that the match was meet', to which she replied 'plainly she might say to her she thought not and that she saw no great joy that the Queen was like to have of it'. 'Yet', her gentlewoman continued, 'such is her affection as I fear me we may have cause to rue for her sake'.[14] Mary 'held her own' against the pressures of her officers in the marriage question. Ultimately it was her decision to make, and she expected all of her attendants to fall in line, with no tolerance for those who 'opposed her will in so important a matter, thus affording others a bad example, and warning them that if they abused her goodness and clemency she would be forced to display her authority, disinclined to do so as she was'.[15]

How far servants were able to participate in high politics was dictated by their royal master or mistress. Elizabeth I was apparently resolved not to engage her ladies and gentlewomen in this capacity, 'commanding them never to speak to her on business affairs'.[16] Certainly these women would facilitate, on the queen's behalf, news and information where it concerned her prospective marriage and the succession, but not without risk of punishment. In 1562, Kat Ashley and Dorothy Broadbelt wrote to the Swedish chancellor, Gyllenstierna, encouraging a match between the queen and Erik of Sweden. Unfortunately, William Cecil managed to seize the letters. Upon learning of their interference, the queen was enraged, regarding them as 'idle cheats'. It was reported that Ashley and Broadbelt, who 'were formerly in high favour with the Queen', had been committed to the Tower.[17] Within a month, they were restored to their former position, indicating that, amidst rumours about her relationship with Robert Dudley, Earl of Leicester, Elizabeth was using her women and the potential of a Swedish match to deflect attention.[18] In no sense were women at court apolitical. Sir Walter Raleigh once remarked that they were 'capable of doing great harm but no good'. Dudley complained in 1569 that the Duke of Norfolk's intentions to marry Mary, queen of Scots had been disclosed to Elizabeth by 'some babbling women' who, Dudley informed the Duke, 'made her highness believe that you and we should seem to enterprise to go through without making her majesty privy, and that the matter was already concluded'.[19]

Servants functioned as an extension of the will of the Tudors, embodying their authority and status. When Henry, Earl of Northumberland and others of Henry VIII's council were sent to arrest Wolsey, the cardinal refused to submit until he had seen their commission. But when Wolsey caught sight of Walter Walsh lurking in the shadows, he turned to him and said, 'I am content to yield unto you... you are a sufficient commission yourself... in as much as you be one of the king's Privy Chamber, for the worst person there, is a sufficient warrant to arrest the greatest peer of this realm, by the king's commandment only, without any commission'.[20] As a groom of the king's Privy Chamber, Walsh was felt by Wolsey to, metaphorically, hold the power, or presence, of Henry himself. This is perhaps why, in 1521, when Edward, Duke of Buckingham was accused of high treason, Henry dispatched Sir William Compton, groom of the stool, with Sir Richard Weston and Sir William Kingston, knights of the body. Accompanied further by two of the king's sergeants-at-arms, they took with them 'secret power' to arrest the Duke, and were advised that they must 'take heed that when the Duke had received the king's letters he should not convey himself, which they wisely accomplished'.[21]

Orders were often communicated by the Tudors through their servants, who were highly respected, even feared. In 1541, the Privy Council sent an unnamed groom of Henry VIII's household to escort a thief to London for trial. This thief was a merchant who had stolen from Charles de Marillac, the French ambassador residing in England, and in consideration of Marillac's 'degree and place', the council deemed it appropriate to send one of the king's own servants to investigate the matter.[22] At the fall of the Duke of Norfolk in 1546, Sir Richard Southwell, John Gates and Wymond Carew, of the king's Privy Chamber, were sent to search his house thoroughly, empty his coffers, ransack the closet, inventory his goods, and take charge of 'his writings and books'.[23] They were also to break the news of the Duke's disgrace to his daughter Mary, Duchess of Richmond, and his mistress Elizabeth Holland. They later informed Henry that the Duchess was 'sore perplexed, trembling and like to fall down', before she 'reverently upon her knees' did 'humble herself in all unto your highness', as if the king himself was there, represented by proxy in his gentlemen.

Servants were particularly useful for governing in the localities. In 1539, Sir Francis Bryan, of the king's Privy Chamber, searched the house of a man suspected of 'counterfeiting a penny of twopence' for 'such manner of tools as were necessary for that feat, whereas nothing was found'. Bryan advised Cromwell that to arrest the 'poor man' would be to his 'utter undoing', and a 'great pity if in this matter he were found without fault'.[24] Sir Thomas Heneage, groom of the stool, was sent to the Privy Council in 1546 to declare 'the King's respite' for a man 'lately condemned in Suffolk for robbery of a church'.[25] Elizabeth I's messenger, Cole, was in 1586 sent to Holborn to search the houses of 'suspected persons' for 'popish relics'; in one house he found 'three sprigs of palm with crosses bound on them', and in another, much to his surprise, 'three Irishmen all in one bed'.[26] A decade later, William Killigrew, Elizabeth's groom, was sent to Plymouth to survey the 'great riches' and 'prizes' which had been taken from Spain.[27] Central to the process of governing the kingdom was empowering servants to wield status, accumulate wealth, and perform administrative and judicial duties at a local and regional level. Placing members of the household in local offices ensured supervision from crown to county. Cardinal Wolsey advised the king in 1519 to 'put himself in strength with his most trusty servants in every shire for the surety of his royal person and succession'.[28] In that same year, the names of several hundred of the king's servants 'in all the shires' were recorded and identified, among them gentlemen ushers, sewers, cupbearers, carvers and grooms of the Chamber and Privy Chamber.[29] Even if not all of these men would have attended upon the king personally, it was in the interests of the crown to swear them as his servants and bind them as agents in the provinces. Strategically, granting servants land, and appointing them as stewards and constables enabled them to settle disputes and enforce law, order and justice. William Brereton, of the king's Privy Chamber, held so many offices in Cheshire that he was described as having 'all the whole rule and governance under our sovereign lord the king's grace'.[30] As many such men were, in fact, required to attend upon their royal master or mistress, they often had to govern from a distance, as is seen when Sir Richard Guildford, Henry VII's servant advised his 'good neighbours' in one local matter requiring his attention that he 'shall see thereto that it shall be done as reason is at my next coming down'.[31] In 1552, Edward VI absolved Sir Richard Blount of his responsibility as collector of customs at the port of Southampton so that he could serve him undistracted and uninhibited in his Privy chamber instead.[32] Albeit lucrative, these additional responsibilities could be burdensome, and difficult to balance with their personal lives. Margaret Thymulby, the wife of Richard Thymulby, Henry VII's gentleman usher, hastily wrote to the king in 1488 to excuse her husband from his recent appointment as sheriff of county Lincoln. Unaware of his new promotion, Richard had already set off on 'certain pilgrimages which he long afore that time had promised', and his wife was left to plead with the king to discharge him.[33]

Men and women serving the Tudors were conscious of the status and dignity accorded to their position. Nicholas Cowley, for instance, warned in 1537 that, as he was Henry VIII's yeoman of the Guard, no man 'should meddle with him'.[34] A few years earlier, James Billingford pretended to be Anne Boleyn's chaplain to extort money from abbeys and priories in Warwickshire, Oxfordshire and Northamptonshire. Billingford was able to take various sums of money, and their horses, even making threats to punish and depose those who did not comply with his demands, 'to the great dishonour and slander of the queen's grace'.[35] A witness to Billingford's extortion later recalled how the 'crafty witted fellow' inferred that he knew the queen personally, and so 'to take care how I meddled with him'. Similarly in 1592, one John Goymer, 'a lewd fellow', claimed to be Elizabeth I's messenger, travelling through the kingdom having 'unlawfully vexed' many of the queen's subjects by extorting 'diverse sums of money from them'.[36]

Servants could be accused of exercising undue influence in government affairs, which were not strictly within their remit. Some felt that attendants in the household of Edward VI manipulated their master. By 1549, Sir Thomas Seymour, the king's uncle, deeply resented the 'governance' that Edward, Duke of Somerset had over the boy king, which, Seymour alleged, was maintained through the close attendance of Sir Michael Stanhope and Sir Richard Page, gentlemen of the Privy Chamber.[37] Somerset's successor, John, Duke of Northumberland, too made strategic appointments to the king's household. His son-in-law, Sir Henry Sidney, had apparently 'acquired so great an influence near the King that he was able to make all of his notions conform to those of the Duke'. Another of Northumberland's agents, Sir John Gates, was known as 'the principal instrument which he used in order to induce the King to something when he did not want it to be known that it had proceeded from himself'. 'All of the others who were in the Chamber', it was observed, were 'creatures of the Duke'.[38] This led to the charge that Edward's ideas, words and actions had been 'rather stirred up in him by gentlemen of his Privy Chamber than grown in himself'.[39] The young king became so frustrated by all this that, one day in 1551, he apparently 'plucked a falcon, which he kept in his private chamber, and tore it into four pieces, saying as he did so to his governors that he likened himself to the falcon, whom every one plucked; but that he would pluck them too, thereafter, and tear them in four parts'.[40]

Nor were concerns about undue power restricted to the households of sovereign kings and queens. When Mary Tudor, Henry VIII's sister, married Louis XII of France in 1514, most of her servants were abruptly discharged by her new husband. 'On the morn next after our marriage', Mary wrote, 'my chamberlain, with all other men servants, were discharged, and in like wise my mother Guildford, with other my women and maidens, except such as never had experience nor knowledge how to advertise or give me counsel in any time of need'.[41] The queen took action especially on behalf of Joan, Lady Guildford, to 'find the means to have her sent back'. She wrote to her brother and to Wolsey of her abject 'discomfort': 'I humbly require you to cause my said mother Guildford to repair hither once again'.[42] Wolsey intervened with Louis, but the king refused to have her reinstated.[43] 'He would not have her about his wife', Wolsey was informed, as 'she began to take upon her not only to rule the queen but also that she should not come to him but she should be with her, nor that no lady nor lord should speak with her but she should hear it, and began to set a murmur and banding amongst ladies of the court'.[44] The king 'has set about her neither lady nor gentlewoman to be with her for her mastery but her servants and to obey her commandments'. Upon hearing the extent of her misbehaviour, Henry was 'pleased that she shall not return' to the French court, and Lady Guildford was forced to retire to England.[45]

Be it polite but opportune exchanges with the Tudors, or hushed, self-seeking whispers in their ear leading to their own advancement, where servants truly thrived was in the politics of patronage. The process by which such politics were conducted, however, is not always transparent. Presumably once state affairs had been transacted, and their domestic duties had been fulfilled, servants presented their own petitions. Servants were often engaged, for instance, in securing pardons from the sovereign. As Henry VII's lord chamberlain, Giles, Lord Daubeney, for instance, would have had ample opportunity in 1495 to make 'instant and assiduous labour' on behalf of Sir William Capel, to obtain for him the king's pardon of more than £1000 in fines for customs offences.[46] In 1522, Henry VIII restored all of the 'forfeited goods, chattels and lands' of Gawin Lancaster 'on the supplication' of Maud Parr, lady-in-waiting to Catherine of Aragon.[47] In 1558, when Sir Thomas Holcroft sought a pardon from Mary I for Dr Edwin Sandys, a Protestant preacher who was arrested during the succession crisis of 1553, he 'procured two ladies of the Privy Chamber to move the queen in it'. Before Holcroft was due to arrive with his petition, he solicited Mary's women 'to put the queen in mind of Dr. Sandys', and 'so they did'. Mary was ultimately convinced that the preacher had been 'sufficiently punished'.[48] 'At the suit of' Elizabeth Stafford, Elizabeth I's gentlewoman, Robert Mallett was pardoned in 1571 for burgling two houses in Devon.[49] When Thomas Throckmorton was imprisoned for recusancy in 1592, he too appealed to those surrounding the queen. Henry Middlemore, his kinsman and a groom of the Privy Chamber, sent a petition on his behalf, emphasising that Throckmorton 'has been thought a man not maliciously affected to the state, nor busy in corrupting order'.[50]

Some surviving grants for offices, licences, leases and more, acknowledge that they were made in response to requests by servants for favour. A licence to export a thousand tonnes of woollen cloth, tin and lead, was granted to a group of men in 1544 'at the suit of' Sir Richard Long, of the king's Privy Chamber.[51] In that same year, the purchase of the manor of Bromeshowe Bury in Essex was permitted by the king 'at the special suit' of John Gates.[52] More enlightening are letters exchanged by servants for the purpose of securing advancement. In 1526, when the rather ruthless William Brereton was pursuing the grant of Shotwick Park in Chester, his brother Randolph urged, 'get your warrant signed in all haste', as he had heard the old and weary incumbent Sir Ralph Egerton looked to secure the patents for his son. 'I would you had not meddled', Randolph remarked, doubting their chances after seeing that Egerton 'speaks fair and every day more gently than other'. 'Give good attendance by yourself and other of your friends about the king,' he advised, 'to the intent to have knowledge what labour Master Egerton makes'. Nearness, and intimacy, was crucial. Egerton may have been treasurer to Princess Mary, but Breteton was a groom of the Privy Chamber, with direct access to the sovereign.[53]

Although the Eltham ordinances of 1526 stated that no servant should attempt to 'advance himself further', 'nor press his Grace in making of suits, nor intermeddling of causes or matters, whatsoever they be',[54] it is quite clear that many of them did. In 1540, Henry VIII's Privy Council had to order both the king's and the queen's servants 'from henceforth' to 'in no wise molest his person with any manner or suit'.[55] This inconsistency between expectation and reality is striking in Elizabeth I's reign too. Robert Cecil once remarked to Sir Robert Cross that he was 'at charge with women to solicit for him and that the queen would give them good words yet they should never effect suit'.[56] However William, Lord Cobham advised a disgraced and ostracised Thomas Wilkes in 1587 to petition the queen 'in all humbleness', urging that 'this must be done with all speed and delivered by one of the maids of the chamber'.[57] Wilkes approached Bridget Skipwith-Cave, who took his petition and delivered it to Elizabeth. 'At the first she wished me not to meddle in it for she would not look upon it', Bridget responded, 'but then I told her Majesty that you were an old acquaintance of mine for which cause I did beseech her highness to read it, and then you should find friends more than I, for to speak unto her Majesty, whereupon her Majesty has promised me to peruse it, and then will I certify you of her answer'.[58] Bridget was not the exception. It was known that Anne, Countess of Warwick, Mary, Lady Scudamore and Blanche Parry, among others, 'in little lay-matters would steal opportunity to serve some friends turns'.[59] A Venetian ambassador regarded Kat Ashley as having 'such influence with the Queen that she seemed, as it were, patroness of all England'.[60] Elizabeth's women would 'effect suit' like Mary I's did before them. In the summer of 1553, Charles V instructed his ambassadors at the Tudor court to inform the new queen of murmurs that her ladies would often 'take advantage of their positions to obtain certain concessions for their own private interest and profit'.[61] Another report reiterated that 'the ladies about the Queen's person are able to obtain from her more than she ought to grant them'.[62]

Persons and petitions alike had to go through servants, who functioned as points of contact and facilitated access to the innermost chambers of royal palaces. Those who visited the court were often received in the Guard and Presence chambers. One Thomas Warley met in Anne Boleyn's Presence chamber with Margery Horsman, her maid-of-honour who had arranged for Warley to receive a kirtle from the queen. When Warley returned there later to thank her, he found that Horsman had 'returned into the Privy chamber, so that since I could not speak with her'.[63] On another occasion, when Thomas Wynter, Archdeacon of York met with the queen, she had kept him 'a long time', and was sent for only upon 'being reminded by her attendants', who received him 'very kindly'.[64] Later Elizabeth I willed Dr John Dee 'to resort oftener to her court', and, as Dee recalled, he was 'by some of her Privy Chamber to give her Majesty to know when I am there'.[65] It was not always so straightforward to catch the eye or ear of the Tudors or their attendants. As one frustrated man vented of Mary, Lady Scudamore, he had been at her chamber 'four times' and 'cannot yet speak with her, for she has been always with her Majesty'.[66] Through the 1580s and 1590s, Sir Robert Sidney too had contacts at court to ensure he remained in the queen's mind and favour while he was away. Chief among them were women serving in the Privy Chamber, like Lady Scudamore, and his aunts, Katherine, Countess of Huntingdon, and Anne, Countess of Warwick, who advanced petitions varying from suits for the office of vice-chamberlain in 1595 to the lease of Oatford Park in 1597.[67] When Lady Scudamore brought Sidney's petition for the wardenship of the Cinque Ports to Elizabeth, the queen 'asked of her, how it came to her hands', and she admitted that it was Lady Sidney, Robert's wife, who 'desired her to deliver it to her Majesty'. Scudamore, asked to report back 'what she observed in her Majesty, while she was a reading of it', found that, although 'she read it all over', she scoffed at the suit 'with two or three pughs'. In 1598, Sidney's agent Rowland White was tasked with securing him a licence granting him leave, and so he approached Sidney's aunt: 'My Lady Huntingdon is at Court. I do daily press her to move her Majesty for your leave, urging the necessity of your return; she promises to do it, and she may yet do it, for her access is good, and she is very gracious with her Majesty'.[68] 'I do very often importune it at her hands, letting her see that your being nearer her Majesty, must be a comfort unto her, and would occasion all them that now trouble her, to give it over', White wrote to Sidney, reassuring his master that 'she protests that she does remember you, and will'.[69] White acknowledged, however, that although the Countess was in the queen's confidence, and 'with her Majesty very private twice a day', regretfully, he 'cannot see what good she does for her friends'.

Servants in the Chamber and Privy Chamber were recognised by their contemporaries as potential patrons. In the 1530s, Arthur, Lord Lisle and Honor, Lady Lisle, residing in Calais, communicated with many of the king's gentlemen through John Husee, their agent in London. Husee regarded Thomas Heneage in particular as 'the trustiest man in the Court'.[70] He repeatedly urged the Lisles to 'write to some one in the Privy Chamber to know the king's pleasure',[71] and to remember Heneage by sending him wine or letters, promising to 'motion' him for their suits.[72] On one occasion, Husee delivered to Heneage eleven dozen quails and a hogshead of Gascon wine, with the accompanying message that his unfortunate master, Lord Lisle, had sustained great losses at the death of Henry Norris, Heneage's predecessor as the king's groom of the stool.[73] Husee expressed his frustrations too when he could 'get no answer' from Heneage, who appears to have been careful not to make too many promises, and often the only assurance he gave was that he would 'do his best'.[74] As Husee remarked, he 'gives fair words, but small comfort'.[75] In one suit, the agent assured Lord Lisle that Ralph Sadler, of the king's Privy Chamber, would 'motion the king's highness in it',[76] and in yet another suit, advised his master that, as the king was 'something sore' and is thus 'seldom abroad', he should 'speak earnestly unto' Sir Francis Bryan to 'move him in it', as he has 'no fellow now in the Privy Chamber' (or, in other words, that he was unrivalled in his influence 'here at the court').[77] When John Fisher, Lady Lisle's chaplain, wished to secure the advowson of Bishops Hanton and the vicarage of Blockley, he wrote to her, suggesting that she might have Lord Lisle write to Henry Norris and others 'of the Privy Chamber' to 'get the king's bill signed'. 'I will be glad for to give to him that does take this pains,' Fisher promised, 'a doublet of satin'.[78] Some openly acknowledged that they would struggle to compete with the influence and favour enjoyed by attendants in the Privy Chamber. In 1534, John Rokewood, reporting to Lord Lisle, doubted the promotion of one Blount against Cornwallis, 'for the King favours Cornwallis much, and the gentlemen of the Privy Chamber also'.[79] On another occasion, a man named Will Tyldesley informed Lord Lisle that he had failed to accomplish his latest suit, and advised that instead 'the way to do it would be first to direct your letters to some of your friends of the Privy Chamber to obtain the King's licence, or else to write to the lord chamberlain, who, I know, will grant your demands'.[80]

In some instances, it was women serving at court who had the advantage.[81] Lady Lisle was advised by Husee in 1537 that, to find preferment for her daughters, Anne and Katharine, to the household of Jane Seymour, it was 'no meet suit for any man to move such matters, but only for such ladies and women as be your friends'.[82] Approaching the Tudors often required great subtlety and timing, and some suits took considerable work and patience to see them through. Margery Horsman, the queen's maid-of-honour, contrived a way for one of Lady Lisle's daughters to be 'seen or known' by her mistress, promising to 'receive her and lay her in her chamber', and to 'bring her with her into the Queen's chamber every day'. 'Madam, your ladyship is not a little beholding unto this gentlewoman', wrote Husee, in recognition of the young Margery's labour in the suit.[83] Within a year, Husee was able to assure Lady Lisle that her patrons in the household promised one of her daughters 'shall be immediately preferred unto the Queen's service at the next vacancy, which is thought shall be shortly'.[84] The opportunity to advance this suit would arise when Eleanor, Countess of Rutland, and Mary, Countess of Sussex, ladies of the queen's Privy Chamber, learned that Jane, who was heavily pregnant, was craving quails. Of this they promptly informed Husee, before receiving and conveying a delivery of two dozen quails to Jane in the spring of 1537.[85] Her ladies, seeing that the queen was unsatisfied with them, then warned the agent to inform Lady Lisle, rather bluntly, that 'those that your ladyship shall hereafter send, let them be very fat, or else they are not worth thanks'.[86] Two months, and presumably, many shipments later, 'the Queen at dinner, while eating the quails,' her agent reported, 'spoke of your ladyship and your daughters before my Lady Rutland and my Lady Sussex'.[87] It was Anne, not Katharine, who was eventually appointed to Jane's household. In this suit 'for her preferment', the queen's servants, in the words of Husee, provided 'counsel'.[88] By 'counsel', Husee meant that they were in a position to know and advise them on how they might ensure a successful outcome to their suit.

Negotiating the personalities, moods and temperaments of the Tudors was key to securing their favour. Shortly after Anne was appointed to serve in the queen's household, her mother began advising her closely on how to remain in Henry VIII's good graces. 'I have declared unto the king's highness all things, as your ladyship willed me to do,' Anne wrote to her at the end of 1539, expressing her gratitude 'for the good and motherly counsel your ladyship does give me, concerning my continuance in the king's favour'.[89] Henry could be affable, friendly, cheerful and gracious, but he could also be ruthlessly cynical, suspicious, and fickle. This became worse still when his health deteriorated and a 'humour' had fallen upon his leg, leaving it swollen and causing him so much pain that he became irritable, and often, cruel. Anne had shown herself reluctant to approach him on account of his ill-temper. 'For I knowledge myself most bound to his Highness of all creatures', Anne wrote to her mother, 'if I should, therefore, in any thing offend his Grace willingly, it were pity I should live.'[90] Lady Lisle sent various gifts and tokens for her to deliver to the capricious king: 'Madam, the king does so well like the conserves you sent him last,' Anne noted, 'that his grace commanded me to write unto you for more of the cognac of the clearest making, and of the conserve of damsons, and this as soon as may be'.[91] Later she presented the cognac to the king, and would report that 'his grace does like it wondrously well'. When the king 'had tasted' the cognac in her presence, Anne was urged to 'move his grace for to send you some token of remembrance'.[92] 'And whereas you do write to me that I should remember my sister', Katharine, for her preferment to the queen's household, Anne assured her mother, 'I have spoken to the king's highness for her'.[93]

Knowing the disposition or state of mind of their royal master or mistress, servants could reassure others that they were secure in their favour, or warn them if they were in danger of falling out of it. John Fowler, Edward VI's groom of the Privy Chamber, recalled how the king's uncle, Thomas, Lord Seymour, constantly pestered him for reassurances of royal favour. Seymour would often ask if Edward 'would say anything of him', and requested that Fowler have the young king 'write some little recommendation with his own hand'. Fowler could only assure him that the king had him 'in memory, as much as he had any nobleman in England'.[94] Blanche Parry, Elizabeth I's gentlewoman, quietly informed the Earl of Leicester in 1566 that her mistress 'much marvelled' that she had not heard from him. The considerate Parry tried to make his excuses with the queen, but she was 'not disposed to hear of anything that may do you good', and thus the gentlewoman urged the Earl 'to send to her before you come'.[95]

Servants were in an advantageous position to judge the likes and dislikes of their royal master or mistress, and as such could advise, for instance, on what gifts would evoke a positive response. Frances, Lady Cobham, of the queen's Privy Chamber, wrote to William, Lord Burghley, with a reassuring report: 'Her Majesty has received your gloves and likes well of them, and willed me to thank you for them. The buttons and the silk wherewith they are garnished pleases her much'. Such gifts often came, rather unsubtly, with a letter or request, though on this occasion the queen probably wished that they had not, as Lady Cobham would tell Burghley: 'Her Majesty has read all your letter, and wished you had not broken so grievous a matter to her, but she spoke not one bitter word'.[96] In 1583, Sir Thomas Heneage, Elizabeth's treasurer, sent her a jewel, and Mary, Lady Scudamore, sent him word on how it was received by their mistress. 'Her highness esteemed much of the jewel', Heneage was duly informed, 'but she esteemed much more of the good will of him that sent it, for whose sake she would wear it till his return on that ear that should not harken to anything that should any ways hurt him that sent it'.[97] The jewel would serve as a reminder to the queen during Heneage's absence of their affectionate relationship.

Serving in the Tudor royal household provided an opportunity to build one's own prestige, reputation and standing with the crown, which in itself drew in clientele. Much of the evidence suggests that contemporaries knew servants to be in a privileged position to advance suits. 'I understand such small matters be easily granted to any of her Majesty's servants that upon any convenient motion become humble suitors for them', one man observed in 1599.[98] After struggling to secure a successful outcome to his suit on behalf of a sick prisoner, another man was a little scornful, remarking that 'if a groom of her Majesty's great chamber had moved it, it would not have been denied'.[99] Indeed some resented the influence exercised by servants. In 1594, Sir William Cornwallis expressed his fury that 'a base merchant's son of Norwich' who had slandered his daughter had been pardoned by the queen of his sentence to punishment by whipping and the cutting off of an ear, merely because, as he saw it, the man had previously lent Mary, Lady Scudamore, £500, and thus by 'putting some purse in her pocket' he had 'gathered around him friends akin to the knave'. Cornwallis was furious that the pardon was 'wrought by a base fellow for such a base respect as lending money or giving some £60, or one hundred marks by such a barbarous brazen-faced woman'.[100] Others felt that their patrons at court were not doing nearly enough to advance their own interests. Lady Scudamore acted on behalf of the Earl of Shrewsbury, declaring in 1592: 'I do offer myself, ladyship and all, to be at your service. I have both presented her Majesty with both your humble duties and showed her your letter at which she has been very merry and very highly contented'.[101] Yet, the following year, Lady Scudamore's disgruntled cousin George, Dean of Lichfield, complained that she did not intervene with enough vigour, and informed the Earl: 'I am afraid that your lordship is not likely to hear in haste from my cousin Scudamore… there is no sure confidence in her'. 'For women be waspish', the Dean continued, 'and will do a man more harm when they be angered than good when they be quiet'.[102] Servants could even be accused of having stalled or frustrated the efforts of those seeking advancement. Henry, Lord Clinton, was convinced in 1585 that his stepmother, Elizabeth, Countess of Lincoln, 'fills the ears of all the Privy Chamber and all her friends about her majesty with most false and slanderous reports which her highness is incensed with to me intolerable grief'.[103] Sir Walter Raleigh apparently once remarked that the ladies of Elizabeth's Privy Chamber 'were like witches', in that 'they could do hurt, but they could do no good'.[104]

Servants did not always have their own axes to grind, but the patron-client system shifted to their advantage when they were courted by those who wished for them to act as intermediaries on their behalf. Few of them would have acted as patrons without some compensation for their efforts. In 1542, Sir Thomas Darcy wrote to John Gates, his fellow in the Privy Chamber, for 'a licence for five hundred wheys cheese'. 'If you can find the means', Darcy stressed, 'I shall give you one hundred marks of money so soon as you give the licence'. If Gates himself could not procure the licence 'for two years at the least', an anxious Darcy urged him 'to make some friend unto the king's grace for it, for if there go none over the sea I know not what we shall do with any cheese, it is the chief thing that we have to make money of'. Darcy also thought it was worth reminding Gates, as he wrote, of 'the horse which you had of me'.[105]

Those who were courted for their favour often received fees, gifts, or bribes, taking full advantage of their position near the crown. In 1557, the Venetian ambassador Giovanni Michieli, eager to win over Mary I, was embarrassed into giving her many gifts 'of no little value'. These gifts were all made at the behest of Mary's gentlewoman, Susan Clarencius, supposedly for the queen's 'need and service', though Michiel was clearly frustrated to find that it was Clarencius herself who was to keep his coach, his horses 'and all their furniture'. 'I had this coach sent to me from Italy from my convenience, and used it all that summer, nor will I from modesty tell what it cost me', Michiel grumbled.[106] In 1595, Anthony Bacon was pursuing Elizabeth I's pardon for Robert Boothe, who had been jailed, fined, and was due to lose his ears. Dorothy, Lady Edmunds was identified as a viable go-between, with some suggestion that she might be bribed with £100. Bacon's agent at court, Anthony Standen, reported that Lady Edmunds 'made no difficulty' with the matter, but she had to first consult with the lord chamberlain, who she found 'wilful but for her sake ready to relent'. It seems that the lord chamberlain pulled Lady Edmunds aside, however, to advise that £100 was not enough, and she would be wise to charge a better fee for her efforts. As Bacon was informed,

> Now here comes in the cogging of this place: she says she must make an express suit thereof to her Majesty and therein plead her ancient and long service for a recompense whereof she must content herself herewith. And that the manner of the queen is to ask what the suit will be worth, so that naming the £100 which is the sum I offered her, she says the queen will not be moved with it for so small a matter to employ her credit and forces she will not.[107]

Standen was struck by the state of affairs at court in which women could wield such influence:

> This ruffianry of causes I am daily more and more acquainted with and see the manner of dealing which grows by the queen's straightness to give these women whereby they presume thus to grange and huck causes.[108]

Some grants were promised for life, and others 'during pleasure', meaning they could be revoked at the whims of the sovereign. In the early years of Henry VII's reign, in around 1488, the king's servants were warned that if they 'endeavour not themselves in giving their attendance according to their duty', the 'divers offices and fees granted to them by his letters patents' would 'be of no better force nor effect but at the King's pleasure'.[109] In 1533, Nicholas Poyntz was looking to shoulder out Thomas ap Guilliam, Henry VIII's yeoman, as keeper of Micklewood, Gloucestershire. The king had granted the chase to ap Guilliam in 1510 'during his grace's pleasure', though more than two decades later, Henry, overlooking his yeoman's interest in the keepership, was persuaded to grant it to Poyntz for life. No doubt ap Guilliam contested this, as Poyntz acknowledged after, knowing well the office was not vacant, that he rather 'should have found some means by gentleness to come by it'. Poyntz assured Cromwell, his patron in this matter, that he would no further 'meddle therein' until the king affirmed his decision.[110]

When the Tudors died, their servants might lose their claim to patronage. Roger Ascham wrote 'a little book of shooting', which Henry VIII 'so liked' that he gave him a patent worth £10 a year, 'but when he lost his life,' Ascham recalled, 'I lost that'. Edward VI renewed the patent, 'which was a great profit to me, save that one unpleasant word, during pleasure, turned me after to great displeasure, for his pleasure went with him, and my whole living went away with them both'. Ascham had 'lost all, and neither looked nor hoped for anything again', but his friends at court petitioned on his behalf for an appointment as Mary I's Latin secretary. To his new mistress, Ascham dared to be bolder still. He wrote out the patent again, this time leaving blank the space for the amount he was due to receive. When asked by the Bishop of Winchester why he had done so, he joked, 'the fault was in the writer, who had done ill besides to leave the vacant place so great, for the old word *ten* would not half fill the room, and therefore except it pleased him to put in *twenty* pounds, which would both fill the vacant place and my purse'. The queen took it in jest, granting him £20 a year 'for life'. In 1567, Ascham wrote once more, this time to Mary's sister and successor, Elizabeth I. Now in his final years, Ascham claimed to 'dislike to ask favours', but 'was urged to it for the sake of my wife and young children', and pleaded with the queen to extend the patent on his 'little book' to be granted to one of his sons after his death, suggesting that he could even reprint it and dedicate it to her. If this was not enough to convince her, Ascham invoked the memory of his long service to the crown:

> If I be not so happy as to leave this poor living to my children, yet will I leave the copy of this poor letter to them, to bear witness with me, in time to come, that although they had a father unfortunate to do them good, he was called and suffered to serve many years in good place, in weighty affairs, and no great fault found in his service, and yet nothing by him obtained to leave behind him to his children.[111]

Likewise, when a servant died, those who depended on them for favour lost a patron. Hugh Fitzwilliam expressed his disappointment that Kat Ashley, whom he recognised was a confidante of the queen, was 'gone', which meant that he had no friends near her 'to make his moan to'.[112]

Power and influence often lay in access to and intimacy with the Tudors. This power circulated through many hands. Servants in the Chamber or Privy Chamber were in a privileged position to engage in such politics, yet, it is important to observe that courtiers, councillors and visitors all bent the royal ear, as did servants in the household 'below-stairs', albeit, we can presume, less frequently. As it was acknowledged in 1582, those who held offices in Elizabeth I's pantry, buttery, cellar, woodyard and more 'most commonly or always approach her Majesty's presence' with a petition in hand.[113]

8

'I pray you pray for me your loving master'
RELIGION, FAITH AND REFORM

The daily routine of religious observances and divine ceremonial saw the Tudors and their servants drawn into their own distinct patterns of piety. Publicly, kings and queens, at least once, often twice or even three times a day, emerged with their attendants and walked in procession from their Privy chamber to their Presence chamber, through their Guard chamber and then by a gallery to the Chapel Royal, where they heard mass before the high altar, gave confession and received penance.[1] On Henry VIII's procession to the Chapel Royal at Christmas in 1531, Eustace Chapuys had hoped to speak with him, but there must have been a fair few hangers-on vying for the king's attention, as the ambassador 'could not obtain either his ear or his eye'.[2] Chapuys later reported in the spring of 1533, the day before Easter Sunday, that Anne Boleyn, by then a queen lacking only a crown, 'went to mass in royal state, loaded with jewels, clothed in a robe of cloth of gold friese'.[3] Mary, Duchess of Richmond, carried her train, and in attendance were as many as sixty young women who conducted her 'to and from the church with the same or perhaps greater ceremonies and solemnities than those used with former queens on such occasions'.[4] For the Maundy Thursday service, the Tudors imitated Christ by washing the feet of poor men and women. A surviving miniature, likely painted by Levina Teerlinc, illustrates Elizabeth I washing the feet of poor women, assisted by her ladies, many of them wearing white aprons, one carrying a large flat plate, another bearing her train, and the rest standing solemnly behind her in procession.[5] If the Tudors went on pilgrimage, they were accompanied by their servants. When travelling from palace to palace, these servants were engaged in almsgiving and poor relief. Jane Dormer, Mary I's gentlewoman, recalled that her mistress 'would sit down very familiarly in their poor houses, talk with the man and the wife, ask them of their manner of living, how they passed, if the officers of the Court did deal with them, as such whose carts and labours were pressed for the queen's carriages and provisions'. The queen once reprimanded her comptroller, Sir Robert Rochester, as 'he had ill officers who gave neither money nor good words to poor men, and that hereafter he should see it amended, for if she understood it again, he should hear it to his displeasure'. 'The next morning the poor men would come for their money,' and Mary warned Rochester 'that they should be paid every penny'.[6]

All of the Tudors had an Almoner, who distributed their alms, and a Confessor, who was responsible for their spiritual welfare, providing them with counsel and hearing their confession for the preservation of their soul. Chaplains held 'matins, masses, and other devotions' for their royal master or mistress and the rest of the household.[7] Servants were required to be in attendance morning, afternoon, evening and night for religious services. The Eltham ordinances of 1526 dictated that 'there should be always some divine service in the court', and 'the King's whole chapel continually attendant upon his person'.[8] Henry VIII's household would typically 'have a mass of our Lady before noon, and on Sundays and holy days, mass of the day, besides our Lady mass, and an anthem in the afternoon'.[9] Sir Richard Blount, Edward VI's gentleman usher, noted that, as soon as the king was awake, he was to inquire 'what time he will go to service in the closet'.[10] Ordinances drawn up for Anne of Cleves and her household in 1551 indicate that services were ministered by one of her own chaplains, who was to be ready at eight o'clock in the morning every day 'in such place as shall be appointed' to say 'such divine service'; and again between nine and ten o'clock 'in her chapel closet to say like service before her grace's gentlewomen and other of her family'; and finally, before five o'clock in the afternoon 'to say like service', and otherwise 'at all times' as was required. Those servants who were absent without licence were to be 'admonished and reconciled', or, for a second offence, discharged from the household.[11] By 1598, many of Elizabeth I's own chaplains had found ecclesiastical promotion, and neglected 'their attendance at the court, and the duties of their places'. To remedy this, the queen appointed one Dr Richard Field 'to preach in that place'.[12] As she became increasingly unwell in her final years, Elizabeth did not appear in the Privy closet, but 'she had cushions laid for her in the Privy chamber, hard by the closet door, and there she heard service'.[13] The sermon that her chaplain, Dr Henry Parry, delivered for her court, was 'so fervent and effectual for her Majesty that he left few eyes dry'.[14] The nature of sermons ranged from the political and religious discourse of John Skip for Anne Boleyn's household in 1536, to the commentary on court fashions by John Aylmer, who preached in 1593 'on the vanity of decking the body too finely'. Elizabeth I was far from impressed, and 'told the ladies, that if the Bishop held more discourse on such matters she would fit him for Heaven, but he should walk thither without a staff and leave his mantle behind him; perchance the Bishop hath never sought her Highness' wardrobe, or he should have chosen another text'.[15]

More privately, the Tudors and their servants would sometimes pray together, recite and debate scripture, engage in theological debate, and read, study or exchange religious books for learning and devotion. A surviving prayer roll bearing Henry VIII's inscription reads, 'William Thomas', a yeoman of his Chamber, 'I pray you pray for me your loving master'.[16] A Book of Hours once owned by Joan, Lady Guildford, contains similar inscriptions from her fellows at court and the Tudors themselves, chiefly her queen and mistress Elizabeth of York ('Madame I pray you forget not me to pray to God I may have part of your prayers') and her sovereign Henry VII ('Madame, I pray you remember me your loving master'). Yet more affectionate were the autographs left by Catherine of Aragon, whom she served as a lady-in-waiting ('I think the prayers of a friend the most acceptable unto God and because I take you for one of mine assured I pray you remember me in yours'), and from the queen's daughter, Princess Mary ('I have read that no body lives as he should do but he that follows virtue and in reckoning you to be one of them I pray you to remember me in your devotions').[17] Katherine Parr's accounts reveal that twelve books 'of the psalm prayers, gorgeously bound and gilt on the leather', at 16s. a piece, were sent by the queen to George Day, Bishop of Chichester, her confessor and almoner, in addition to three copies of the same sent to William Harper, clerk of the queen's closet, presumably for use by her household attendants.[18] In 1547, Nicholas Udall remarked that 'instead of cards and other instruments of idle trifling', the dowager queen Katherine's attendants had 'continually in their hands either psalms or homilies, and other devout meditations, or else Paul's epistles, or some book of Holy Scripture matters, and as familiarly both to read or reason thereof in Greek, Latin, French, or Italian, as in English'.[19] Their activity caught the attention of the rest of her household staff and the wider court. Francis Goldsmith, her gentleman usher, in 1544 felt that every day was like a Sunday in the queen's 'holy' household 'where Christ is daily celebrated'.[20] Anthony Cope, her vice-chamberlain, in 1547 praised Katherine's 'gracious intent and godly purpose in the reading and study of holy Scripture'.[21]

The Tudors were responsible for keeping their servants constant and conspicuous in their piety. The 'good' master or mistress, in the words of William Latymer, Anne Boleyn's chaplain, ruled their servants 'in most godly wise and princely manner' to uphold strict moral order and virtue in their households. Anne apparently 'began immediately after her royal coronation to convert her whole thought, imagination and endeavour to the godly order, rule and government of such as was committed to attend her Highness in all her affairs'.[22] As queen, she 'kept her maids and such as were about her so occupied in sowing and working of shirts and smocks for the poor';[23] 'yielding herein example to others to the like endeavour', she kept an English bible in her chambers for her servants 'to read upon when they would', and even urged her chaplains to 'exhort them to fear God,' and 'cause them daily to hear the divine service'.[24] The martyrologist John Foxe, whose account was informed by women who served the queen, wrote that Anne 'carried ever about her a certain little purse, out of the which she was wont daily to scatter abroad some alms', engaging her attendants in poor relief, urging them to 'command my alms liberally' and to 'take special regard in the choice of such poor people as shall be found most needy'.[25] It is difficult to determine if Tudor royal households in this period were 'godly', pious and virtuous, if it was judged as such by its contemporaries, or if this was merely constructed later. Much of the evidence which survives is determinedly one-sided. The most descriptive accounts for Anne and her servants' religious activity were composed during the reign of Elizabeth I, Anne's daughter, and as such may have been written in an attempt, firstly, to rehabilitate or retrieve her reputation, and secondly, if indirectly, influence the Elizabethan religious settlement.[26] It is significant that these accounts of Anne Boleyn are strikingly similar to those on Catherine of Aragon by Catholic authors, who invoked the same imagery and rhetoric. Nicholas Harpsfield, a Catholic priest writing in Mary I's reign, described Catherine 'in much prayer, great alms, and abstinence', and 'when she was not this way occupied, then was she and her gentlewomen working with their own hands something wrought in needlework costly and artificially, which she intended to honour of God to bestow upon some churches'.[27] The Catholic polemicist Nicholas Sanders had Catherine 'present every morning in church for six hours together during the sacred offices', and 'in the midst of her maids of honour, she read the lives of saints'.[28] Certainly these authors intended to preserve strictly the most idyllic image and 'pious' representations of these queens in the reigns of their respective daughters, Elizabeth and Mary.

Many servants continued to live and serve through decades of tumultuous religious change, but more than a few of them were prepared to risk or even resign their position for their faith. Amidst Henry VIII's break with Rome, marking the beginning of the Reformation in England through the 1520s and 1530s, Sir John Gage, the king's vice-chamberlain, abruptly left court. His friend and fellow attendant, Sir William Fitzwilliam, observed that Gage had 'departed from the king's highness after such a sort, as I am sorry to hear'. Henry reluctantly granted him a licence to be relieved of his duties and to return home, and so his servant 'took his leave of him, with the water standing in his eyes'. Fitzwilliam was clearly upset too, urging Cromwell to be 'a means unto' Henry 'for the obtaining of the king's his grace's favour' for Gage, and 'the bringing of him unto the room and state he was before'. The pious and disillusioned Gage, Fitzwilliam commented, was 'more disposed to serve God than thou world, yet there is such honesty in thou man that I dare warrant you next God he loves thou king above all things'.[29] It would be reported the following year that Gage had 'renounced his office and gone to a charterhouse, intending, with the consent of his wife, to become a Carthusian'.[30] He would return to the king's service by 1540. Gage kept his distance once more during Edward VI's reign, but when Mary I became queen and reinstated Catholicism, he was appointed as lord chamberlain of her household. His career reveals the potential impact of the Reformation on the lives of men and women serving at court.[31] Similarly, by 1536, Jorge de Athequa, Bishop of Llandaff and formerly Catherine of Aragon's confessor, felt that 'he could not live a Catholic life' in England 'without endangering his conscience'. Athequa was determined to leave, but was 'so clumsy about it, and took so little precaution, that he was discovered, arrested, and sent to the Tower'. Like Athequa, Dr Ferdinand de Victoria, Catherine's physician, was eager to escape. The king, suspecting that Victoria would soon depart, tried to oblige him to remain by appointing him to serve in his own household. The physician was reluctant, excusing himself as 'there might be cause for people to think and speak badly of him' for 'entering the king's service so soon after the late queen's death'.[32]

Although Henry VIII was radical in refusing papal authority and dissolving the monasteries, he was fairly orthodox in his faith. His court was expected to align their own beliefs with those of their sovereign, as reflected in a near-contemporary poem, *A Groom of the Chamber's Religion in Henry VIII's Time* (1618), by Sir John Harington:

> One of King Henry's favourites began
> To move the King one day to take a man
> Whom of his chamber he might make a Groom.
> "Soft," said the King, "before I grant that room,
> It is a question not to be neglected,
> How he in his religion stands affected."
> "For his religion," answered then the minion,
> "I do not know what's his opinion;
> But sure he may, talking with men of learning,
> Conform himself in less than ten day's warning."[33]

Although the use of scripture and new learning to support the king's 'Great Matter' was adopted through the 1520s and 1530s, Henry himself was seemingly ambivalent towards reform, and his reign was characterised by confusion and uncertainty as to what constituted 'heresy'. Strict laws forbade, for instance, the purchase and possession of prohibited books of a heretical nature. Cardinal Campeggio remarked in 1529 that 'certain Lutheran books, in English, of an evil sort, have been circulated in the King's court'.[34] Anne Boleyn had in her chambers a copy of William Tyndale's *Obedience of a Christian Man*, which she had lent to one of her maids, Anne Gainsford, some time in 1529. George Zouche, one of the queen's servants, 'plucked' the book from the maid, which was then snatched from Zouche by Dr. Richard Sampson, Dean of the king's Chapel, who confiscated and delivered it to Wolsey. A fearful Anne Gainsford 'wept', because 'she could not get the book back from her wooer'. She knew that possession of the book in question 'was enough to make a man a heretic, and reading of it a dangerous article against any in these days'. Wolsey sent for and examined Zouche, who informed him that 'it pertained to one of the queen's Chamber'. But before the cardinal could report it to Henry, the queen herself went to him. 'Upon her knees she desires King's help for her book', and even 'besought his Grace most tenderly to read it'.[35] Some years later, in 1536, the queen entrusted William Latymer, her chaplain, and Joan Wilkinson, her silkwoman, to purchase and import what were, potentially, forbidden books to her chambers.[36] Latymer was apprehended upon his return from Flanders.[37] Clearly there were limits to how far servants could engage in and advocate for reform. Whereas many would have outwardly conformed, as an overzealous, or even unorthodox faith, could risk attracting hostility and incurring the king's wrath, behind this conformity, a reformist zeal, which may otherwise be seen and judged as heretical, could be practised, and potentially hidden.

An intensely personal faith shared between a royal master or mistress and their servants could attract the attention of the wider court and kingdom. In 1536, Christopher Askew, Henry VIII's gentleman usher, was examined by his Privy Council.[38] Some three weeks earlier, Askew had been sent by Thomas Cromwell to Lincolnshire to gather intelligence on a popular uprising against the dissolution of the monasteries.[39] On his journey, Askew was urged by the abbess of the Benedictine nunnery of Clementhorpe in York to move the queen, Jane Seymour, to prevent its dissolution, promising him £30 'for his labour if the matter were brought to'. Jane was known to be strictly orthodox, and thus the abbess of Clementhorpe had Askew act as a go-between to solicit the queen for her protection. Askew had to go through her servants, and rely on them to move the request on his behalf. This the abbess must have known, as the insurgents in Yorkshire, working alongside her, urged Askew to bring the matter to the queen's council and 'bid him offer… money to them'. Askew travelled to Windsor Castle and arrived at the queen's chambers. He met with Sir Edmund Bedingfield, Jane's chancellor, and William Paget, her secretary, and 'showed unto them' the matter of Clementhorpe. He told them that the abbess would give 300 marks to the queen, which 'she may yet have if you think… meet for her grace to take them'. When Askew advised how the insurgents might convey the 300 marks safely from York, assuring them of their bribe, the queen's servants 'promised to move the Queen's grace'. Askew told 'the same tale' to Margery Horsman, her maid, who, rather cautiously, 'asked of him what communication he had with the queen's council'.[40] After the Pilgrimage of Grace, Jane was solicited by Sir Robert Constable, one of the leading Yorkshire rebels, to move the king for his pardon. Constable wrote to his son, Marmaduke, begging him 'to entreat my Lord of Rutland', Thomas Manners, the queen's lord chamberlain, 'to be mean unto the queen her grace of pity to sue unto the king his majesty to pardon me my life with as poor a living as may be to the intent that may all my life time lament my offences'. The rebel trusted that Manners would, like Jane, be sympathetic to his cause and move the matter: 'if he can get my Lord of Rutland and him both to labour unto her grace then… all shall be well'. 'I intend to live by God's grace who leaves no good deed unrewarded', 'if you offer a sum of money', Constable advised, 'you shall be no loser'.[41] It is unknown if Jane, or the queen's servants, intervened, but the Benedictine nunnery of Clementhorpe in York was dissolved in 1536, and Constable was executed for treason in 1537. 'At the beginning of the insurrection', Jane, profoundly upset, apparently 'threw herself on her knees before the King and begged him to restore the abbeys, but he told her, prudently enough, to get up', warning her 'not to meddle with his affairs'.[42]

The prosecution of heresy at the Tudor court intensified in the 1540s, and many servants faced punishment. At Windsor, in the summer of 1543, a group of men were found guilty of heresy under the Six Articles and were burnt at the stake. At a trial held in Berkshire, an accusation was levied against certain of the king and the queen's attendants for having 'abetted, aided, favoured, counselled and consented' the guilty parties in committing these heresies. Foulke Langley, Katherine Parr's yeoman, 'had lain at Windsor all the time of the business and had got knowledge what number were privily indicted', before reporting back to Sir Thomas Cawarden, of the king's Privy Chamber.[43] He learned that Cawarden, along with his fellows Philip Hoby, gentleman usher, Edmund Harman and Thomas Sternhold, grooms, Thomas Weldon, master of the household, William Snowball, yeoman cook, and many of their wives too, were all to be indicted by the Six Articles.[44] Be it on the orders of the queen, or acting on his own initiative, Foulke's presence at Windsor protected them, as the indictments were intercepted and seized by Cawarden. All those accused were pardoned, though Hoby and Weldon had already spent time imprisoned in the Fleet earlier that year for adhering to the views of a cleric 'known to be of evil opinions touching the Sacrament'.[45] Three years later, in the summer of 1546, Sir George Blagg, of Henry VIII's Privy Chamber, too was vulnerable to charges of heresy. Blagg had apparently been overheard saying that 'the good Lord's body could not in any means be minished nor repaired'. Musing what would happen if the consecrated bread were eaten by a mouse, it was 'in his opinion' that 'it were well done that the mouse were taken and put in the pix', a vessel containing the bread for mass.[46] For these remarks against the sacrament Blagg was arrested and condemned to be burnt alive. Henry was 'sore offended', but not by Blagg. He was furious that these investigations 'would come so near him, and even into his Privy Chamber, without his knowledge'. Blagg was immediately pardoned by the king, who summoned him shortly thereafter. 'Ah! My pig,' Henry welcomed him affectionately, to which Blagg replied, 'if your majesty had not been better to me than your bishops were, your pig had been roasted here this time'![47]

Not all servants were protected like Blagg. In 1539, Lancelot, one of the king's guard described as being 'of no less godly mind and disposition, than strong and tall of body', was burnt at the stake merely for showing sympathy for two of his friends accused of heresy.[48] The following year, a young Mandeville, groom to Anne of Cleves, was burnt in St. George's Field, by Southwark, 'for heresy against the sacrament of the altar'.[49] Another man named John Bettes, probably the yeoman serving in the queen's household through the 1540s, was condemned to death for violation of the Six Articles.[50] Shortly after the execution of Thomas Cromwell in 1540, John Lascelles, the king's sewer, idly asked Jonson and Maxey in the king's chambers 'what news there were pertaining God's holy word, seeing we have lost so noble a man which did love and favour it so well?'[51] In 1546, the same Lascelles would be executed for his views on reform, signing a letter from prison as 'late servant to the king, and now I trust to serve the everlasting King, with the testimony of my blood in Smithfield'.[52] Punishments for charges of heresy were not always so severe. Richard Morison, of Edward VI's Privy Chamber, was regarded as 'a learned and lettered man, and well thought of for his proficiency in the new theology', but a few years earlier, in Henry's reign, Morison was reportedly 'deprived of his place' in the king's household, as 'he had presumed too far in certain writings to find fault with our Holy Father the Pope'.[53]

Some servants dared to engage in activity which could be construed as heresy at court, right under the nose of their sovereign. In 1546, Thomas, Duke of Norfolk, was brought before the Privy Council and examined 'for disputing indiscreetly of Scripture with other young gentlemen of the Court' in the queen's chambers.[54] The Duke, 'assured of the King's clemency if he would frankly confess' his 'indiscreet talking of Scripture matters', was soon released.[55] That the Duke had disputed scripture in Katherine Parr's chambers was significant. The queens' lodgings had become an environment wherein forbidden books were read and exchanged, and the debate of scripture encouraged between her servants. There were reports circulating at court that the queen's ladies had 'infected' her with heresy.[56] A royal proclamation was issued to purge books which had 'sundry pernicious and detestable errors and heresies', in possession of anyone, 'what estate, degree, or condition, soever they or he be'.[57] Katherine's chambers were to be searched to uncover 'what books, by law forbidden, she had in her closet',[58] some of which were thought to have been sent to the queen by Anne Askew, a Lincolnshire gentlewoman and known heretic who was acquainted with her servants. When Askew was arrested and tortured in 1546, she was examined as to their involvement as agents of radical religious dissent.[59] The king's councillors specifically named and questioned Askew on the queen's ladies and gentlewomen, Catherine, Lady Suffolk, Mary, Countess of Sussex, Anne, Countess of Hertford, and Joan, Lady Denny, of whom she stated, 'if I should pronounce any thing against them, that I were not able to prove it'. All that Askew admitted to under torture was having received money, ten shillings from 'a man in a blue coat', apparently from the Countess of Hertford, and eight shillings delivered by a man 'in a violet coat', sent from Lady Denny.[60] Askew could not have been mistaken in that the king's councillors were targeting the queen's servants: 'they did put me on the rack,' she felt, 'because I confessed no Ladies or Gentlewomen to be of my opinion'.[61] Engaging in theological debate, prayer sessions and the study of scripture in the queen's chambers, attending sermons from visiting preachers and possessing forbidden books on the new religion, Katherine and her servants were drawn together by their commitment to defining, developing and advocating for reform.[62] The queen 'at all times convenient', would 'have private conference touching spiritual matters' in her chambers. 'Every day in the afternoon for the space of an hour, one of her said Chaplains in her Privy chamber made some collation to her and to her Ladies and Gentlewomen of her Privy Chamber, or other that were disposed to hear', Foxe recorded, 'in which sermons, they oft times touched such abuses as in the church then were rife'.[63] The queen, accompanied by her servants, would exhort the king, as

> she did with all painful endeavour apply herself by all virtuous means, in all things to please his humour... sometimes of herself would come to visit him, either at after dinner or after supper, as was most fit for her purpose. At which times she would not fail to use all occasions to move him, according to her manner, zealously to proceed in the reformation of the Church.[64]

It is not known if the queen's servants had yet been interrogated by the king's council. Certainly this was their intention, and their testimony would have been taken to secure a conviction against their mistress. Only Katherine's ladies and gentlewomen, as those who were 'privy to all her doings', could produce the evidence that the prosecution required. Foxe observed that the king's councillors knew that 'the better to bring their purpose to pass, because they would not upon the sudden but by means deal with her, they thought it best, at the first, to begin with some of those Ladies whom they knew to be great with her'. Anne Parr, Countess of Pembroke, the queen's sister, Maud Parr, Lady Lane, her cousin, and Elizabeth, Lady Tyrwhitt, all of whom served in her Privy Chamber, were to be apprehended, questioned, and their coffers searched, 'whereby the Queen might be charged' and 'carried by barge by night unto the Tower'.[65]

Servants whose personal faith did not align with that of the sovereign had to be incredibly cautious. Katherine and her servants had endangered themselves by their activity in the queen's chambers. A warrant for her arrest was produced, but a draft of the articles was mislaid, and 'some godly person', namely Thomas Wendy, her physician, brought it to the queen. Like Foulke before him, Wendy protected her by taking this document, not, to his sovereign, but to his mistress. When Katherine learned of it, 'for the sudden fear thereof, she fell incontinent into a great melancholy and agony, bewailing and taking on in such sort, as was lamentable to see'.[66] Her physician, 'for the comforting of her heavy mind, began to break with her in secret manner, touching the said articles devised against her' and 'exhorted her somewhat to frame and conform herself unto the king's mind'. The queen panicked, 'commanding her ladies to convey away their books which were against the law'. 'The next night following after supper', ladies of the queen's Privy Chamber, Lady Herbert and Lady Lane, 'who carried the candle before her', accompanied Katherine 'unto the king's bed chamber', where, by pleading ignorance and acting with the utmost deference, the queen was able to convince Henry of her innocence. When Wriothesley later confronted the queen to arrest her, Henry intervened: 'Knave! Arrant knave, beast and fool!' the king berated him.[67]

Household piety could prove to be a strong, compelling force on its members. During the reign of Edward VI, the reformist agenda had developed, yet the king's sister, Princess Mary, and many servants of her household, were defiant in their Catholic faith. The ambassador Van der Delft noted in 1547 that Mary was 'firm and constant in her good attachment to our ancient faith, and never allows a day to pass without hearing two, three or four Masses, and every night has prayers in her chapel'.[68] In 1549, the Act of Uniformity mandated Protestant services, as opposed to traditional Latin mass, but Mary continued to celebrate it in her court at Kenninghall. 'It is a pleasure to see how well kept and well ordered is her household in the observance of our ancient religion', Delft reported in 1550, noting that 'her servants are well to do people and some of them men of means and noblemen too whose boast is to be reputed her servants, and by these means they continue to practise the said religion and hear God's service'.[69] Mary had been issued a dispensation 'to practise the ancient religion, observance of the sacraments and divine service with her whole establishment and household'.[70] Although the king and the council felt it pragmatic to tolerate Mary's faith, they became increasingly concerned that she was abusing the privilege, accommodating more than her household servants. By the end of 1550, the king's council were losing patience. Mary was summoned for refusing to cease celebration of Catholic mass. Significantly, the princess made her entry into London with her household, and each of the gentlemen and ladies in her entourage bearing 'a pair of beads of black',[71] a rosary, a display of religious defiance. Frustrated by her obstinacy in advocating for the 'old religion', Edward wrote to his sister Mary chastising her for continuing to break the laws of the realm, remarking 'you would be angry to see one of the servants of your household, of those nearest to you, openly disregarding your orders; and so it is with us, and you must reflect that in our estate it is most grievous to suffer that so high a subject should disregard our laws'.[72] The king's council were set to indict Francis Mallet and Alexander Barclay, Mary's chaplains, for preaching heresy against the king's laws. The following year, Mallet was apprehended and imprisoned in the Tower for having 'persisted and persuaded certain others of the King's subjects to embrace his naughty opinions'.[73] Mary hastily wrote to the council defending him, protesting that 'he did it by commandment'. She insisted that no one should find themselves in danger 'for saying Mass in my house', urging the council to discharge her chaplain and 'set him at liberty'.[74] Whereas Mallet, remaining stubborn and reluctant to conform, was brought before the council, his fellow Barclay was pardoned for adhering to their demands.

Servants who put themselves at risk for their faith had to rely on the protection of their royal master or mistress. By the summer of 1551, the king's council summoned Princess Mary's officers, Robert Rochester, Francis Englefield, and Edward Waldegrave, to answer questions regarding the errant activity of her household. At first, Mary tried to excuse Rochester from attending the summons, but his absence was, the council warned, 'under penalty of incurring the King's displeasure', and when the 'malignant' Rochester eventually did attend, they 'reproved him bitterly'. The council felt that it was by their 'instigation and persuasions' that Mary was encouraged in her religious orthodoxy. So great was their influence that they charged these men with ensuring the Act was enforced in Mary's household. They were to forbid her chaplains to celebrate the 'old religion' and warn her servants 'to absent themselves' from any such service.[75] This the officers were reluctant to do, arguing that they could not give any commands to or against Mary as their royal mistress. They reminded the council that they merely managed her household and its 'temporal' goods, and 'as for her religion and conscience she asked nobody's advice', so that 'not one of her ministers dared broach the matter in her presence'.[76] Of course, the council urged that they must regard their loyalty first to the king, and when they arrived back at Mary's household bearing the council's instructions, the princess regarded it 'very strange and unreasonable that her ministers and servants should wield such authority in her house'.[77] She disregarded their orders and warned them sternly 'not to meddle with religious or her conscience'.[78] Mary sent them back with a letter addressed to the king, maintaining that her servants should not be made to 'move' her, as she wrote, 'in matters touching my soul'.[79] Edward's council insisted again that her officers must declare the king's orders by 'virtue of their allegiance' to him, but Rochester and Waldegrave resisted, stating that they would 'rather endure whatsoever punishment or imprisonment the Lords should think meet for them', while Englefield remarked that 'he could neither find in his heart nor in his conscience to do it'.[80] This staunch loyalty shown by Mary's officers, to their mistress and to the 'old religion', was striking. Unsurprisingly, they were all arrested and imprisoned in the Tower for their 'ill' behaviour, having 'manifestly disobeyed' their sovereign. A concerned Mary would plead for their release, particularly Rochester, her comptroller, giving a crude description of her undertaking his duties, which were at once beneath her station and above her capacity:

> I take the account myself of my expenses, and how many loaves of bread be made of a bushel of wheat... my father and mother never brought me up with baking and brewing, and to be plain with you I am weary of mine office, and therefore, if my Lords will send my officer home they shall do me pleasure.[81]

Only when the king threatened to discharge Mary's entire household did she rethink her obstinacy. Her officers were shortly released from the Tower, and the princess petitioned her brother to permit her to celebrate Latin mass, but in her Privy chamber.[82] After many such years of being 'sorely troubled and distressed', and her household caught 'in so dangerous a pass',[83] Mary eventually became queen. She was able to reinstate Catholicism both at court and in the wider kingdom, much to the relief of her loyal attendants.

Servants faced pressure to conform throughout the rest of the Tudor period. Sir John Gates, gentleman of Edward VI's Privy Chamber, was taken as Mary's prisoner in 1553 after proclaiming Lady Jane Grey as queen. Shortly before his execution,

Gates was brought to the chapel within the Tower to hear mass. There he was urged by a priest that, if he was to receive the sacrament, he not only had to believe that it was 'the body and blood of our saviour Christ', but also had to openly acknowledge his mistakes in promoting heresy under the late king. 'I confess we have been out of the way a long time, and therefore we are worthily punished', Gates said, 'and, being sorry therefore, I ask God forgiveness therefore most humbly, and this is the true religion'.[84] On the scaffold, moments before death, Gates declared that he was 'the greatest reader of the scripture', not, 'to aid the glory of God', but 'arrogantly to be seditious, and to dispute thereof, and privately to interpret it after my own liking and affection'.[85] Mary kept a strict eye also on her sister Elizabeth, who was suspected of 'having lent an ear to the heretics'.[86] The queen even told the Imperial ambassador, Simon Renard, that she believed Elizabeth 'had not a single servant or maid of honour who was not a heretic'.[87] Sir Henry Bedingfield, Mary's councillor and Elizabeth's custodian, was charged with ensuring that the princess and her household only attended divine services in Latin, not English. With an English primer in her hands, Elizabeth remarked, 'I know the queen's majesty does not use it, and therefore unless my lord chamberlain will assent to it, it shall not be used for me'.[88] Outwardly, Elizabeth was anxious to reassure the queen, promising to 'dismiss those of her servants who were suspect'.[89] She necessarily distanced herself from their actions, but how far she encouraged them in private remains unclear. Although the princess dutifully attended Latin services, some of her household refused to attend. Mary was not comforted. She wrote to Bedingfield and advised him to discharge Elizabeth Sandes, one of her sister's gentlewomen whom she regarded as 'a person of an evil opinion', and 'not fit to remain about her'. Bedingfield agreed that Sandes was 'a woman to be looked unto for her obstinate disposition'. The princess was greatly upset by Sandes' departure, and her absence was reportedly 'not without great mourning'.[90] John Foxe later wrote that Sandes was 'displaced from her room' and forced into exile to avoid persecution for her beliefs.[91] And she was not the only one who left Elizabeth's household so abruptly. Foxe recalled that Robert Horneby, of her Privy Chamber, 'being willed to come to mass, refused to do so'. He was summoned by the Privy Council and committed to the Marshalsea. Horneby may have anticipated that his faith would eventually get him into trouble, as he petitioned 'many times' for a licence to absent himself from the household, his excuse being that he wished to 'seek remedy for a disease which he has, as he says'.[92] It was thought that he was 'not unlike to have sustained further danger', but eventually Horneby was fortunate enough to be released.[93] Many of Elizabeth's attendants, together with those who had served the late king Edward, were either banished on suspicion of committing heresy, or fled the country for fear of persecution. Upon Elizabeth's accession, one of Mary's ladies grumbled that the new queen would 'not be well-disposed in matters of religion, for I see her inclined to govern through men who are believed to be heretics and I am told that all the women around her definitely are'.[94]

Some servants did adapt to survive, serving peacefully and keeping the conflict of their faith within, where it could be tolerated. It was observed, for instance, in 1555, that one Sir Peter Carew was 'well disposed towards the service of the King and Queen', while 'his conscience is still, however, influenced by his religion'.[95] Others were less cautious, and attracted attention for their faith. Edward Underhill, gentleman pensioner to Mary I, and known to some contemporaries as a 'hot gospeller', was imprisoned in Newgate in 1553 for drafting a pamphlet which denounced the Pope and all papists. During his examination, Underhill declared, 'I have offended no laws, and I have served the Queen's Majesty's father and brother a long time; and in their service have spent and consumed part of my living, never having, as yet, any preferment or recompense; and the rest of my fellows likewise, to our utter undoings, unless the Queen's Highness be good unto us'. While imprisoned, Underhill met Brystow, who went on to serve as one of Mary's guardsmen, and kept his Protestant faith a secret, 'for else,' he said, 'he should not have found such favour as he did at the Keeper's hands', recognising that 'to such as love the Gospel, they were very cruel'.[96] Underhill was eventually released, and although he was formally discharged from his office, he continued to be paid his wages by Sir Humphrey Radcliffe, the lieutenant of the gentlemen pensioners who 'always favoured the Gospel'.[97] Evidently Underhill had his sympathisers within the queen's household, though he had his share of antagonists too. At the outset of Wyatt's rebellion in 1554, the band of pensioners were commanded to stand guard. Underhill 'thought it best, in like sort, to be there, lest by my absence I might have some quarrel picked unto me'. Upon arriving at Whitehall, he was met with the 'rank papist' John Norris, of the queen's Privy Chamber, who, upon seeing Underhill's name on the check roll for attendance, struck it out saying, 'that heretic shall not be called to watch here!'[98] Still Underhill faithfully donned his armour and went to defend the queen against Wyatt's advancing forces. A year later, when Underhill arrived at Winchester for the celebrations of Mary's marriage with Philip of Spain, he was challenged again by Norris, as Underhill recalled:

"What!" said he unto me; "what do you here?"

"Marry, sir!" said I, "what do you here?"

"Eh!" said he, "are you so short with me?"

"Sir!" said I, "I must and will forbear for the place you be in; but if you were in the place you were in, of the Outer Chamber, I would be shorter with you! You were then the doorkeeper; when we waited at the table. Your office is not to find fault at my being here. I am at this time appointed to serve here, by those that be in authority; who know me, as well as you do!"

"They shall know you better!" said he, "and the Queen also."

At this stage, John Calveley, a fellow gentleman pensioner, intervened, urging Norris to show 'good faith', for Underhill had 'served of long time', and was 'ready to venture his life in defence of the Queen's Majesty'. A frustrated Norris remarked, 'I perceive you will hold together!' 'Else we were worse than beasts,' Calveley responded, 'if we would not, in all lawful cases, so hold together; he that touches one of us, shall touch all.' Underhill would be challenged once more, this time by the Earl of Arundel, who branded him an 'arch-heretic' and, perusing the check roll of gentlemen pensioners, questioned the lieutenant Radcliffe, 'what does he here?', to which he replied, 'I know no cause why he should not be here, he is an honest man. He has served from the beginning of the band and was as forward as any to serve the Queen, in the time of Wyatt's rebellion'. It was clearly felt by Calveley and Radcliffe that Underhill's faith was irrelevant, as he had long proven himself to be loyal to the crown by his actions.[99] The same grace was shown to Sir Thomas Cornwallis in Elizabeth I's reign. Although precautions were being taken in 1596 against invasion by seizing the arms and horses belonging to any recusants, an exception was made for Cornwallis, whose loyalty was so dependable that it was not deemed necessary to treat him in the same manner. Cornwallis, the Privy Council observed, was 'an ancient and true servant unto her Majesty, and notwithstanding his difference in religion hath never been touched with any suspicion of disloyalty or ill affection to her Majesty and the State, but has always carried himself as a dutiful and faithful subject'.[100]

9

'Honest and moderate play'
COURT CULTURE AND PASTIME

Servants engaged in all manner of 'vain' and 'idle' pastimes at the Tudor court. In the early years of Henry VIII's reign, the king's Privy Chamber was dominated by a tightly knit circle of boisterous bachelors with whom he spent much of his time in leisure. The young king was lively, energetic, and always seeking out physical challenges in sport, like jousting, wrestling, tennis and, in the winter, even snowball fights.[1] Who better to compete with in such pursuits than his own attendants? They would participate chiefly in hunting, hawking and archery. Richard Pace observed Henry would arise early, 'and hunts till 9 or 10 at night', remarking that his master 'spares no pains to convert the sport of hunting into a martyrdom',[2] while Thomas Heneage reported that 'His Grace, every afternoon, when the weather is anything fair, does ride forth on hawking, or walks in the park, and comes not in again till it be late in the evening'.[3] So often would the king's servants accompany him when he went hunting or hawking that the court was left 'disgarnished' and his pastimes were often 'hindered, and impeached'.[4] In 1551, Edward VI recorded games of archery in which he participated with his household. 'A challenge made by me,' the young king recalled, 'that I, with sixteen of my chamber, should run at base, shoot, and run at ring with any seventeen of my servants, gentlemen in the court'.[5] The following year, Edward wrote to his friend Barnaby Fitzpatrick, contrasting the experience of his court hunting during the summer progress with the grim reality of war which engaged Fitzpatrick while he was stationed in France:

> For whereas you all have been occupied in killing of your enemies, in long marchings, in pained journeys, in extreme heat, in sore skirmishings, and divers assaults, we have been occupied in killing of wild beasts, in pleasant journeys, in

good fare, in viewing of fair countries, and rather have sought how to fortify our own then to spoil another man's.[6]

Henry VIII's queens and their attendants would occasionally accompany the king in his pastime. Catherine rode with the king to Shooter's Hill for the May Day celebrations in 1515. The queen and her ladies joined Henry and his lords 'to take the open air', and they were treated to an elaborate display by archers, led by 'Robin Hood', that 'much pleased the king, the queen and all the company'.[7] 'The Queen intends to hunt tomorrow four miles hence in a little park', Pace observed in the summer of 1518.[8] Indeed hunting was not exclusively a masculine preserve. One afternoon in 1565, Elizabeth I 'went hunting' and 'killed two fat bucks'. She 'went so hard that she tired everybody out, and as the ladies and courtiers were with her they were all put to shame'.[9] Whenever the Tudors would 'walk privily, in parks, orchards, gardens, or galleries',[10] they were trailed by their servants. While Princess Elizabeth was under house arrest in 1554, her custodian Sir Henry Bedingfield wished to know if she was still 'to have liberty to walk in the garden when so ever she does command'. Mary I granted that, 'for her recreation', her sister was permitted 'to walk abroad and take the air in the gardens', provided Bedingfield was himself always present in her company. He later recalled that, on one particularly sunny day, the princess dragged him and her gentlewomen all around the grounds trying to find shade.[11]

Tudor queens and princesses had their own recreation to enjoy with their ladies and gentlewomen.[12] Catherine of Aragon kept her servants occupied with needlework. In 1527, when the queen was visited by cardinals Wolsey and Campeggio, she 'came out of her Privy chamber with a skein of white thread about her neck', and excused herself: 'but to make answer to your request I cannot so suddenly, for I was set among my maidens at work, thinking full little of any such matter'.[13] Of Anne Boleyn's handiwork, George Wyatt wrote that many of the 'rich and exquisite works' which adorned Hampton Court were 'for the greater part wrought by her own hand and needle, and also of her ladies'. This queen apparently encouraged 'those about her daily to work in shirts and smocks for the poor'.[14] Some distinction was made between pastime which was deemed appropriate for women, and that which could be seen 'vain', even 'illicit'. Embroidering fine shirts and wall hangings, for instance, would keep idle hands busy. In the midst of king's 'Great Matter', Catherine of Aragon was accused of exhorting her attendants far too often 'to dance and pass time'.[15] Conversely, William Forrest, who served the queen's daughter Mary as her chaplain, remembered Catherine directing them in pastime which she felt was 'meet' for women:

> With stool and needle she was not to seek
> And other practices for ladies meet;
> To pastime at Tables, Tick-tack or Gleek,
> Cards, Dice, or vain toys accustomed yet,
> She thought not seemed for women discreet,
> But were incitements to sin and vice,
> Wherefore she gave her to other exercise.
> The youth that to her were associate,
> As upon her, their mistress, to attend,
> Using touches light and elicited,
> She thereof would them most straightly defend,
> With other means if they list not amend,
> So that in that part (which was marvellous)
> Her Court was as it had been Religious.[16]

Some ordinances forbade 'unlawful games' at court, while others warned against 'immoderate and continual play'.[17] There was an incident in 1598, when Ambrose Willoughby, Elizabeth I's squire for the body, interrupted a game of cards in the Presence chamber between Sir Walter Raleigh and Henry, Earl of Southampton. It must have been quite late at night, as the queen had already gone to bed, and the squire 'desired them to give over' and finish their game. 'Soon after he spoke to them again,' it was reported, 'that if they would not leave he would call in the Guard to pull down the board'. The noblemen left, but the Earl 'took exception at him, and told him he would remember it'. Later, the Earl cornered Willoughby in the gardens and 'struck him', while the scrappy squire 'pulled off some of his locks'. The queen rightly backed Willoughby, who was merely doing his job by enforcing the ordinances of the household.[18]

All of the Tudors gambled, and their servants made for convenient chancers. The Eltham ordinances of 1526 stated that Henry VIII was 'contented, that for some pastime', his attendants 'shall use honest and moderate play, as well at the chess and tables, as at cards', though his chambers were not to be used for 'frequent and intemperate plays, as the groom porter's house'.[19] Be it cards, dice, tennis, archery, or bowls, almost any pastime could settle a wager, and Henry himself frequently gambled with his gentlemen. Between 1529 and 1532, the king played cards and dice with Richard Hill, his sergeant of the cellar, and lost money in varying amounts from £11 8s. 4d. to £22 10s.[20] At card games, Henry would sometimes enlist Hill to play alongside him as his partner at the table.[21] The sergeant also played bowls with Anne Boleyn in 1532, on which occasion he won £7 7s. 6d.[22] In 1519, Henry Courtenay, Earl of Devon, played shuffleboard in the king and queen's chambers with their attendants, and laid out various sums for 'playing money' against Sir Christopher Garneys, Henry Sherbourne and Arthur Pole. The Earl lost 13s. 4d. to William Welsh 'at shooting' in Greenwich, and 8s. to William Carey on a game of tennis at Richmond. Some of the king's servants would be accused of encouraging him too far in his incessant gambling 'which has made him lose of late a treasure of gold'.[23] Edward VI owed as much as £143 17d. for 'money lost in play' and, in one instance, he wagered ten yards of black velvet on a tilt with Sir Thomas Wroth, of his Privy Chamber, and lost.[24] His gentleman pensioner Edward Underhill later recalled how he was once 'conversant' with and kept the company of 'shifters' and 'dicers' at the young king's court, before he 'fell to reading' and, 'following the preachers', abandoned both the habit and 'the wickedness of those men'.[25] Anne of Cleves regularly played cards with her gentlewomen, as her accounts reveal that while she was queen she frequently laid out, for instance, 33s. 4d. for 'playing at cards', and the next day, 40s. 'for cards', and 20s. for 'groats to play', delivered to and kept in the hands of one of her chamberers, usually Anne Joscelyn.[26] There are similar entries in the accounts of Elizabeth of York, as 13s. 4d. was conveyed by Joan, Lady Guildford, and 6s. 8d. on another occasion by Elizabeth Lee, her gentlewoman, for 'playing at dice'.[27]

Some servants probably gambled more than they could afford. One visitor to Elizabeth I's court witnessed the lords and ladies in her Presence chamber 'playing at various tables for high sums of money'.[28] George, Earl of Shrewsbury, wrote to his wife from court in 1568 to comment that 'it is every night so late before I go to my bed, being at play in the Privy Chamber at primero', a card game, 'where I have lost almost a hundred pounds and lacked my sleep'.[29] Roger Manners, Elizabeth's squire for the body, wrote to the Earl of Rutland in 1583 to thank him 'for the £20, which this day is sore wasted at decoy', another card game.[30] In contrast, Sir William Petre, Mary I's secretary, appears to have been rather more restrained, and only occasionally laid out small sums while socialising or awaiting an audience with his royal mistress. These varied from 7s. 6d. 'lost at cards' in the Presence chamber at Westminster, to 13s. 4d., which he had to lend from William Rice, Mary's groom, after arriving at

Hampton Court unprepared 'to play at passdice with the Queen'. Petre also sent for 4s. from his privy purse to play at cards with Susan Clarencius, the queen's gentlewoman, at her home in Hutton, and 5s. 'to play at cards' in 1548, when Petre hosted Mary at his home, Ingatestone Hall.[31]

Servants often engaged in reading, writing, and idle conversation with artful and witty repartee. As one man warned of Elizabeth I's court, 'you should be here a month before you could learn to speak to one and not offend the other'.[32] Music and poetry were central too, as the Tudors retained bands of minstrels, trumpeters, choirs and more who performed in the Presence chamber or the Great Hall, much to the enjoyment of the rest of the court. In 1583, Elizabeth I tasked her secretary, Sir Francis Walsingham, to recruit a company of 'very skilful and exquisite actors' for her household. These players were 'sworn the Queen's servants', and granted 'wages and liveries as Grooms of the Chamber', to be treated as her own attendants, always on hand to stage entertainment for their mistress.[33] Some servants were already renowned for their talents. Stephen Hawes, Henry VII's groom, was also a poet whose verses reflected on life in the king's court.[34] Philip van Wilder, a Dutch composer and lutenist, served Henry VIII in his Privy Chamber, and was sent on occasion by the king to the royal children to instruct them in the instrument. Prince Edward wrote to his father to thank him for sending Wilder, 'who is both eminent in music and a gentleman', so that he might 'become more expert in striking the lute'.[35] In fact, more than a few attendants who served the Tudors in their households occupied this dual role, performing both domestic duties and musical compositions. A young Mark Smeaton, who was skilled in the virginals, was clothed, rewarded and cared for by Henry VIII before he became a groom of the king's Privy Chamber.[36] Giles Duwes, Princess Mary's gentleman waiter, was also a lutenist, though his will reveals that he had many instruments in his repertoire, like regals, virginals and clavichords.[37] In 1554, Giacomo Soranzo, the Venetian ambassador, noted that Mary, now queen, 'takes pleasure in playing on the lute and spinet, and is a very good performer on both instruments', and that 'before her accession she taught many of her maids-of-honour'.[38] Elizabeth I's maids too were occupied in 'all kinds of music, which they use only for recreation sake when they have leisure and are free from attendance upon the Queen's Majesty'.[39] It was reported in 1575 that one of Elizabeth's grooms enjoyed 'extreme favour with her Majesty on account of his being an excellent musician'.[40]

The Tudors sometimes acted as patrons for their servants so that they could chase more fulfilling pursuits. Giles Duwes recalled that he was commissioned by Mary to write a book, and he 'dared not' refuse her order, 'because of mine obedience that by any service or sacrifice that to her I may do, fulfilling her most noble and gracious commandment'.[41] Some servants even dedicated their works to their royal master or mistress in hope of preferment. Thomas Sternhold, Edward VI's groom, dedicated a collection of psalms to the king shortly after his accession:

> Trusting that as your Grace takes pleasure to hear them sung sometimes of me, so you will also delight not only to see and read therein yourself, but also to command them to be sung to you of others: that as you have the psalm itself in your mind, so you may judge my endeavour by your care.[42]

All of the Tudors had their own fools, who told jokes, sang songs, and staged comedic performances. These men and women had the privilege of familiarity without deference, providing the household 'above-stairs' with entertainment. Will Somers was Henry VIII's fool from 1525, and he was quite dear to the king. His humour could lighten the king's mood, especially in his later years when he struggled with his sore leg. The jokes Somers told were so outrageous that he would sometimes incur the king's anger. Presumably for a skit, Katherine Parr laid out money for three geese and a hen for her fool, Jane. While serving the queen, Jane was befriended by Princess Mary, who paid for her shoes, smocks, a coffer, needles, 'for shaving her head' and at 'the time of her sickness'.[43] Evidently both Will and Jane were cherished members of the royal household, as they feature alongside Henry VIII, Jane Seymour, and the king's three children in the magnificent Tudor family portrait, c. 1545.[44] Those servants who knew the sensibilities of their royal master or mistress too provided great merriment and cheer. 'To cause the king to laugh', Henry Winslow, Henry VII's gentleman usher, wore a paper trapper to a joust in 1494, and 'thereupon painted two men playing at dice and certain others written', which one joyless writer felt were 'not worthy here to be rehearsed'.[45]

Some servants were accused of having a little too much fun during their time at the Tudor court. Sir William Knollys moaned that, late in the evening, Elizabeth I's maids-of-honour 'used to frisk and hey about in the next room', which kept him awake. Apparently one night, having lost all patience with their laughing, Knollys dared to intrude on the maids, wearing only a nightshirt and a pair of spectacles on his nose, and issued them with a stern warning.[46] Dr Richard Croke, the young Henry, Duke of Richmond's tutor, complained in 1527 that his household was so unrestrained that they kept their master from his studies. His attendants, Croke claimed, had taught the prince to act with 'impunity', and 'do all they can' to make him dislike literature and 'despise' Croke's authority as his tutor. He blamed Richmond's comptroller, Sir Richard Cotton, for having 'forbidden Croke to have access to the prince, even at the hours of teaching', in favour of 'buffoons' who 'sing indecent songs before him'. Cotton obviously felt that Croke was 'too severe', far too inclined to be harsh in his methods, and thus would interfere whenever the tutor would scold the young prince. On the other hand, Croke felt that Cotton was treating the young prince too lightly, excusing his faults, encouraging him to sleep in late, and too often taking him out hunting, shooting or other outdoor activities 'which fatigues him for his lessons'.[47]

Many servants participated in pageants, masques and other dances. Henry VIII's enthusiasm for such festivities and merriment at court saw an increase in the frequency in which these events were staged. The chronicler Edward Hall kept a close eye on such events and recorded them in exquisite detail. In 1510, Henry and twelve of his men 'came suddenly in a morning, into the Queen's chamber' at Westminster, 'all apparelled in short coats... with hoods on their heads, and hosen of the same, every one of them, his bow and arrows, and a sword and a buckler, like outlaws, or Robin Hood's men', before 'certain dances and pastime' were made. Amusingly, Catherine of Aragon and her ladies were 'abashed, as well for the strange sight, as also for their sudden coming'.[48] During a pageant held in 1511, a few riotous and unwelcome guests 'ran to the pageant, and rent, tear, and spoiled' it, even 'to the king, and stripped him into his hosen and doublet', while 'the ladies likewise were spoiled'. After 'the king with the queen and the ladies returned to his chamber', where 'all these hurts were turned to laughing and game... and so this triumph ended with mirth and gladness'.[49] At a masque staged at Elizabeth I's court in 1600, eight of the queen's ladies and gentlewomen, 'prettily and richly attired', were 'delicate' as they danced altogether. Mary Fitton, Elizabeth's maid, 'went to the queen and wooed her to dance'. 'Her Majesty asked what she was', to which Fitton replied, "Affection". "Affection! Affection is false," the queen remarked, before she too then 'rose and danced'.[50]

Tudor royal households were centres of hospitality and sociability. Servants were responsible for ensuring all chambers were well kept, particularly if they were staging elaborate banquets for courtiers, councillors, noblemen and women, or ambassadors and dignitaries to enjoy. Ordinances for Princess Mary's household in 1525 mandated that her gentlemen, yeomen, grooms and pages had to give their 'due attendance every one as to his room and place', to see that 'the chambers be always serviced as the time and case shall require', and especially 'when there shall be access or recourse of noblemen or other strangers repairing unto that court or that it be as festival days or times or other things requisite'.[51] Later in 1531, when Mario Savorgnano, the Venetian ambassador, visited Mary at Richmond, he was greeted first by the princess, before she then 'turned to her attendants', among them six maids-of-honour, 'desiring them to treat us well, and withdrew into her chamber'.[52] Such occasions strengthened social and political bonds between the royal master or mistress and those who visited them. When Anne Boleyn 'received the king at dinner in her chamber' in 1533, with 'many other lords and ladies' in attendance, Henry VIII was 'so much occupied with mirth and talk' and 'engaged in play and conversation with the ladies' that 'he scarcely talked to the rest of the company' and 'said little which could be understood'![53]

The Tudors often held jousts and tournaments, wherein combatants, many of them royal attendants, fought with swords or lances while mounted on horseback. At a tournament in 1494, Henry VII's master of the horse Sir Thomas Brandon was notable for breaking many lances, recovering from nearly coming off his horse, and ultimately winning the prize of a gold ring with a ruby.[54] Many of Henry VIII's men shared in the 'lusty, young and courageous' king's enjoyment 'in feats of chivalry'. He was always 'delighted to set forth' Sir Francis Bryan and Sir Nicholas Carew, two of his gentlemen servants, at the tilts in 1515. Bryan even lost an eye during the jousts, and the damage was so severe that he wore an eyepatch from that day on. Nicolo Sagudino, a Venetian envoy, reported on a joust which, 'being ended, a beam was brought, some twenty feet in length, and was placed on the head of one of his Majesty's favourites', Carew, 'who was one of the jousters, and he ran a long way with the beam on his head to the marvel of everybody'.[55] At the Field of Cloth of Gold in 1520, in preparation for the 'jousts, tournaments and other feats of arms, as well on horseback as on foot intended to be made', galleries and tents were constructed specifically 'for the Queens' ladies, nobles, and all other comers, as shall resort to see the said feats'.[56] At one joust, the two queens exchanged greetings and began 'talking and amusing themselves, surrounded by great personages and their favourite ladies'.[57] When it began to rain, both Henry and Francis 'ascended the ladies' stages and too amused themselves'.[58] On another occasion, the kings 'passed the time partly on horseback, and partly with the ladies'.[59] It was only 'after salutations' were 'made to the Queens being by their stages', and 'the reverence done to the Queens and their ladies', that 'the king's had their spears ready'.[60] 'For love of them', it was observed, 'each of the jousters endeavoured to display his valour and prowess, in order to find more favour with his sweetheart'.[61] The presence of women was meant to elevate the competitive spirit and encourage the men in their feats.

Ladies and gentlewomen servants were situated at the centre of a chivalric court culture, in which knights would, feigning their love, woo them with dances, poems, songs and gifts and other favours in an unending pursuit for their affection.[62] At a masque held in the autumn of 1518, twelve 'ladies disguised' with twelve 'knights disguised' together 'danced at one time and after they had danced, they put of their visors, and then they were all known', and all the company 'had high cheer' until two o'clock in the morning.[63] Men and women at court sometimes exchanged letters and tokens, as Elizabeth Blount and Elizabeth Carew did in 1514 with Henry and his favourite, Charles Brandon, Duke of Suffolk. Brandon was frustrated by the lack of attention he received from the queen's maids, and wrote to the king reminding him to tell them 'the next time that I write unto them or send them tokens they shall either write to me or send me tokens again'.[64] Sir Edward Baynton, Anne Boleyn's vice-chamberlain, reported to her brother, George, in the summer of 1533, that, 'as for pastime in the queen's chambers', there 'was never more'.[65] 'If any of you that be now departed have any ladies that you thought favoured you, and somewhat would mourn at parting of their servants,' Baynton continued, 'I cannot perceive the same by their dancing and pastime they do use here, but that other take place, as ever has been the custom'.[66] These interactions, or 'fantasies' as Baynton describes them, between the queen's women and 'their servants', gentlemen at court, represent *amour courtois*, or the 'courtly love' tradition. For many servants, participation in this tradition was merely a fun distraction, and did not necessarily denote romantic or sexual feelings. This much is clear in the account of Giles Duwes, Princess Mary's tutor, who imagines his nine-year old mistress drawing names on Valentine's Day. When the young princess drew the name of the aged and ailing Sir Ralph Egerton, her treasurer, she did not hesitate to take him as her 'husband adoptif', even jesting, as his 'wife', that he took better care of his gout than he did of her.[67]

The 'courtly love' tradition ran through the Devonshire manuscript, an anthology of nearly two-hundred poems of courtly verse, and other riddles and 'tokens', many of which were composed and circulated by women in Anne Boleyn's innermost circle.[68] The manuscript illustrates a courtly circle-in-action, led by Lady Margaret Douglas, Mary Shelton and Mary Howard, Duchess of Richmond, three of Anne's servants. It is a material witness to how men and women interacted with one another in the queen's chambers. By their literary expression, annotation and circulation of the manuscript, the queen's servants provide a view not only of the pastime enjoyed and pleasure taken in 'poetical fancies' and amorous repartee,[69] but also of the impassioned and unrestrained environment in which even Anne herself incautiously flirted with gentlemen at court. Thematically, forbidden, or improper love, loyalty, and fidelity, are contextualised by the scandals which arose in the queen's chambers. Lady Margaret Douglas conducted her liaisons with Thomas Howard, the younger son of the Duke of Norfolk, in secret. But when their affair was discovered, it was the queen's servants who were examined: John Ashley, Anne's sewer, apparently 'perceived love between them' for at least 'a quarter of a year', while Thomas Smith, clerk of the council, remarked that often the Duke 'would watch until my Lady Boleyn was gone and then steal into her chamber'.[70]

Flirting at the Tudor court was rampant. The kind of flirtations typical in this period are captured by an account describing an interaction between Thomas Wyatt and Anne Boleyn, when she was one of the queen's maids, wherein Wyatt

> in sporting wise caught from her a certain small jewel hanging by a lace out of her pocket, or otherwise loose, which he thrust into his bosom, neither with any earnest request could she obtain it of him again. He kept it, therefore, and wore it after about his neck, under his cassock, promising himself either to have it with her favour or as an occasion to have talk with her, wherein he had singular delight, and she after seemed not to make much reckoning of it, either the thing not being much worth, or not worth much striving for.[71]

The flirtation between Elizabeth I and Sir Robert Dudley, her master of the horse, led Alvaro de la Quadra, the Spanish ambassador, to report in 1559 that he had heard 'some extraordinary things about this intimacy, which I would never have believed'.[72] Another observed that Dudley had 'come so much into favour that he does what he likes with affairs and it is even said that her Majesty visits him in his chamber day and night'. Their interactions raised more than a few eyebrows and whisperings at court, with one claiming 'that his wife has a malady in one of her breasts and that the Queen is only waiting for her to die so she can marry Lord Robert'.[73] Only a queen's most intimate attendants could testify to her virtue. In that same year, the Imperial ambassador Baron Breuner set out to investigate Elizabeth's chastity for the Holy Roman Emperor, who was pursuing a prospective match between her and one of his sons. He commissioned François Borth, who was on 'friendly terms with all the ladies of the bedchamber and all other persons who have been about the Queen'. Borth noted that these women did 'swear by all that is holy that her Majesty has most certainly never been forgetful of her honour'. Nevertheless, Kat Ashley was so concerned about the affection Elizabeth had shown towards Dudley that she 'fell at Her Majesty's feet, and on being questioned, implored her in God's name to marry and put an end to all these disreputable rumours'. She urged that the queen's actions would lead to 'much bloodshed in the realm'. Fearing that the reputation of her mistress would come to harm, Ashley apparently remarked 'rather than that this should happen she would have strangled her Majesty in the cradle'. Perhaps a little extreme, and the queen did not share Ashley's concerns, as she felt no one could pay any heed to such rumours 'seeing that she was always surrounded by her ladies of the bedchamber and maids-of-honour, who at all times could see whether there was anything dishonourable between her and her Master of the Horse'. In other words, Elizabeth's women could and did vouch for her chastity. The attendants of Catherine of Aragon and Prince Arthur were called upon to testify, not for, but against the queen's virginity, when Henry VIII wished to annul their marriage in the late 1520s. Both Arthur and Catherine's servants were examined to prove that, in 1501, the day after their wedding, 'this lusty prince and his beautiful bride were brought and joined together in one bed naked, and there did that act'. As the chronicler Edward Hall recorded, Arthur's 'familiar servants, which had then neither cause nor reward to lie or fain, declared openly that in the morning he called for drink, which he before times was not accustomed to do'.[74] Sir Anthony Willoughby, one of Arthur's attendants, would later recall that the young prince emerged from his Privy chamber and said, 'Willoughby, bring me a cup of ale, for I have been this night in the midst of Spain', before remarking, 'Masters, it is good pastime to have a wife', which, to Willoughby, meant that Arthur and Catherine had consummated their marriage the night before. To substantiate that the prince and princess 'lived together as man and wife', this account was supplemented by further testimony taken from the rest of Arthur's attendants, like the groom William Thomas, who stated that he often conducted the prince from his chambers to Catherine's bedchamber, and back again in the morning.[75] Catherine's attendants, presumed to be 'well informed of what passed', were to be cross-examined as to what they knew of the consummation, or non-consummation, of the marriage between Arthur and their mistress. It would appear some effort was made to contact those of her household who had, many years earlier, returned to Spain, like Catalina of Motril, 'who used to make her bed' and 'attend to other secret services of Her Highness' chamber', Maria de Rojas, who 'used to sleep in the queen's own bed', and Catalina Fortes, who was 'much in her confidence'.[76]

Flirting at court inevitably gave rise to the problems of sexual immorality. When Edward VI sent Barnaby Fitzpatrick to France in 1551, he advised him to 'behave himself honestly, more following the company of gentlemen, than pressing into the company of the ladies there', and to apply himself in 'honest games' such as hunting, riding, shooting and tennis, and 'not forgetting sometime, when you have leisure, your learning'.[77] A year later, the young king acknowledged Fitzpatrick, 'in avoiding all kind of vices', and pursuing only pastimes 'that be honest and meet for a gentleman', had left Edward 'not a little glad'.[78] Fitzpatrick responded to the king in a letter promising always to abide by his instructions and advice.[79] Whereas promiscuity, or even adultery, would rarely touch a man's honour and reputation, women serving at court were wholly vulnerable to such charges. A queen's household had to be the epitome of morality. Anne Boleyn acknowledged the potential for 'wantonness', 'pleasures' and 'licentious liberty' in her chambers, and was acutely aware of such dangers, urging her chaplains, as Latymer recalled, 'to omit nothing that may seem to appertain to my honour': 'in this wise you may preserve my court inviolate'.[80] Even if the character and demeanour of women was irreproachable, their virtue remained the subject of scrutiny and gossip. 'You may imagine whether, being an Englishwoman and having been long at court, she would not hold it a sin to be still a maid', Chapuys mused at Jane Seymour's apparent virginity upon her marriage to the king.[81] Jane may have been eager to set herself apart from her predecessor and rid the queen's household of its supposedly wayward influence, by consciously and carefully constructing the image of her attendants as gentle and virtuous. If Anne's household was flirtatious and given to vanity, Jane's would, by her rigid enforcement of discipline and decorum, maintain an outwardly virtuous and incontestably high moral standard. Anne's maid-of-honour, Besse Harvey, was discharged, and wrote to Sir Francis Bryan, gentleman of the king's Privy Chamber, asking 'why she was discharged of the Queen's service', soliciting him to find her preferment. Bryan 'sent her word that he had moved it', but 'the King bid him meddle with other matters'.[82] Perhaps Besse, whose reputation was far from beyond reproach, was discharged, and kept out of the queen's household on account of Jane's rigidly enforced morality. A woman whose reputation had been brought into disrepute was unfit to attend upon the queen.[83] 'To serve God and to be virtuous', it was observed, was 'much regarded' in Jane's household.[84]

How their servants led their own lives, in what they said, what they did, where they went and with whom, even what they wore, reflected upon the Tudors as their royal masters and mistresses. This is perhaps why several of Elizabeth I's attendants were punished for their transgressions. Mary, Lady Cheke, of the queen's Privy Chamber, was married to Henry Mackwilliam, gentleman pensioner, but in 1569, she and Thomas, Earl of Ormond, were temporarily banished from court 'for having been surprised together in a secret and suspicious place'.[85] Helena, Marchioness of Northampton, one of Elizabeth's ladies, and Thomas Gorges, the queen's groom, married in secret in 1576. When the queen learned of it, Gorges was imprisoned, and the Marchioness was exiled, left a 'poor, desolate, and banished creature'. The Marchioness knew well that the only way to restore favour was to attend court, 'if it be but to see her Majesty', as she wrote begging the Earl of Sussex to 'remember my sorrowful cause to her Majesty that if any hope be left I may receive some relief'.[86] Eventually Elizabeth's heart warmed, and both her attendants were permitted to return. In 1581, Anne Vavasour, the queen's maid, became pregnant out of wedlock. Elizabeth, who was 'greatly grieved with the accident', sent her to the Tower once she had given birth to a son.[87] When Mary Fitton was appointed as Elizabeth I's maid-of-honour in the 1590s, courtier Sir William Knollys wrote to her father and his 'very loving friend' Sir Edward Fitton to assure him: 'I will with my counsel advise your fair daughter, with my true affection love her and with my sword defend her if need be. Her innocence will deserve it and her virtue will challenge it at my hands, and I will be as careful of her well doing as if I were her true father'.[88] Knollys himself, however, soon became infatuated with the young maid, and in spite of his promises to her father, it seems he did little else but pine for her. By 1601, Fitton was being pursued by William, Earl of Pembroke. To visit him undetected, she would apparently 'put off her head attire and tuck up her clothes and take a large white cloak and march as though she had been a man to meet the said Earl out of the Court'.[89] Their affair was soon uncovered, as Mary was 'proved with child', and although she swore that the Earl had promised to marry her, it was reported that he 'utterly renounces all marriage'. 'I fear they will both dwell in the Tower awhile', one man observed, 'for the queen has vowed to send them there'.[90] Ultimately, both were discharged from court, and although the queen had the Earl imprisoned in the Fleet, he could not be persuaded to marry her maid.[91]

10

'Expert in outward parts'
WAR, SECURITY AND DIPLOMACY

Tudor royal households functioned for the protection and security of the crown. Upon the accession of Henry VII in 1485, as the chronicler Edward Hall wrote, his reign was burdened

> with troubles and mischiefs before past, remembered that it was wise to fear and provide for the crafty wiles and lurking traps of his secret enemies, remembering all me for the most part imbrued and exercised in planting of division and sowing dissention, can not lightly leave their pestiferous appetite and seditious occupation.[1]

Entries to royal palaces, and the doors to their chambers, were closely guarded. The 1494 ordinances for Henry VII's household dictated that, once the king retired for the evening, his attendants 'must see that the watch be set'.[2] All households employed yeomen of the Chamber for this purpose, but the crown also retained yeomen of the Guard, established by Henry VII 'for the safeguard and preservation of his own body,' being 'hardy, strong and of agility to give daily attendance on his person'.[3] They were described at the reception of Catherine of Aragon in 1501 as 'strong, valiant, and bold men' who were 'evermore standing by the ways and passages upon a row in both the sides where the King's Highness should from chamber to chamber, or from one place to another, at his goodly pleasure be removed'.[4] At the celebrations for the birth of Prince Henry in 1511, crowds of onlookers in attendance managed to breach and lay their hands on their sovereign, at which time 'the king's guard came suddenly, and put the people back, or else as it was supposed more inconvenience had ensued'.[5] Gentlemen Pensioners, a band of royal guardsmen armed with spears and poleaxes, were instituted in 1509 as the 'spears' and 'chosen from men of noble blood'. 'Unexercised in the feat of arms', they had to be rigorously trained.[6] Refounded in Thomas Cromwell's ordinances at the end of 1539, and led by a captain, Sir Anthony Browne, these men, like the Guard, were stationed around the court for the safety and security of the crown. For the reception of Anne of Cleves at Greenwich in 1540, sure to be a joyous and potentially riotous occasion, the gentlemen pensioners were stationed strategically 'in such parts of the house as shall be meet to keep order'.[7]

Although the Tudors had their own bodyguard, they were flanked too by the rest of their entourage. Precautionary measures were taken, but those employed by the crown still had to be constantly vigilant. In 1525, when Henry VIII, chasing his hawk, attempted to vault over a muddy ditch with a pole, it suddenly broke and he fell in head first. If the heroic Edmond Mody, the king's footman, had not immediately 'leapt into the water' and pulled up his head 'which was fast in the clay', it was thought that his master would have drowned.[8] Later, in 1537, fearing that his only son might be vulnerable to disease, or worse, assassination, Henry drew up instructions for Prince Edward's household holding them responsible for 'the keeping, oversight, care, and cure of his Majesty's and the whole realm's most precious jewel the Prince's grace'. These servants were required to exercise 'all diligent and honest heed, caution, and foresight', which 'ought to be taken to avoid (as much as man's wit may), all practices and evil enterprises, which might be devised against his grace'.[9] More specifically, they had to ensure that only they had the opportunity to 'touch his grace's person, cradle, or any other thing belonging to his person, or have any entry or access into his grace's Privy chamber'.[10] John, Duke of Northumberland's increasing concern for security in 1550 led him to restate the duties of the Privy Chamber, urging them to be 'diligent in their office' and always present to surround and protect the boy king.[11] Richard Blount, Edward VI's gentleman usher, observed that 'if the King's Majesty remove to any strange house', his servants must be sent ahead 'to see that all the roofs and floors be strong and sure', and 'that his bed chamber especially, and all other his privy chambers have no back doors into gardens or courts'.[12] 'Great care' was taken in 1567, as Elizabeth I 'ordered all the keys of doors leading to her chambers to be taken away, and the only entrance is by one door'.[13] In 1594, William Cecil tightened security around the queen by proclamation, declaring that 'her Majesty forbids all persons that are not servitors upon the council or upon other lords and ladies or gentlemen attending on her Majesty, to forbear to come to the court or near to the court'.[14] All back gates were locked shut, the names of all those admitted at the front gate written down, and if any intruders were found in the vicinity of the court without permission or reason, they were to be thrown in prison.[15]

The Tudors were to be protected by their servants from eating food which had been poisoned, or wearing clothes which had been tampered with. It was their responsibility to ensure there had been no 'intermeddling' by 'other persons having no office there, in such wise as no danger may follow'.[16] In around 1563, William Cecil was so worried about the potential for poisoning that he drew up a memorandum specifically regarding the food that Elizabeth I ate and the clothes that she wore. Cecil urged that the queen's apparel, and 'all manner of things that shall touch any part of your Majesty's body bare, be circumspectly looked unto, and that no person be permitted to come near it, but such as have the trust and charge thereof'. The queen's gentlewomen were the caretakers of her clothes, giving no one else the opportunity to place within them some harmful substance. 'No foreign meat or dishes' were to be served to the queen 'without assured knowledge from whom the same comes'.[17] At a state occasion in 1600, it was observed that, as the dishes were brought into the Presence chamber, one of Elizabeth I's ladies 'after kneeling three times, took a piece from each dish to be tasted'.[18] These fears were longstanding, and the threat of poison to the Tudors ever present. In 1533, the Pope feared that Catherine of Aragon was particularly vulnerable, and warned that, unless her servants were 'trusty and devoted', she 'ought to quit England at once lest they should administer poison to her'.[19] The Imperial ambassador Eustace Chapuys was concerned that Princess Mary had only one maid in her retinue, and 'the usual practice of making her taste the Princess' food as a precaution has been done away with, which is equivalent to opening the gate to the perils and insidious dangers from which God Almighty might preserve her'.[20]

Servants could be armed at short notice as a precautionary or reactionary measure to bolster the court and to aid in the defence of the kingdom. In 1556, for instance, Mary I's Privy Council ordered, 'upon consideration of the state of things at this time', that all of the queen's officers and servants be summoned 'to enquire what armour and weapon each of them have, giving them straight charge and commandment in their Majesty's names that every of them do prepare such armour and weapon'.[21] The following year, Mary wrote to Henry, Lord Arundel, her steward, and appointed him as Lieutenant General, with directions to muster and arm all of her servants and their tenants.[22] The queen was taking no chances after the outbreak of Wyatt's rebellion in 1554, at which military support in her household proved crucial to secure her position. When Wyatt's forces pushed into Southwark, Edward Underhill, one of the gentlemen pensioners, recalled how they

> were commanded to watch in armour that night at the court... we came up into the chamber of presence with our poleaxes in our hands, wherewith the ladies were very fearful; some lamenting, crying, and wringing their hands, said "Alas, there is some great mischief toward; we shall all be destroyed this night! What a sight is this, to see the queen's chamber full of armed men; the like was never seen nor heard of.[23]

One chronicler recorded that, within the court, as the rebels drew nearer, 'there should you have seen running and crying of ladies and gentle women shutting of doors and such a shrieking and noise as it was wonderful to hear'.[24] Another report stated that some of the guard apparently came home with 'their coats turned, all ruined, without arrows or string in their bow, or sword, in very strange wise', which was 'very displeasing to the queen and council'.[25] Sir John Gage, the queen's lord chamberlain, led around a thousand guardsmen, among others, to push back Wyatt's forces at Charing Cross. But when the rebels approached, many on the queen's side panicked and 'were so frightened that they folded in at the gates in such haste that old Gage fell down in the dirt and was foul arrayed'.[26] Gage, dragging his frail body up and out of the mud, was 'so amazed' that he and others cried 'Treason!', suspecting their own side had abandoned the queen for Wyatt.[27]

The Tudor royal household provided crucial military assistance, as their servants formed the nucleus of a standing army whenever it was deemed necessary. At the onset of the Pilgrimage of Grace in the autumn of 1536, upon learning that 'certain lewd persons have lately made insurrection' against the king's 'evil counsellors', Henry VIII wrote to members of the English nobility and gentry, ordering each of them to immediately rally their 'servants, tenants, and friends to repress the evil disposed persons lately assembled'.[28] Chief among those whom the king could depend on for this support were his own attendants, especially those who were 'well furnished with men', or those 'who have lands or rule thereabouts' and thus themselves commanded large retinues.[29] As local officeholders, if not landowners, servants had the authority to unite men in their respective jurisdictions and lead them into battle. It was remembered of Henry Norris, that for all the fees he accumulated from the local offices he held as groom of the stool, 'the leading of the men, whenever it took place, was what he regarded'.[30] For the Pilgrimage of Grace, Sir John Gage, vice-chamberlain, rallied 50 men in Sussex, while Sir Edward Neville and Sir Thomas Cheney, gentlemen of the Privy Chamber, provided 200 men each in Kent, Sir Nicholas Carew a further 200 men in Surrey, and Sir William Paulet, comptroller, 100 men in Hampshire.[31] Stationed in Nottingham and preparing to march to Doncaster against the rebels, Thomas, Earl of Rutland, the queen's lord chamberlain, requested that the king send to him 'a man that is expert in wars'. Henry had already sent Roger Radclif, of his Privy Chamber, to join him, and would insist that the Earl not doubt his abilities and 'in all things to use his advice and counsel'.[32] Having directed his groom Walter Walsh in the days prior 'to prepare and furnish to attend and wait upon us in our intended journey against the rebels', rallying some 200 men to the cause, Henry wrote to him again, this time to express his gratitude and instruct his garrison to stand down, to remain 'in such a readiness as upon reasonable warning you may be with us at such time and place', if or when they were required to rise again.[33] Sir William Fitzwilliam, treasurer of the Household, later told that he came 'with such diligence' when summoned by the king that he brought with him 'neither bed, coat, gown', nor any 'other apparel, save only such as I have daily on my back'.[34]

Indeed servants were urged always 'to be in readiness', as time was sensitive in suppressing rebellion or waging war.[35] The lists of men mustered, for instance, for the Boulogne expedition in 1544, indicate that servants in the Henry VIII's Chamber, Privy Chamber, Household and Stable brought with them horsemen, billmen, pikes and archers, with numbers varying from a rather more humble following of one to many hundreds of men each in their armies, which together amounted to a powerful and surely quite an intimidating force.[36] The most trusted servants would undertake roles which were central to military strategy. In 1545, the king sent Sir Edward Bellingham, of his Privy Chamber, to Henry Howard, Earl of Surrey. The king assured the Earl that he had 'special trust and confidence' in Bellingham to communicate 'matters of great importance, touching the advancement of our affairs, and annoyance of our enemies'. He urged Surrey to consult with Bellingham to consider 'by what means and with what numbers the enemies' fort may be taken, surprised or won'. If the Earl intended to take the fort, the king advised that Bellingham, of 'good experience and forwardness', should be assigned to a post fit for the 'place whereto we have called him', as a gentleman of the Privy Chamber, 'and give him occasion to declare that earnest service which we are well assured he means, and will not fail to see executed'.[37]

If the king was at war, so too was the queen and her household. While Henry VIII led the charge on a military campaign in Tournai in 1513, Catherine of Aragon was appointed as regent and Captain General during the king's absence. Catherine wrote to Cardinal Wolsey that, while the men were 'encumbered' with war, she and her gentlewomen were 'horribly busy with making standards, banners and badges'.[38] An emerging crisis soon required more decisive action from the queen. Within weeks, James IV of Scotland had invaded England. This saw Catherine determined to travel north to meet the threat.[39] Although the queen herself would not take up arms, she rallied her household in response, preparing a reserve army. Warrants were drawn up granting £100 to William Bulstrode, her gentleman usher, 'for the conveyance of the ordinance with the queen's grace northwards', and £36. 14s. 4d. to Owen Holand, her squire, 'for the conveying of 1500 almain rivets northward'.[40] An additional warrant signed by the queen ordered the suits of armour to be delivered to Holand, 'to be conveyed in our journey'.[41] The next day, Thomas Howard, Earl of Surrey, leading the English army, triumphed over James IV and his men in the Battle of Flodden. The Scots were defeated, and their king was dead. His disfigured corpse was taken to Catherine, who wished to send it proudly to her husband. This grim task might have been left to her unfortunate yeoman, John Glynne, but the queen ultimately sent the Scottish king's blood-stained surcoat instead:

> My husband, for hastiness, with Rogecrosse I could not send your Grace the piece of the King of Scot's coat which John Glynne now brings. In this your grace shall see how I can keep my promise, sending you for your banners a King's coat. I thought to send himself unto you, but our Englishmens' hearts would not suffer it.[42]

In 1544, Katherine Parr was appointed regent while Henry was at war in Boulogne. The queen and her council, among them her own servants, communicated with the king and the front line concerning military provisions they required, and any advancements they made.[43] One report brought by Sir William Herbert, of the king's Privy Chamber, reassured the queen that Boulogne had been captured 'without effusion of blood';[44] another informed her that the king's men served 'with such diligence'.[45] The spirited optimism of early dispatches sent back home continued in spite of some casualties. More than a few unnamed servants on the king's side were reportedly 'slain', while George Harper, squire for the body, and John Culpeper, gentleman waiter, 'were hurt with the same shot'.[46] Sir Christopher Morris, master of the ordnance, was hurt by a handgun, 'but he demeaned himself very valiantly before, and killed all the master gunners of Boulogne'.[47] Some of those who were captured would be ransomed.[48] 'One of the scout watch' was apparently 'hanged for being absent when the Frenchmen came'.[49] Sir Anthony Browne, with an army of several hundred, marched on an abbey defended by the French. It was observed that, although 'divers of our men, both horse and foot, were taken and slain', the heroic Anthony 'won it by fire'.[50] The presence of the king's servants, embodying the spirit of their master, surely did much to boost morale among larger garrisons on the battlefield.[51]

The 'Household', or household 'below-stairs', too participated in war campaigns. Likely dating to either 1513 or 1544, a surviving map of an army encampment reveals that many tents were erected for various departments, such as the pantry, pastry, kitchen, ewery and scullery, who administered provisions to Henry VIII and his army. These tents circle the king's lodging, established at the centre of the camp and thus easily accessible for these attendants. On the far-right side of the map, some men, presumably the yeomen, grooms and pages 'below-stairs', are shown to be conveying baskets of bread and turning a pig on a spit. Undoubtedly, these men, probably unarmed, not only kept Henry in the comfort and estate to which he was accustomed as sovereign, but replenished stocks of food and drink to the relief of the king's army.[52]

Servants often acted as ambassadors, sent on diplomatic errands to forge alliances and prevent bloodshed on behalf of their royal master or mistress. The staff of the Privy Chamber in particular were entrusted with confidential, sensitive missions abroad. In 1505, when a widowed Henry VII was contemplating a new match with Joan, queen of Naples, it was understood that he could not contract a marriage 'without being first certified by his ambassadors and envoys as to the person and appearance of the said Queen'. The king would not take her 'if she were ugly, and not beautiful'.[53] He dispatched James Braybrooke and Francis Marzen, grooms of his Privy Chamber, to inquire further. They reported back of the potential bride in uncomfortable, almost excruciating detail, concentrating foremost, as they were instructed, on her appearance and, crudely enough, her financial estate, which was meagre.[54] Before Braybrooke and Marzen, there was Matthew Baker, Henry VII's esquire of the body, who was regularly dispatched to France to meet with Louis XII. He had to apologise to the French king on one occasion in 1502 for struggling to convey his master's words: 'Your grace knows well that I am no clerk, but a man more familiar with war', to which Louis remarked, 'I like this better, for we understand each other well'.[55]

As a gesture of friendship and hospitality, Henry VIII and Francis I exchanged personal servants, and each monarch treated them as if they were his own. A set of instructions for Sir Richard Jerningham, Henry's gentleman of the Privy Chamber and new ambassador to France in 1520, required him to thank Francis I for 'his comfortable words and pleasant messages' sent 'as well by letters of his own hand as by sundry of his familiar servants of his Privy Chamber'.[56] Jerningham would report to Henry that Francis welcomed him into his own Privy Chamber, and was treating him well.[57] His predecessor, Sir Richard Wingfield, too had been sent as one of the king's 'right trusty and near familiars' for the 'perseverance of fraternal love on both parts'.[58] Like Jerningham, his successor at the French court, Sir William Fitzwilliam, was required to keep his master informed of all that occurred while he was there. Understandably, Fitzwilliam was anxious that he would be outed as a spy. He felt it necessary to remind Wolsey not to name either himself or his informant to the French ambassador in England.[59] The cardinal promised to send Fitzwilliam a cipherer to communicate more sensitive matters,[60] as he appears to have lacked the specific skill of one of his fellows in 'household' diplomacy: Sir Francis Bryan, often sent abroad as an envoy, was also one of the king's cipherers, for which he received an additional 50 marks a year.[61] By 1526, it was acknowledged that gentlemen of the Privy Chamber should be 'well languaged, expert in outward parts, and meet and able to be sent on familiar messages, or otherwise, to outward princes, when the case shall require'.[62] Diplomatic missions required 'great dexterity', 'great caution', and 'great secrecy'. Sir Thomas Cheyney, for instance, was expected to subtly undermine the peace agreed between Francis and Charles V, Emperor of Spain in favour of a much more personal and assured alliance with Henry, but without disparaging the Emperor, and in such a manner that it would 'appear as their own suggestion'.[63] Cheyney must have been able to speak French, as one of the instructions laid to him was to congratulate Francis 'not as an oration, but as a familiar, friendly and kind message' to be 'well couched in the French tongue'.[64] Sir Thomas Cheyney wrote a letter to Henry while on embassy in France in 1522:

> In my last letters is mentioned of the French King's commandment to me, that I should use myself at all hours in his Privy Chamber, as I do in yours. Yet, that

notwithstanding I would not be so presumptuous upon his first commandment so to do, wherefore this morning he sent Morrett to my lodging to bring me to him. At my coming, the King was but lately risen, and in his night gown was looking out a window. Please it Your Grace, that when I came into his said chamber, and that he was ready to the washing of his hands, the towel was brought to the Great Master, and so he took it to me, and made me give it to the King, saying, that your Grace used him so, at his being in England.[65]

This exchange of servants cut through formalities. As Cheyney performed the more intimate and personal duties required of the Privy Chamber, his presence physically in the French court facilitated a closer relationship between the two kings.[66] This goodwill between Henry and Francis continued when Sir John Wallop was sent to France as an ambassador in 1528. In one report, Wallop wrote back to Henry, 'how be it, to be plain to Your Grace, I had much care to understand him', he admitted, 'for he has lost the most part of his upper teeth'![67]

Careful consideration was taken as to which servants were best for the mission. Thomas Magnus, Henry VIII's chaplain, and Roger Radclif, his gentleman usher, were sent to Scotland in 1524, as Wolsey regarded them as

> right meet persons for this purpose, the one to give good and wholesome advice in plain and secret manner to the Queen, and the other pleasantly and dulcetly to handle himself with the King, and both to help to the furtherance and conducing of all such things as may sound to the establishment of perfect intelligence between both Princes may and shall do great stead in advertising the King's Grace from time to time of the very truth and certain of the proceedings doings and successes there.[68]

Ralph Sadler, of the Privy Chamber, was sent to Scotland in 1537 to visit the king, James V, and Margaret, queen of Scots and Henry VIII's sister. Crucially, Margaret felt she was able to confide in Sadler, Henry's 'secret servant'.[69] Instructions for Sadler from the king required him to address how his sister was being treated by her husband, Henry Stewart (and in particular how he was mismanaging her finances). Of course, this had to be done 'rather gently' and 'with such dexterity' as to not cause any conflict.[70] A few years later, in 1540, Sadler visited Margaret again, and was able to report that the queen was better treated, though she still complained that her brother did not write more often, 'for it had been a small matter to have spent a little ink and paper upon her'.[71] Anthony Ashley, Elizabeth I's clerk of the Privy Council, was the queen's own 'special choice' to join Sir Francis Drake and Sir John Norris on their journey to Spain in 1589, as his mistress regarded him as 'trusty' and 'well qualified with knowledge, authority, learning, and discretion'. Ashley was entrusted 'to keep a true journal in writing of all public actions and proceedings' and report back to the queen.[72] Later, in 1598, Sir William Cecil was to travel to France accompanied by three or four of the queen's men, though he was hesitant when selecting his companions, knowing well his mistress would notice their absence. 'Before I resolve of any of her Majesty's ordinary servants,' Cecil wrote, 'I desire to know her pleasure, that I may not give offence by carrying any away'.[73]

All men and women in service would have been conscious of the dignity required of their position, but this was especially true for those acting as ambassadors and chosen representatives of the realm. Cecil reminded Anthony Ashley before he was to depart on his 1589 mission that the queen had 'by her princely wise speeches to yourself informed you how to behave yourself in this service'.[74] A few decades earlier, in 1551, Cecil had written to Barnaby Fitzpatrick, Edward VI's ambassador in France, urging him to remember that he carried with him the king's reputation:

> I beseech you that you will think, wheresoever you go, you carry with you a demonstration of the King's majesty, coming *á latere suo*, and bred up in learning and manners with him. With your conversation and modesty let them therefore believe the good reports of the King to be true; and let them perceive what the King is, when one brought up with him *habeat virtutis tam clarum specimen*. This I write boldly, as one that in you will our master's honour and credit.[75]

Fitzpatrick no doubt appreciated Cecil's advice, which he regarded as 'more fatherly than friendly'.[76] Sir William Pickering, the resident ambassador in France, wrote to Cecil regarding Fitzpatrick: 'I assure you his good and gentle nature so much inclined to virtue promises the utter performance of all that your letter requires at his hands'.[77] Some time later Pickering wrote again: 'I assure your lordship that his demeanours have been such towards all men since his coming here, his fashions so sober and discreet in every place, that he has got great praise in this court, and all men his well willers that know him'.[78] Henry II of France even wrote to Edward directly to express his satisfaction with Fitzpatrick's conduct.[79] Likewise, Sir Philip Hoby, of Edward's Privy Chamber, made such a good impression when he was sent to Spain in 1548 that Charles V loathed to send him home. Edward initially wrote to the Emperor asking him to 'grant him favourable access to your person and benevolent audience, as the perfect and mutual friendship binding us requires, and that you may place all trust and confidence in what he shall expose to you from time to time on our behalf, as you would in ourself were we with you in person'.[80] Hoby previously served Edward's father Henry VIII in his Privy Chamber, and was first dispatched to Spain in 1538, when he had quickly developed rapport with the Emperor.[81] It was thought that Hoby had 'gained the favour' of Henry 'by his skill in languages, and he was in the habit of serving the King in the entertainment of foreigners'.[82] By 1550, the young king summoned Hoby back to England, asking the Emperor to grant him licence to 'return hither, being desirous of employing his services in certain affairs within this realm'.[83] Charles, however, was reluctant to let him leave, and wrote back weeks later that the 'modest and becoming' Hoby had behaved so 'dutifully where our service was concerned', that 'we would desire him to continue to reside here', albeit accepting that he would grant him leave if Edward wished him to return.[84] Hoby was eventually recalled, and in his place was sent Richard Morison, as the king observed, for the 'fostering and continuance of our good friendship and ancient alliances'.[85]

Not all servants acting as ambassadors were felt to have conducted themselves in the manner appropriate to their station. Sir Francis Bryan and Sir Nicholas Carew were reprimanded in 1519 for dishonouring the king while on embassy in France, where they 'rode disguised through Paris, throwing eggs, stones and other foolish trifles at the people'. Back at court, some judged the ambassadors to have returned 'all French, in eating, drinking and apparel, yea, and in French vices'.[86] Nor were missions led by servants always successful. In 1568, Henry Middlemore, Elizabeth I's groom, was entrusted to represent his mistress and communicate her wishes as her special ambassador 'to learn the state of the troubles in Scotland'.[87] Mary, queen of Scots, however, was rather more concerned with why Elizabeth had not visited herself, and although Middlemore tried to make excuses for her, Mary remained unconvinced.[88]

Reports would indicate that, while on embassy, servants were generally well-received and treated honourably. Sir Ralph Sadler wrote in 1540 that, upon his arrival, he was set to reside in 'a mean lodging', but James V soon intervened and turfed out the Bishop of Ross to accommodate him in a much more fitting and 'fairly furnished' abode. Sadler acknowledged too that he was 'right well entertained of the King'.[89] However, by 1543, as relations began to break down between England and Scotland, Sadler complained that 'there was never so noble a Prince's servant as I am so evil treated as I am amongst these unreasonable people, nor I think never man had to do with so rude, so inconstant, and beastly a nation as this is'.[90] Sometimes servants were homesick, and begged for leave to return. In 1539, Cheyney wrote to Cromwell 'to move the king's majesty' for his return, 'for I lie here at no little charge', Cheyney remarked, 'and can do his highness no service'.[91] Visiting ambassadors and dignitaries to the Tudor court in England were received generously too. Thomas Wyseham, Henry VIII's groom, was tasked in 1515 with accommodating the French ambassadors and their horses, drawing up a bill thereafter for his 'costs and charges', among them 40*s.* for meat and drink, 6*s.* 8*d.* for their beds and lodgings, and 7*s.* 10*d.* for hay.[92] In 1520, a young Princess Mary's household received visitors from France in her Presence chamber, where 'goodly cheer was made unto them', and they were served 'strawberries, wafers, wine and hippocras in plenty'.[93] In 1529, Sir John Russell entertained Eustace Chapuys, the Imperial ambassador, while they waited for the king to arrive. Chapuys saw through Russell's adulation, however, remarking later that the king's servant had told him 'all manner of agreeable things respecting the good impression I had made upon the King, his master, and other flattering remarks about my person, such as the courtiers of this country are in the habit of saying to any new ambassador'.[94] On the morning of his departure in 1545, Chapuys, as he reported, 'hardly had time to rise from the chair in which I was being carried', before he was approached by the queen, Katherine Parr, accompanied by four or five of her gentlewomen attendants, who greeted him for a more intimate audience. Chapuys felt 'from the small suite she had with her, and the haste with which she came' that 'her purpose in coming was specially to speak to me'.[95]

Consorts, princes and princesses sometimes sent their own attendants out of the kingdom. Francisco Felipez, Catherine of Aragon's sewer, was frequently sent to Spain on behalf of the queen. In 1527, Charles V wrote to Inigo de Mendoza, the resident Imperial ambassador in England, acknowledging that Mendoza's letters, along with one written from his aunt, Catherine, 'were brought by Francisco Felipez, who, in virtue of his credentials from the Queen herself, informed us verbally of the state of her affairs'. Felipez was able to relate to Catherine's nephew all of the 'scandalous' details of the king's 'Great Matter', to which the Emperor, appalled, resolved that they 'cannot desert the Queen, our good aunt, in her troubles'.[96] Going abroad on diplomatic missions could be treacherous. In a list of expenses drawn up shortly after the death of his mistress in 1536, Felipez reminded the king that, in France, as he recalled, 'my horse fell and my arm was broken'; on another occasion, as he travelled to and from Aragon, he was robbed of £186 15*s.* by a man named Depontez and his band of eighty men.[97]

Although ambassadors were male, they could be accompanied by their wives, particularly if they were abroad for longer periods of time, like when Sir Nicholas Throckmorton was joined by Anne, Lady Throckmorton, on embassy to France in the 1560s.[98] These women occasionally went on errands on behalf of their royal mistress. Elizabeth Brooke accompanied her husband when he went on embassy in 1554, and Mary I asked that she purchase a looking glass, or 'a glass of crystal' which was 'garnished with jasper'.[99] Sometimes women serving the crown were drawn into diplomacy. At the Field of Cloth of Gold in 1520, their contemporaries focused their reports on their physical appearance and attire, but there is evidence that the ladies and gentlewomen in attendance were engaged in the summit in ways which were more than merely decorative. At a banquet, Francis I was 'received in the most courteous manner possible'.[100] Catherine of Aragon's ladies and gentlewomen were accomplished, and well-rehearsed, in welcoming and entertaining guests, as they did in the queen's chambers in England. 'When that dinner was done', Francis 'passed the time in the banqueting chamber with dancing among the ladies'. With his cap in his hand, he passed from one end of the chamber to the other, kissing the queen's attendants, 'saving four or five that were old and not fair'.[101] How Catherine and her ladies reacted to this faux pas cannot now be known, though presumably women at court often had to bite their tongue to keep up appearances. They dined again with Francis in the queen's chambers two weeks later, and the king staged a masque. Catherine's ladies and gentlewomen were 'apparelled in masking clothes with vizors on their faces gorgeously beseen', and they all 'danced to the sound of fifes'.[102] Such occasions facilitated close interaction between the English and the French courts, so that they 'shall see and converse together familiarly, to the end that it may engender between them an amity more firm and stable'.[103]

Women serving the crown often created an amicable, relaxed environment for 'pleasant' pastime and diplomatic conciliation. Their hospitality and sociability in 'making merry' at formal and informal gatherings in the queen's chambers usually required a certain grace and gaiety, but not always. At a tournament held at Guînes for the Field of Cloth of Gold in 1520, one of the queen's ladies 'took a large flask of wine, and putting it to her lips, drank freely, and then passed it to her companions, who did the like and emptied it'. 'Not content with this, they drank out of large cups, which, during the joust', it was observed, 'circulated more than twenty times amongst the French lords and those English ladies'! The Mantuan ambassador in attendance stood aghast, remarking a few days later that these ladies 'were neither very handsome nor very graceful'.[104] It may be that this unflattering report of the queen's attendants drinking freely, and without ceremony, hardly perpetuated an image of virtue, or magnificence. The French lords too were partaking in the merriment, suggesting that these women were engaging in the 'performance' of familiarity required of diplomacy, embracing fully the spirit of the summit, a celebration of peace. The chronicler Edward Hall regarded only their 'good behaviour from day to day since the first meeting'.[105] The bishop John Fisher, whose account survives in a sermon preached shortly after the summit, was in attendance on the queen's side, and as such was an eyewitness to all these festivities. Though Fisher condemned the cost, extravagance and wastefulness of the summit, of the 'fair ladies' he testified only to their 'sumptuous and gorgeous apparel', and their active participation in 'such dancings, such harmonies, such dalliance, and so many pleasant pastimes'.[106] That neither Hall nor Fisher made mention of any disorder by the women suggests that their behaviour was seen, at least by the English camp, in good cheer. By their beauty, charm, gaiety, and, occasionally drunken diplomacy, these women encouraged friendship and goodwill, or at least, eased tensions and deflected attention from irreconcilable differences between the two countries.[107]

11

'It is hard trusting this wily world'
CONSPIRACY, INTRIGUE AND TREASON

Servants in the Tudor royal household were often caught up in the unpredictable, sometimes precarious, even perilous machinations of monarchy. The Tudor court was characterised by pride, flattery, avarice, intrigue and corruption. 'It is hard trusting this wily world', one man sighed, 'every man here is for himself'.[1] A disgruntled Sir Edward Neville, who had served Henry VIII for many years, uttered to Sir Geoffrey Pole shortly before his death in 1538 that 'the King keeps a court of knaves here that we dare neither look nor speak', and that he 'would rather any life in the world than tarry in the Privy Chamber'.[2] His fellow, Sir Anthony Denny, regarded the court in 1540 as 'a place so slippery… where you shall many times reap most unkindness where you have sown greatest pleasures, and those also ready to do you much hurt, to whom you never intended to think any harm'.[3] In that same year, the French ambassador Charles de Marillac remarked that 'the ministers seek only to undo each other to gain credit, and under colour of their master's good, each attends his own'.[4] It was not only the men at court who had to watch their backs. Before the arrival of her daughters, Anne and Katharine, in 1537, Honor, Lady Lisle, was warned by her agent in London that 'the court is full of pride, envy, indignation and mocking, scorning and derision'.[5] Eleanor Bridges, Elizabeth I's maid-of-honour, commented to Edward, Earl of Rutland in 1574 that 'the court is as full of malice and spite as when you left'.[6] Shortly after her appointment as a lady of the queen's Privy Chamber, Elizabeth, Lady Wolley, assured her father that, although she had 'a good beginning at court', she promised that she would 'live very warily amongst them'.[7]

The potential for conspiracy against the Tudors was very real. The Privy chamber and bedchamber in particular became the focus for intrigue. All chambers were searched regularly for intruders, but more than a few known incidents reveal that security measures were sometimes lacking. The vulnerability of the royal body was made apparent when courtier Pierre de Chartelet one night in around 1562 managed to sneak into the bedchamber of Mary, queen of Scots, where he 'was found lying under the Queen's bed with his sword beside him and his dagger about him'.[8] On another occasion it was reported that Chartelet had, again, in her bedchamber, 'retired himself to a secret corner', and when Mary was left alone with only two of her gentlewomen, he approached with 'such force, and in such impudent sort, that the Queen herself was fain to cry for help'.[9] Chartelet was later beheaded for his actions. In 1566, David Riccio, Mary's secretary, was brutally murdered in her private chambers. Such incidents must have been shocking and terrifying to not only Mary but her cousin Elizabeth. In 1594, an assassination plot hatched between a few Irish gentlemen was uncovered, whereby one of them intended to 'serve some person about the Queen's Privy chamber', taking advantage of the intimacy of their position, 'and then manage to way-lay her in some progress, and kill her with a sword or a dagger, at a gate or narrow passage'.[10] It is rather telling that Thomas Lee, conspiring in 1600 to 'step unto the Queen', Elizabeth, 'and kneel before her, and never rise till she had signed a warrant' for the release of the Earl of Essex, intended to do so 'about supper time' when he knew well she 'was attended with only a few ladies'. At the door of the queen's Privy chamber, Lee, bearing his weapon, was ultimately 'thrust back by the clerk of the kitchen, and apprehended on suspicion'.[11]

All servants were obliged to disclose 'with diligence' if they had heard any person 'speak or use any evil or unfitting language' against their royal master or mistress.[12] If they knew of acts of treason, 'malice and falsehood', 'libels' or 'seditious bills' found 'in or about the court', Elizabeth I's subjects were encouraged to confer 'secretly' with 'some of her Majesty's councillors, or other her faithful servants attendant about her person'.[13] In 1581, for instance, a conspiracy to assassinate Elizabeth engineered by John Payne, a Catholic priest, was uncovered and disclosed by George Eliot, a yeoman of her Chamber, who had recanted his own Catholic faith. Eliot warned that this 'horrible treason' was 'shortly to happen'. He informed the Earl of Leicester that, upon asking Payne 'how they could find in their hearts to attempt an act of so great cruelty', the priest responded that to murder the queen 'was no offence to God, nor the uttermost cruelty they could use to her'.[14] Functioning as 'points of contact' for the rest of the kingdom, servants were often conduits for others to inform against their fellow subjects. William Oxenbridge, Anne Boleyn's groom porter, reported treasonous words spoken in the parish of Rolvynden, Kent to Thomas Cromwell in

1535. 'Knowing that I was the queen's grace's servant', as Oxenbridge wrote, a man named William Lawless had informed him that the vicar of the parish had preached 'you shall not follow the saying of evil princes, nor evil rulers, but rather put on your harness and fight against them.'[15] In that same year, Thomas Smith, Henry VIII's servant, had heard a priest utter words 'upholding the supremacy of the Pope as head of the Church on earth'.[16] Likewise in 1537, William Barke, groom of the Chamber, overheard John Creke falsely claim that the king was dead, and as a result, Creke was sent to prison.[17] The following year, William Harrison, of the king's Privy Chamber, overheard the abbot of Pershore in conversation at his table speaking words 'sounding to treason'.[18] There were some concerns among servants that, upon disclosing treasonous activity, the Tudors might 'shoot the messenger'. As one unfortunate fellow in Henry VII's service warned, 'you would be wary how you break to him any such matters, for he would take it to be said but of envy, ill will and malice'. 'Then should anyone have blame and no thanks for his truth and good mind,' he continued, 'and that have I well proved heretofore in like causes'. This man recalled one such instance, when he disclosed the intrigues of one Lord Lovell to the council. They brought him before the king, who was incredulous, 'angry and displeased', much to his servant's frustration, who vowed, 'I shall no more tempt him while I live in such causes'. Another remarked that it was 'a great pity that the king did not trust his true knights better, and to give them credence in such things as they should show for his surety, for great hurt may come by that mean'.[19]

Tudor royal households could rally together in times of crisis. In 1549, when Sir Thomas Seymour was arrested on suspicion of pursuing a marriage with Princess Elizabeth without first obtaining the consent of the Privy Council, two of Elizabeth's attendants, Kat Ashley, her gentlewoman, and Sir Thomas Parry, her cofferer, were interrogated by Sir Robert Tyrwhitt on their knowledge of Seymour's intentions. Tyrwhitt suspected that Elizabeth, Ashley and Parry had all anticipated his questioning, rehearsing their answers beforehand and promising 'never to confess to death'.[20] Ashley and Parry were soon imprisoned,[21] as was Ashley's husband, Sir John Ashley, who had warned his wife that Elizabeth 'did bear some affection' for Seymour, and had noticed that their mistress 'would blush when he were spoken of'.[22] Kat Ashley was kept in uncomfortable isolation in the Tower. 'Pity me,' she said, 'and let me change my prison, for it is so cold that I cannot sleep, and so dark I cannot see by day, for I stop the window with straw as there is no glass'. Ashley and Parry eventually disclosed that Seymour had been with Elizabeth in her bedchamber, had even tickled and kissed her, and that the princess herself 'wished both openly and privately' that they would be married, words which she knew were a 'great folly'.[23] These confessions were shown to Elizabeth, who, remarkably, held her nerve, refusing to implicate her attendants. 'In no ways she will confess that our Mistress Ashley or Parry', Tyrwhitt reported, 'willed her to any practice with my Lord Admiral, whether by message or writing'.[24] Ashley was discharged from Elizabeth's service, though she remained in the Tower. Elizabeth took this 'heavily', and 'wept all that night', which so struck Tyrwhitt that he would remark 'the love that she bears her is to be wondered at'.[25] Fearing that her gentlewoman would, like Seymour, be condemned to death for committing treason, Elizabeth would plead for her release. 'She has been with me a long time, and many years,' the princess wrote, 'and has taken great labour, and pain in bringing of me up in learning and honesty'.[26] Much to the relief of them both, Ashley was eventually released from the Tower.

Servants took the responsibility of protecting the Tudors very seriously, even to the point of sharing in their troubles and anxieties as if they were their own. Both Princess Elizabeth and her household were suspected of complicity in Sir Thomas Wyatt's rebellion in 1554, which proposed to overthrow Mary I and replace her with her sister. When Elizabeth was summoned to court to answer to these accusations, she feigned illness, and the staff of her household composed a remarkable letter on her behalf to the queen's Privy Council excusing her absence:

> May it please your good lordship, that albeit we attend here on my Lady Elizabeth's grace, our mistress, in hope every day of her amendment, to repair towards the Queen's Highness, (whereof we have, as yet, none apparently likelihood of health) yet, considering this dangerous world, the perilous attempts and the naughty endeavours of the rebels, which we daily hear of against the Queen's Highness, our Sovereign Lady, we do not forget our most bounden duty, nor yet our readiness in words and deeds to serve her Highness by all the ways and means that may stand in us, both from her grace, our mistress, and of our own parts also. Which thing, although my Lady's grace, our said mistress, has before signified unto the Queen's Highness of her behalf by message, it might, nevertheless, seem to your good lordship, and the Lords of the Council, some negligence that we did not make you also privy hereunto; We have, therefore, thought it our duty to declare this unto your lordship. Most humbly beseeching the same to prescribe unto us the Queen's pleasure and yours herein, or in anything else, wherein we may serve her Highness. And we, according to our most bounden duties, shall not fail to perform the same

always to the uttermost of our lives. Our Lord knows it, to whose blessed tuition we commit you.[27]

The letter evokes genuine concern for Elizabeth, as her household attempted to shield their mistress from submission. Unfortunately, Mary's suspicions persisted, and she had her sister imprisoned in the Tower, and at other times, under house arrest. Throughout this tumultuous period, Elizabeth was comforted by her servants. One night at Richmond, the princess called one of her gentleman ushers to her presence and 'desired him, with the rest of his company to pray for her', 'for this night,' she confided, 'I think to die.' 'God forbid that any such wickedness should be pretended against your Grace', the gentleman consoled her, before he himself 'burst out in tears'. He frantically approached Elizabeth's custodians and begged them to declare the matter: 'whether any danger is meant towards my mistress this night or no that I and my poor fellows may take such part as shall please God'. Later still the princess 'desired her gentlemen and gentlewomen to pray for her, for that she could not tell whether ever she should see them again'.[28] Elizabeth and her household had become so emotionally bonded that they felt her peril deeply. Strikingly, one of the custodians, Sir Henry Bedingfield, wrote that, when the princess was first taken to the Tower, her servants were found 'lying about' at the gates, almost as if they were staging a protest, refusing to let their mistress to be alone.[29] Later at Woodstock, the princess remained under house arrest, and her cofferer, Parry, much to Bedingfield's concern, kept a household near at hand at which many of Elizabeth's attendants had gathered. Bedingfield felt that their presence constituted a threat to order and undermined Mary's authority. He had been advised by the queen and her council to ensure Elizabeth did not 'have conference with any suspected person out of his hearing, nor that she does by any means either receive or send any message, letter or token to or from any manner of person'. Bedingfield urged, however, that his 'poor wit and endeavour' could only stretch so far, as Elizabeth's attendants, especially the gentlewomen and grooms of her Privy Chamber, had 'full opportunity to do such matter as is afore prohibited'.[30] He reported also that, 'political as they be', he 'could get no knowledge of their doings',[31] suspecting that 'daily and hourly' her cofferer, and others of her attendants, 'may have and give intelligence' to the princess.[32] Elizabeth's household were so committed that, in spite of orders from the Privy Council to disband, they continued to stand together and support their mistress.

Servants who were accused of crimes, petty or serious, treason or otherwise, could themselves be protected by the Tudors. Henry, Duke of Richmond, wrote to Thomas Cromwell in 1534 on behalf of his gentleman usher, Thomas Delaryver, who had been 'wrongfully' and 'only of malice' accused of hunting and killing a stag belonging to the Abbot of Byland in York. The Duke sent Delaryver to Cromwell and solicited him to, as the Duke wrote, 'hear my said servant speak' so that he might 'more evidently make unto you further relation of the truth'.[33] When Thomas Knyvett, Elizabeth I's groom of the Privy Chamber, was accused of killing a servant of the Earl of Oxford in the summer of 1582, he petitioned the lord chancellor, Thomas Bromley, to allow his case to be heard in a 'privy session', as opposed to a more public trial. When the queen heard that Bromley had refused her servant's request, Sir Christopher Hatton, her vice-chamberlain, wrote in haste that she 'marvelled not a little'. Elizabeth proceeded to put pressure on the chancellor to reconsider Knyvett's cause, for whom she 'looked for justice'. 'You know who he is, and where he serves, and therefore,' the queen remarked, 'in a cause so important as this, you might have restrained the malice of his enemies well enough'. Hatton urged Bromley, 'it is very necessary to take care to please the Queen in this case, for, in truth, she takes it unkindly at your hands that she should be strained to meddle and be seen in this matter'.[34] Indeed Elizabeth was meddling, as all of the Tudors did when seeking special treatment for servants they had grown to be particularly fond of. Yet Bromley did not find Knyvett's request to be 'reasonable'. Although the upright chancellor himself acknowledged that he 'would be loath to offend' the queen, he resisted her pressure, and dealt with her patiently, replying that he 'never knew', and 'never heard' of 'any such commission granted', and advised her vice-chamberlain that for Knyvett 'her Majesty's pardon be needful, though the matter of itself require it not'.[35] So high was Knyvett in Elizabeth's favour that, a year later, when one of Knyvett's own servants was killed by one of the Earl of Oxford's men, probably in retaliation, she backed her groom again, and ordered that the incident be closely investigated. Observers at court attributed the queen's continued hostility to the Earl to her affection for Knyvett. It was suggested that her mind had been framed, and her 'opinion' of the Earl distorted by Knyvett, who, as her intimate servant, had the opportunity to declare the matter to his mistress first.[36]

Servants could make a personal plea to the crown for mercy, either for themselves, or on behalf of those who were suspected of committing treason. The abandoned 1556 plot against Mary I led to many arrests, and subsequently, petitions to the queen's household pleading for mercy. 'Move mistress Clarencius for me', John Bedell urged his wife, knowing that Susan Clarencius, as a gentlewoman of the Privy Chamber, could bend the ear of her mistress.[37] Anne, Lady Bray, whose husband too was imprisoned for his alleged involvement in the plot, 'went to the Court' and spoke with Sir Robert Rochester, Mary's comptroller, 'who gave her very fair words, and made her fair promises'. Although Lord Bray was eventually released, one Edward Lewkenor, the queen's groom porter who was also implicated, was not shown the same mercy, and would die in prison.[38] A few years later, in 1559, Frances Bridges, serving in Elizabeth I's Privy Chamber, was accused of 'conferring with wizards' and other 'fantastical practices', intending to poison her husband, George Throckmorton, gentleman pensioner, for his 'entire and perfect love', to make him remain faithful to her. Her mother, Elizabeth Grey, who also served the queen, had to appeal on her daughter's behalf to stop her from being prosecuted. It is unclear if Throckmorton was genuinely concerned, but the supposed witnesses later admitted that he had threatened them to depose that his wife 'went about his destruction'.[39] In 1599, when Richard Bancroft, Bishop of London, had 'greatly offended' Elizabeth I for 'certain printing, preaching and prayers' engaged in London, he knew well that, to ease the queen's displeasure, 'next my prayers and most faithful service to her,' he had to 'rely for a time' upon 'the favour of my good friends at the court'.[40] There was no guarantee that these pleas would be successful. Miles, Henry VIII's groom of the Chamber, was unable to prevent his father from being hanged for his part in the Pilgrimage of Grace in 1537, but he proceeded to appeal to Thomas, Duke of Norfolk, to retrieve his possessions.[41] Shortly after Thomas Wyatt's rebellion in 1554, his wife Jane, Lady Wyatt, appealed to Mary I for clemency on his behalf. Sir Edward Hastings warned her that 'she should find the Queen in no mood', but Lady Wyatt pressed her anyway, and 'found indeed some sharp answer, whereat she, shrieking and sinking down, the Queen perceiving it, turned back and said she would have mercy on her, and to her ladies, I think I must save both or lose both'.[42]

Due to the sensitivity of their position, all servants had to be cautious in what words they spoke, and to whom. Shortly after Mary I's coronation, rumours began to circulate that her predecessor, Edward VI, was not actually dead. In 1554, Robert Rowbotham, the queen's yeoman, was arrested for 'his lewd talk that the king's majesty deceased should be yet living'. His words constituted treason, though he was forgiven and, after a brief incarceration, he was reinstated.[43] That same year, William Cox, serving in Mary's household 'below-stairs' as an officer of her pantry, was temporarily discharged when he was found to be in possession of 'a lewd bill surmising that king Edward was still living'.[44] Richard Smith, Mary I's yeoman of the Guard, too was imprisoned 'for spreading abroad lewd and seditious books'. Within a few months, 'his coat being first taken from his back, and he discharged of his service', Smith had inexplicably 'by secret means' managed to fenagle his way back into the Guard, on a wage of 16d. a day!'[45] This deception was uncovered the following year, as the queen's Privy Council ordered that the slippery Smith must be 'no more accepted for her Majesty's servant'.[46]

The nature of the evidence means that it is often difficult to know if servants ever even spoke the words they were alleged to have uttered. In 1591, a Catholic priest named Thomas Pormant was interrogated and tortured by Richard Topcliffe, an esquire of the body in Elizabeth I's household. Pormant claimed that, while in his custody, Topcliffe bragged of his intimacy with the queen, declaring that 'he himself was so familiar with her Majesty that he has very secret dealings with her'. So intimate was Topcliffe with the queen that he had apparently seen her legs, and even felt them 'with his hands above her knees'. What is more, Topcliffe had allegedly put his hands 'between her breasts and paps, and in her neck'. Elizabeth is supposed to have said, 'Be not these the arms, legs and body of King Henry?' At both Pormant's trial and his execution, Topcliffe vehemently denied the priest's accusations. Unfortunately for Elizabeth, this account, as incredible as it is, was circulated by other Catholic priests to defame the queen.[47]

The most politically astute of servants kept their eyes and their ears open at all times. It appears that many of them, be it carelessly or intentionally, often leaked, or traded, potentially sensitive information that perhaps they should not have. In 1510, when Francisca de Cáceres, Catherine of Aragon's gentlewoman, was caught acting as an informant for the Imperial ambassador, Luis Caroz, she was 'forbidden to enter the Palace' by the queen.[48] Caroz reported that Cáceres had been put out of the queen's service and that Catherine refused to see her. 'She is so perilous a woman that it shall be dangerous', the queen later remarked, 'I have no more charge of her'.[49] The ambassador urged for Ferdinand I of Spain to send a letter recommending that she be reinstated, as he regarded her as 'skilful' and emphasised that 'as soon as she is in the palace, she will herself recover her place, and, even if she does not recover it, she will render the greatest services'. 'For now, having nobody there', Caroz complained, 'I do not know, as I ought to know, what passes there'.[50] In 1541, the French ambassador Marillac sent Francis I an extensive report on Princess Mary, which he acknowledged was written with 'the assistance of a woman who has served in her chamber from her infancy'. This gentlewoman disclosed intimate details on her appearance, health, demeanour, activities and pastimes.[51] Later, in 1555, when Mary, now queen, was suffering from a 'phantom' pregnancy, her gentlewoman Susan Clarencius was to inform Marillac's successor Antoine de Noailles 'that the Queen's state was by no means of the hopeful kind generally supposed, but rather some woeful malady'.[52] The Imperial ambassador Baron Breuner had a spy at Elizabeth I's court, who in 1559 had 'learnt from her ladies and maids-of-honour that her Majesty had been quite melancholy alone in her room of nights and had not slept half an hour', and in the mornings she 'was quite pale and weak'.[53] In 1560, the London merchant John Dymock pressed Kat Ashley, Elizabeth's gentlewoman, on who the queen was to marry. Ashley 'solemnly declared that she thought the Queen was free of any man living'. Her husband, John Ashley, master of the jewel house, related to Dymock the following day that 'the Queen would rather not marry'.[54] Yet another ambassador, Bernardino de Mendoza, considered Henry, Lord Howard, to be a valuable informant in 1581, as he 'is friendly with the Ladies of the Privy Chamber, who tell him exactly what passes indoors'.[55]

Some servants were guilty of abusing their office for financial gain, and those who were caught were charged with corruption, usually amounting to treason. Counterfeiting in particular seems to have been a recurring problem. In 1538, Edmund Coningsby, Henry VIII's groom of the Chamber, confessed to forging the king's sign manual and privy signet. He was convicted at Guildhall, and sentenced to be hanged, drawn and quartered at Tyburn.[56] 'When he had heard his judgement', Coningsby begged to be allowed to speak in confidence, swearing it to be in the king's interest to hear him out.[57] Sir Richard Gresham permitted him to write a letter to Cromwell, but it soon became apparent that, as Gresham observed, 'he knows nothing', and that he was merely stalling in the vain hope that he might be pardoned. Desperate, Coningsby revealed that the old bishop of Lincoln owed him £400 and 'he will give to the king's highness for to have his pardon'. This, Gresham remarked coldly, 'is worth nothing', and 'so I have put him to execution and God pardon him'.[58] In 1578, Elizabeth I's messengers were found to have counterfeited on warrants the hands of the lord chamberlain and secretary, defrauding the queen of £3000. They were sentenced to stand on a pillory at Westminster 'on certain days appointed, and then to have their ears cut off'.[59] Likewise the 'lewd' Anthony Nixon and John Norbury, Elizabeth I's servants, were apprehended and imprisoned in 1592 for 'going about the country with false warrants whereunto they had counterfeited the hands' of the queen's Privy Council 'and thereby terrifying many of her Majesty's good subjects, have extorted from them good sums of money'.[60] Christopher Porter, Elizabeth I's messenger, was interrogated in 1600 for having had three stamps made, counterfeiting the names of Sir Robert Cecil and two others. To excuse his behaviour, Porter claimed that, having 'suspected that others had heretofore deceived her Majesty by such practices', he was determined to prove their guilt, and commissioned the stamps so that they could be compared with other bills already submitted.[61]

Embezzlement often proved to be all too tempting for servants who had privileged access to the royal bounty. Sir Giles Daubeney, Henry VII's lord chamberlain, was severely punished for appropriating as much as £8000 of the king's money in Calais for his own use. He was discharged from his office as lieutenant of the garrison and had to pay back £2000 to the king.[62] One man said of Daubeney that 'he loves the king as well as any man can do living, but it has been seen in times past that change of worlds has caused change of mind'.[63] Slightly more petty but no less serious, Richard Cotton, Henry, Duke of Richmond's comptroller, was accused in 1527 of having diverted provisions like foodstuffs meant for the young prince's household for his own profit.[64] At the end of 1548, Sir William Sharington, Edward VI's gentleman of the Privy Chamber, was caught embezzling money from the Bristol Mint. He tried to extricate himself from this treasonous activity, urging his co-conspirator, Sir Thomas Seymour, as he later testified, 'I could not justify my doings in the mint'.[65] But it was too late. Sharington was charged with having 'made a profit for himself of £5000 by coining money', and was sentenced to death. He would be pardoned, however, saving his own neck by pinning the blame on Seymour, who was found to have 'defrauded' and 'deceived' the king not only by concealing but 'by all means' aiding and assisting Sharington in committing treason.[66]

Conspiracy and intrigue were an altogether more dangerous game when it was not money at stake, but power. An embittered Sir Thomas Seymour, who had been consigned to the outer circle by Edward, Duke of Somerset, engaged John Fowler, Edward VI's groom, to secretly communicate with his master, and ultimately, to take 'the government of the King's Majesty'.[67] Rallying the disaffected at court 'by kindness and gifts', Seymour was accused of having sought to win the favour of the king through his attendants.[68] The council later charged him with corrupting 'the nearest about his Majesty's person' with money, rewards and 'fair promises' to 'allure his Highness to condescend and agree to the same your most heinous and perilous purposes'.[69] Increasingly impatient, all this culminated in a failed attempt by Seymour to seize the young king from his bedroom. Armed with a pistol, Seymour broke into the privy garden and approached Edward's bedchamber. He had not anticipated, however, that Edward's dog would be lying outside the door waiting for him. As the dog attacked, its barking woke a gentleman of the Privy Chamber sleeping at the foot of the king's bed, his 'faithful guardian', who cried out, 'Help! Murder!' The king's bodyguards soon arrived, and Seymour was arrested. What made this incident all the more disturbing was that Seymour had apparently 'obtained from one of the king's chamberlains, who was privy to his design, a key, by means of which there is the nearest access by a door to the royal bedchamber, which he entered in the dead of night'.[70] The Privy Council later condemned Seymour, for he 'would have laid his hands upon the person of the King's Majesty, and have taken the same into his order and disposition (if by God's grace and wisdom he had not been prevented), to the great peril and danger of his Majesty and the subversion of the state of the whole realm'.[71] For all this Seymour would ultimately be executed for treason in 1549.

Fearing the worst, the Tudors sometimes came to suspect their own servants were acting against their interests. Henry VIII himself was often suspicious, urging Wolsey in 1519 to 'make good watch on the Duke of Suffolk, on the Duke of Buckingham, on my lord of Northumberland, on my lord of Derby, on my lord of Wiltshire and on others which you think suspect'.[72] Indeed Henry's nearest attendants were subject to his paranoia. Sir John Wallop, gentleman of the king's Privy Chamber, was 'accused of sundry notable offences and treasons' in 1541.[73] It is unclear what Wallop had done that constituted treason, though one report suggested it was because he had 'said something in favour of Pope Paul'.[74] 'Considering his long service done unto us', Henry ordered that Wallop should neither be committed to 'any common ward or prison', nor 'suffer any act or thing to be done or published' against him.[75] The king was anxious that Wallop should be 'secretly examined of such things as were objected against him',[76] to prevent any 'infamy, slander or dishonour'. Henry was quite aware that just a whisper of scandal, even if the accused would later be proven innocent, could see a man's 'good name' brought into disrepute.[77] Sir Richard Long, Wallop's fellow in the king's household, was sent to escort him from Sittingbourne to Southwark. Long was required, somehow, without arousing Wallop's suspicion, to retrieve any letters he had in his possession, along with locating the rest of his papers, so that these could be searched for evidence. In spite of all this underhanded, covert action, Wallop was tipped off. As he later told the king, 'if he had thought himself, to have offended Your Majesty he would rather come home and put himself in to Your Highness' hands, than to live abroad with slander to be noted a false man to Your Grace'.[78] Wallop decided to 'yield himself as prisoner', and at dinner with Long, 'weeping', declared openly 'that nothing grieved him so much' that his master 'should think that he was a false man'.[79] The distressed Wallop soon arrived in London and was promptly lodged in the Tower, before he was brought before the Privy Council 'assembled to declare what was laid unto him, and to hear what he could say for himself'. At first, Wallop maintained his innocence, but presented with letters he had written to a known traitor of the crown, 'he cried for mercy, acknowledging his offences', and made a 'most earnest and hearty protestation' that his actions were not from any 'evil mind or malicious purpose'.[80] In that same year, Sir Thomas Wyatt too was arrested and led through the city to the Tower 'so bound and fettered that one must think ill'.[81] Early reports suggested that, 'with the exception of words, which elsewhere than here would not have been noticed, nothing has been proved against him'.[82] One man accused him of being a papist, guilty of 'communing' with traitors and sharing 'intelligence' with Reginald Pole. He was also supposed to have spoken ill of the king, remarking 'that he feared that the King should be cast out of a cart's arse, and that by God's blood if he were so he were well served'.[83] A 'manacled' Wyatt composed his *Defence*, in which he disregarded the accusations laid against him as mere 'tales', the 'cunning whereof, made by learned men, weaved in and out to persuade you and trouble me ...may both deceive you and amaze me, if God put not in your heads honest wisdom to weigh these things'. He begged that those in charge of prosecuting him 'be not both my judges and my accusers, that is to say that you aggravate not my cause unto the quest'.[84] The king granted that Wyatt should be released, but on 'rather hard conditions'. First, Wyatt had to 'confess the guilt for which he had been arrested', and second, he would 'resume conjugal relations with his wife, from whom he had been separated for upwards of fifteen years'. If he were found to have continued his relations with those women 'that he has since loved', he would 'suffer pain of death and confiscation of property'.[85] The Privy Council recorded that Wyatt confessed 'in a like lamentable and pitiful sort as Wallop did', excusing himself as suffering from 'rage and foolish vainglorious fantasy, without spot of malice'.[86] Ultimately, it was 'at the great and continual suit of the Queen's Majesty', Katherine Howard, that the king decided to forgive and pardon both Wallop and Wyatt, the former 'for his leadership in war', the latter 'for his wit', and both of them 'for their great services past and to come'.[87]

Not all servants, however, were shown the same grace. Both John Radcliffe, Lord Fitzwalter, Henry's lord steward, and Sir William Stanley, lord chamberlain, were accused in 1495 of plotting in favour of Perkin Warbeck, the Yorkist pretender to the English throne. The evidence laid against Stanley was fairly circumstantial, he having once uttered 'that he would never fight nor bear armour against the young man', Warbeck, if he were indeed the son of Edward IV, but this was quite enough to secure a conviction. That Stanley had been uncovered as a conspirator was so alarming that Henry, at first, refused to believe it, and 'could in no wise be induced nor persuaded'. Only once it was 'openly proved' was the king 'greatly dismayed and grieved', especially 'considering first that he had the governance of his chamber, and the charge and comptrollment of all such as were next to his body, and also calling to remembrance the manifold gratuities, which he had received at his hand'. Examined by the Privy Council, Stanley, perhaps in hope of mercy, 'nothing denied, but wisely and seriously did stipulate and agree to all things laid to his charge'. The chronicler Hall mused on how the 'sincere and faithful' Stanley, who had always been shown 'special favour', could bear such 'hatred and spite' for his master.[88] His suspicion was that the lord chamberlain 'began to grudge and disdain' the king when he was not elevated as Earl of Chester. Stanley's support for Warbeck constituted treason, and he was beheaded in 1495. Lord Fitzwalter too was arrested and attainted for treason for supporting Warbeck. He was executed in 1496 after failing to escape his imprisonment at Guînes castle.[89] Such incidents saw Henry VII increasingly concerned about the loyalties of his attendants. A few years later, Warbeck, held under house arrest in the custody of William Smith and James Braybrooke, escaped Westminster Palace. The following day he was seized by royal guardsmen. It was unclear how he managed to escape, but the Venetian ambassador suggested that the king's servants, Smith and Braybrooke, were involved.[90] Smith had supposedly encouraged the escape, though it could be that, unknowingly to Warbeck, this was actually done on behalf of the king, who needed an excuse to throw him in the Tower. All this came from a longstanding fear of conspiracy against the crown. As early as 1487, a plot to murder the king's councillors was uncovered. Many of Henry VII's own attendants were implicated, and at least four of them were hanged on Tower Hill. Shortly after, Parliament enacted a statute, 'occasioned by envy and malice of the King's own household servants', which empowered officers, like the steward, treasurer and comptroller, to investigate if any person 'admitted to be his servant in his house, sworn and his name put into the check roll of his household, what so ever he be serving in any man's office or room reputed had and taken', had ever been involved in 'any confederacies, encompassings, conspiracies, imaginations with any person or persons, to destroy or murder the king'.[91]

Paranoia and anxiety for the Tudors over the 'doubleness' of servants was not necessarily unfounded. Rarely would servants publicly oppose, criticise or betray their royal master or mistress, and their performance of routine duties, tasks and functions might conceal their duplicity. Perhaps the most disturbing was the case of Dr Roderigo Lopez, who had been serving as Elizabeth I's physician for nearly thirteen years when he was accused in 1594 of being a double agent for Philip of Spain. 'I have discovered a most dangerous and desperate treason', the Earl of Essex wrote to the queen. Lopez was arrested on suspicion of conspiracy to poison the queen and examined by both William Cecil and the Earl of Essex, who was determined to prove that the physician was guilty.[92] His answers were convincing, and although at first it appeared he might be found innocent, he was eventually committed to the Tower and, perhaps under the strain of interrogation, confessed 'more than enough' to incriminate him. At his trial for high treason, Lopez was described as a 'perjuring murdering traitor', who 'undertook to poison her, which was a plot more wicked, dangerous and detestable than all the former'. It was observed that Lopez 'was so careful that he never wrote anything himself', nor did he communicate with his co-conspirators directly. As Elizabeth's physician, Lopez was in a dangerously intimate position, with a claim to access the queen's person and advise her not only on what medicines to take, but also what she should eat and drink. It was all the more unsettling that the accused was 'her Majesty's sworn servant, graced and advanced with many princely favours, used in special places of credit, permitted often access to her person, and so not suspected, especially by her, who never fears her enemies nor suspects her servants'. The King of Spain was 'paying him for it', and had apparently sent Lopez a ring, promising to grant him 'honours and rewards'.[93] One report stated that Lopez had been assured of fifty-thousand crowns for the act, and was 'greedy to perform it', every day asking 'When will the money come? I am ready to do the service'. This, the jury determined, was proven by witnesses, intercepted letters, and Lopez's confession, which he now retracted and, once again, maintained his innocence. The physician even claimed to have misled his alleged accomplice by promising that he would 'minister the poison in a syrup', knowing 'her Majesty never doth use to take any syrup' to avoid such dangers. Lopez was clearly flustered under intense questioning. According to an anonymous report, he would confess to and deny the charges 'almost in the same breath'.[94] He was eventually found guilty and was sentenced to be hanged, drawn and quartered. Although Elizabeth, who clearly had some affection for Lopez, was not convinced, and intended to forestall his execution by delaying the signing of his death warrant, unfortunately for Lopez the prosecution proceeded against him anyway and he was executed on Tyburn Hill weeks later.[95] The suggestion that a servant as intimate as Lopez could be so sinister in his intentions led to 'great speech', or murmuring, 'at this time both at the court and city'.[96] 'There was never so wicked, devilish and hateful a treason so closely, cunningly and smoothly conveyed', it was reported, 'by such as had means with least suspicion to carry it'.[97]

The Tudors recognised the potential for servants to act in their own interests as their agents, or 'double' agents. When Henry VIII was pursuing an annulment from his marriage to Catherine of Aragon, he attempted to bring Francisco Felipez, her sewer, into 'more firm confidence', knowing well that he was 'privy unto the queen's affairs and secrets'.[98] The king arranged for Felipez to be 'taken by enemies', or 'secretly to be stopped and molested in some part of France', before paying his ransom to gain his trust. Henry made it clear that, for his plan to work, it must not be 'in anywise known' that Felipez's arrest had been orchestrated by his own hand.[99] It is unlikely that Felipez's allegiance could be won, however, as he was staunchly loyal to the queen. On the other hand, Robert Shorton, Catherine's almoner, was persuaded by Wolsey to disclose private conversations that he had overheard in the queen's chambers. Although Shorton had shown himself reluctant, the cardinal reminded him that 'his obligation to be true and faithful' was to the king, not the queen, and that it was the king who was responsible for his preferment.[100] Wolsey would be accused of having 'gathered unto himself the most subtle witted' of the queen's servants, who were 'fit for his purpose', and 'made her sworn to betray the Queen, and tell him what she said or did'.[101] These servants were apparently susceptible to the cardinal's influence, and could be bribed with gifts, financial rewards or other inducements. 'In like manner, he played with the ladies and gentlewomen', and 'whosoever of them was great, with her he was familiar, and gave her gifts'. 'By these spies, if ought were done, or spoken in Court against the Cardinal,' Tyndale observed, 'of that he had word within an hour or two'.[102]

It was difficult for consorts, princes and princesses to judge who could and could not be trusted when their households were subject to the authority and surveillance of the sovereign. Through the late 1520s and 1530s, Catherine of Aragon was essentially 'surrounded by spies in her own chamber'.[103] The queen would be forced to contrive a way of communicating with her family and friends cloak-and-dagger. Catherine's daughter Princess Mary too was isolated, and by 1536, according to Chapuys, was 'so eager to escape from all her troubles and dangers that if he were to advise her to cross the Channel in a sieve she would do it'. The ambassador communicated with the princess by a man 'in whom she trusts' to acquaint her with a plan to help her leave England. Mary was effectively kept under house arrest, surrounded by attendants who had been appointed by her father, Henry VIII. Incredibly, the princess suggested that she might be able to escape undetected 'if she had something sent her to drug some of her women with'.[104] This plan was never put into action, and Mary's situation soon eased, but in 1550, the princess once again came under increasing pressure, this time from Edward VI and his council, prohibiting her from publicly celebrating mass in her household. A new plan was hatched for Mary to escape by a small boat with Jehan Dubois, an Imperial envoy, but Robert Rochester, her comptroller, intervened, stressing to Dubois 'that he saw no earthly possibility of bringing my Lady down to the water-side without running grave risks'. Rochester was uneasy, suspecting that Mary was being watched carefully, not only outside of, but from within her own household, 'which was not so free of enemies to her religion as she imagined'.[105] When Dubois eventually arrived to escort Mary to the boat, he found her unprepared, and frantic. Her comptroller had heard that Dubois' boat was likely to be impounded. Foreseeing disastrous consequences, Rochester cautioned his mistress, who became anxious, saying 'What is to become of me?' After conferring with her comptroller, and a lady of her bedchamber 'keeping the door', the three of them decided it was much too risky to leave.[106] News of the plan soon reached the king, who dispatched Sir John Gates, of his Privy Chamber, 'to stop the going away of the Lady Mary'.[107] On this occasion it would appear that Mary's true attendants had indeed prevented their mistress from falling into 'great danger'.

Outwardly, servants acting as 'double' agents necessarily concealed competing claims on their allegiance, and when their duplicity was uncovered, the dynamics between master or mistress and servant could be shaky, tense, and surely, a little awkward. In 1540, when Henry VIII obliged Sir Wymond Carew, Anne of Cleves' receiver-general, to intercept the letters addressed to and received from her brother William, Carew was to read them and report back to the king, which he did.[108] Carew was instructed by the Duke of Suffolk to spy on his mistress, but when Anne learned of his involvement, she became, in the words of Carew, 'bent with her women to do me displeasure'. She began to mistrust him, 'for as I suppose she has had knowledge how I procured... such letters as was sent to her', Carew reported. He must have felt that Anne had lost faith in him, as he begged to be discharged from her service.[109]

Information was powerful, and their intimate knowledge of the Tudors made servants dangerous. When Anne Boleyn was arrested on suspicion of committing adultery in 1536, her ladies and gentlewomen were at the centre of the scandal. Anne was accused of 'following daily her frail and carnal lust',[110] but the evidence was inconclusive. 'There is much communication that no man will confess anything against her', wrote Sir Edward Baynton, Anne's vice-chamberlain. 'It would', Baynton suggested, 'much touch the King's honour if it should no further appear'. To substantiate the charges laid against her and secure a conviction, the ladies of her Privy Chamber and 'others of her side were examined'.[111] Lacking anything like proof, the case against Anne rested on their compliance. These women were interrogated as to her when and whereabouts, whom she was with and what she said. Elizabeth Browne, Countess of Worcester, we are told, admitted that the queen's brother, George Boleyn, as well as Mark Smeaton and Henry Norris, of the king's Privy Chamber, 'spent many nights with her, without having to pursue her'.[112] Jane, Lady Rochford, her sister-in-law, revealed that the queen had told her 'the King had neither the skill nor the virility to satisfy a woman', or rather that 'the King was impotent'.[113] Bridget, Lady Wingfield, had apparently confessed on her deathbed what she knew of Anne's misconduct before her marriage to the king, and this confession led the judge John Spelman to remark of the queen that it was thought 'there was no such whore in the realm'.[114] As they were her most intimate servants, their testimony carried weight. Thomas Cromwell reported that 'the Queen's abomination was so rank and common' that 'her ladies of her Privy Chamber, and her chamberers' could not 'contain it within their breasts'.[115] It is clear from Anne's indictment that her servants, be it willingly or reluctantly, provided full and frank statements, which were quite enough to condemn their mistress to death, placing them firmly on the side of the king.[116]

Although servants posed a genuine threat to the Tudors for what they knew, some of them could be better trusted to keep their secrets. Margery Horsman, Anne's maid-of-honour, appears to have frustrated the efforts of the prosecution when she had shown herself reluctant under interrogation to provide evidence. Baynton, the queen's vice-chamberlain, cooperated directly with the king's council, and was tasked with extracting testimony from Anne's servants. He admitted that he struggled to wrest a confession from Horsman. 'I have mused much at ...mistress Margery,' Baynton wrote, 'which has used herself strangely toward me of late being her friend as I have been'. 'She must be of counsel therewith', Baynton observed, noting that there 'has been great friendship between the Queen and her of late'.[117] The 'strange' conduct that Horsman was exhibiting, as Baynton reports, was her reluctance to implicate Anne. Although the queen's vice-chamberlain and her maid had been familiar, perhaps even on friendly terms, the arrest of their mistress had created a rift between them, reflecting the divergence of their allegiances and interests.

The disastrous, sometimes grave consequences for the Tudors who were surrounded by servants in whom they could not trust is obvious. While Anne Boleyn was imprisoned in the Tower in 1536, she was attended by four or five gentlewomen who were appointed by the king and instructed to report back 'every thing' that the queen said.[118] 'I think much unkindness in the king to put such women about me as I never loved', Anne remarked, 'but I would have had of my own Privy Chamber, which I favour most'.[119] Kingston assured her that 'the king took them to be honest and good women', or, in other words, that these women could be trusted to watch and inform against her.[120] Certainly, the queen spoke unguardedly. She was manifestly nervous, increasingly anxious, desperately trying to make sense of her fall. Anne began rehearsing in great detail, if indiscreetly, incidental conversations that took place in her chambers with the gentlemen with whom she was accused. Anne confided in Margaret Coffin that, a few days before her arrest, she had asked Henry Norris, a gentleman of the king's Privy Chamber, why he did not go through with his marriage to her cousin, Madge Shelton, to which Norris 'made answer he would tarry a time'. 'You look for dead men's shoes,' Anne scolded, 'for if ought came to the king but good, you would look to have me'. Norris was clearly horrified, fearing that 'if he should have any such thought he would his head were off'. The queen knew she had misspoken, and fearing that her words could be misconstrued, urged Norris to swear an oath to her almoner that she was a good woman.[121] Anne recalled for Isabel Stonor another conversation she had with Mark Smeaton, groom of the king's Chamber. The queen had 'found him standing in the round window in her Presence chamber and asked, 'why he was so sad'. He answered that 'it was no matter'. Here Smeaton's pitiful state must have vexed the queen, as she then she said scornfully, 'You may not look to have me speak to you as I should do to a nobleman, because you be an inferior person', to which he replied, panic-stricken, before taking his leave, 'No, no, madam, a look sufficed me, and thus fare you well.'[122] Unfortunately for Anne, her words were reported back to Kingston, and then to Cromwell, substantiating the charges of adultery and treason laid against her in a damning indictment. Within two weeks of her arrest, Anne stood trial. She was found guilty of high treason and was condemned to death. A few days later, Anne was taken from her lodgings within the Tower of London to a nearby scaffold, where her head was stricken off with a sword.

Servants had to possess the skill to manoeuvre circumstances adverse, difficult, and dangerous to their advantage. Many of them had the instinct to preserve oneself and one's own position at court, adapting through periods of change. Some of the women who served Anne may have felt that they had no choice but to turn against their mistress in 1536. Others may have been eager to furnish to crown with evidence, knowing their interests would be protected. This is corroborated by the investigation into Katherine Howard's adultery in 1541. Katherine was accused of concealing from the king her 'familiarity', or indiscretions prior to the marriage, with Henry Mannox and Francis Dereham, two male attendants with whom she had served at Lambeth and Horsham. The king's councillors had no difficulty in extracting from her servants testimony to substantiate these allegations. A woman named Mary Hall, who served at Lambeth with Katherine and first brought the matter to the king's attention, was not only spared, she was protected. 'She is, as an encouragement to others to reveal like cases,' the Council assured, 'not to be troubled'.[123] Katherine Tylney, the queen's chamberer, was questioned as to 'whether the Queen went out of her chamber any night late'.[124] At Pontefract, Morton would recall that the queen, 'being alone with Lady Rochford, locked and bolted her chamber door on the inside' and insisted that 'neither Mrs. Lovekyn nor no other should come into her bedchamber'.[125] Tylney added only that, at Lincoln, she and Morton 'were sent back' on two occasions when the queen went to Lady Rochford's chamber.[126] They were careful not to incriminate themselves, insisting that they had 'heard or saw nothing of what passed', though their testimony of bolted chambers and backstairs meetings meant that the prosecution could convincingly levy the charge of the queen having held 'illicit meeting and conference'.[127] Wriothesley later acknowledged that Tylney 'has done us good service',[128] indicating that she may have been offered a reprieve for her cooperation. Faced with complex, often unprecedented crises, the outcome of which would affect their lives and careers directly, servants were forced to act or react in one way or another, to align, or realign their loyalties, to survive.

12

'Natural passions of grief'
DEATH, MOURNING AND MEMORY

The Tudors died surrounded by their most intimate attendants, who comforted them to their last breath. In 1553, when Edward VI lay dying at Greenwich Palace, the young king, praying alone in his bed, apparently 'turned his face, and seeing who was by him,' said, 'Are you so nigh? I thought you had been further off'. 'We heard you speak to yourself, but what you said we know not,' Dr George Owen, his physician, responded. Edward smiled, before uttering his last words: 'I am faint. Lord have mercy upon me, and take my spirit'.[1] 'This young prince who died within my arms, had almost caused death to penetrate his dart even into my one soul', Sir Henry Sidney, of the king's Privy Chamber, later recalled.[2] Edward VI's mother, Jane Seymour, died at Hampton Court in 1537 when she succumbed to an illness which had afflicted her since giving birth to the prince days earlier. The queen was surrounded by her ladies, one of whom, Eleanor, Countess of Rutland, likely informed her husband, Thomas, the queen's lord chamberlain, that her mistress had been 'very sick' the night before. 'Her confessor has been with her Grace this morning,' the Earl of Rutland wrote to Thomas Cromwell, 'and has done that, to his office appertains, and even now is preparing to minister to her Grace the Sacrament of Unction'.[3] Her attendants were blamed for the late queen's illness: 'Our mistress,' Cromwell reported, 'through the fault of them that were about her, which suffered her to take great cold, and to eat things that her fantasy in sickness called for, is departed to God'.[4]

Upon the death of their royal master or mistress, servants fell into a state of mourning, though there remained important duties yet to fulfil. Firstly, the body itself had to be prepared for burial. For Catherine of Aragon, it was prescribed that 'the corpse must be cered, trammelled, leaded, and chested with spices'.[5] Sir Edward

Chamberlain, the king's comptroller, and Sir Edmund Bedingfield, lord steward of Catherine's household, were instructed to 'close the body in lead, the which must needs shortly be done, for that may not tarry'.[6] Within a few days, Bedingfield wrote again to Cromwell to report that the 'bowelling and cering is already done in the best manner'. 'The leading and chesting', Bedingfield assured him, 'is prepared for, and shall be finished with all speed'.[7] Shortly after her death, an unnamed groom of the chandlery, who had served the late Princess Dowager, was tasked with embalming and cering, or wrapping, the body of his mistress, before it was enclosed in a chest. A grim, if honourable, last act of service. Giovanni Carlo Scaramelli, the Venetian ambassador, wrote in the days following Elizabeth I's death in 1603 that 'the body of the late Queen, by her own orders has neither been opened, nor indeed, seen by any living soul save by three of her ladies'.[8] This was meant to preserve the queen's dignity, but Elizabeth Southwell, who had served briefly as her maid-of-honour, later claimed that Sir William Cecil had her body opened anyway. In her account, which has been dismissed as Catholic propaganda, Southwell recalled that she was appointed as one of six ladies and gentlewomen to watch over their mistress, whereupon she witnessed that 'the body', which was 'fast nailed up in a board coffin with leaves of lead covered with velvet', did 'break with such a crack that split the wood lead and cerecloth'.[9]

Typically, once the royal body had been prepared, it was placed in a coffin in the Privy chamber 'under the canopy of State', where 'it rested seven days, without any other solemnity than four flambeaux continually burning'.[10] Servants attended vigil masses and kept watch over their master or mistress. In 1547, Henry VIII's coffin was placed in the Privy chamber at Whitehall, while in 1509, his father Henry VII's corpse was 'sumptuously prepared', before it was 'brought out of his Privy chamber' in turn to the Presence chamber, the Great Hall and then to the Chapel, resting for three days in each, with his household in mourning 'giving their attendance, all the service time'.[11] Shortly after Mary I's death in 1558, her body was taken to her Privy chamber, and 'there was attendant every day gentlewomen which did pray about the same with lights burning, and watch every night, with dirge and mass every day', until the coffin was moved to the chapel, where there continued 'a solemn watch both of lords, ladies, gentlewomen, which ladies sat within the rails of the hearse'. Others of Mary's household too gathered bearing torches and 'continued in prayers all night till the morning'.[12] Some years earlier, in 1537, Mary herself had attended vigil masses for Jane Seymour. A 'goodly watch' was kept over the late queen 'all the night long', and by morning, those attendants who 'continually did kneel about the corpse', lit only by torches, were relieved of their duties and 'departed to their breakfast provided for them'.[13] When Elizabeth I died in 1603, the queen's coffin 'came by night in a barge from Richmond to Whitehall' accompanied by 'a great company of Ladies attending it where it continued a great while standing in the withdrawing chamber'. Anne Clifford remembered that her mother was among the women who surrounded the corpse, and that she sat up 'with it two or three nights', though, as she recalled, 'my Lady would not give me leave to watch by reason I was held too young'.[14]

Letters of summons were sent to members of the upper ranks of English nobility to attend royal funerals. Preparations were made for Catherine of Aragon's funeral within days of her death in 1536.[15] Henry VIII wrote to Grace, Lady Bedingfield, the wife of Sir Edmund Bedingfield, who the king had entrusted to remain with the queen at Kimbolton Castle. Henry informed Grace that he intended for Catherine's body to be conveyed from Kimbolton and buried at Peterborough Abbey 'according to her honour and estate' as Princess Dowager. The king understood that it was 'requisite to have the presence of a good many ladies of honour', and so he wrote to Lady Bedingfield: 'you shall understand that we have appointed you to be there one of the principal mourners; and therefore desire and pray you to put yourself in readiness'.[16] Other letters of summons have not survived, but John St. John wrote to Cromwell on behalf of his wife, who was also appointed to be one of the mourners. He petitioned for the king's pardon to excuse his wife from this duty, for she was 'lately sick of breeding of young bones', or, in other words, that she was suffering from an illness from her recent pregnancy. St. John also advised that, as he was himself in the service of the late queen's daughter, Princess Mary, 'all such horses and servants' that his wife 'should be furnished with' for the occasion remained with him.[17] Those appointed to mourn Catherine were to travel to Kimbolton, where, her steward and her household would do all he could 'for the entertainment of such personages of honour as repair hither by commandment'.[18] For each of the Tudors, the rest of the funeral cortège was made up of their servants, irrespective of their rank. The special bond they had formed with their royal master or mistress was respected, and highly regarded. Their names are prominent in the surviving accounts of funerals for the Tudor royal family; indeed, these records are sometimes the only trace that these men and women were ever in their service.

Servants took part in a solemn, public procession, in which they flanked the hearse carrying the body to the chapel. In 1509, Henry VII's body was placed in a chariot covered with black cloth and cushions of fine gold, which travelled from Richmond

Palace to St George's Field, before heading through the city of London and on to Westminster, trailed by 'all the king's servants, in black'.[19] In 1557, the day before Anne of Cleves' funeral, a grand procession set out from Chelsea, first retrieving the corpse, before heading towards Westminster Abbey. Her body was transported on a hearse, with men and women in front, behind, and at either side of her. A near-contemporary sketch illustrates that, at the head of the hearse, there was prepared seats with cushions covered with black cloth specifically for the old Duchess of Norfolk. The next day, nine ladies and gentlewomen, the principal mourners, were 'to be at the church by seven of the clock in the morning' to attend the first masses for the funeral service. Led by Lady Peckham, her train borne by Mistress Hall, both 'having their hoods on their heads', these women arrived 'at the west door', where they lit their torches, 'proceeded to the hearse' set within the abbey, and 'took their places accordingly'.[20]

Servants honoured the Tudors by participating in their funerals, paying their respects and praying for the souls of the deceased. During the ceremony, they made offerings, and each, in turn, laid palls upon the hearse, before listening to a sermon. At Elizabeth of York's funeral in 1503, those in attendance rose up and, 'going up to the offering', laid out money, for some a piece of gold, others, an angel, an old English gold coin. Elizabeth, Lady Stafford, one of the queen's servants, together with the rest of her ladies 'two and two together' offered 'groats a piece'. Following this, thirty-seven palls in total were laid, representing the queen's age at her death. When Lady Mountjoy received a pall, she took it to the foot of the hearse, and after 'she had done her obeisance' she 'kissed it and laid it along the corpse'. Then Richard, Bishop of Rochester, delivered a sermon lamenting 'the great loss of that virtuous Queen'. Their duty of service ceased, symbolised by the ceremonial breaking of staffs of office. At the end of the service, when Elizabeth's body was interred, the queen's lord chamberlain broke his staff and 'cast it into the grave', as did her gentlemen ushers with their rods.[21] The funeral ceremonies and burials of the Tudors were sad, sombre occasions. At Prince Arthur's funeral in 1502, one man was so moved 'to have seen the weepings when the offering was done', that he felt 'he had a hard heart that wept not'.[22] 'Wonder it were to write,' the chronicler Hall recorded of Henry VII's funeral in 1509, 'of the lamentation that was made for this Prince amongst his servants'.[23] At one of the vigils for the dead for Anne of Cleves in 1557, four of her gentlemen and eight yeomen participated, 'but no gentlewomen for that they were not well at ease' to 'watch the corpse all night', suggesting they were so troubled with grief they could not fulfil this office.[24]

The nature of the surviving source material is such that we can rarely know the depths of their inward feelings or emotions in mourning, but it is apparent that the death of a Tudor king or queen would have been deeply felt by their servants. When Elizabeth of York died in 1503, Henry VII withdrew to mourn, but remembered to send by Sir Charles Somerset and Sir Richard Guildford 'the best comfort to all the Queen's servants that has been seen of a sovereign Lord with as good words'. Some accounts reveal an outpouring of emotion from those who were grieving. In Elizabeth I's final days, Noel de Caron, the Dutch ambassador, 'never thought to live to see so dismal a day' when he reported that, between the coffer chamber and the queen's bedchamber, he saw 'great weeping and lamentation among the lords and ladies, as they passed to and fro'.[25] Albeit undoubtedly exaggerated in accordance with contemporary literary and cultural conventions, a Latin epigraph on Katherine Parr composed by John Parkhurst, her chaplain, recorded that, upon the death of their 'most gentle mistress' in 1548, her servants were struck with bitter grief. 'For the departed,' Parkhurst wrote, 'we her household flow with watery eyes'.[26] Neither Anne Boleyn nor Katherine Howard had a funeral, and both were buried with little honour or ceremony in the chapel of St Peter ad Vincula, within the walls of the Tower of London and close to the place of their execution. This does not mean, however, that their tragic end was not mourned by those who knew and served them. Moments before Anne's execution in 1536, her ladies on the scaffold were reportedly 'half dead themselves', describing them as 'bereft of their souls, such was their weakness'. The queen 'consoled her ladies several times', as one of them 'in tears came forward to do the last office and cover her face with a linen cloth'.[27] At least one account corroborates this, recording that they then 'withdrew themselves some little space, and knelt down over against the scaffold, bewailing bitterly and shedding many tears'.[28] Immediately after her head was stricken off with a sword, it was taken up by one of her ladies and 'covered with a white cloth', while the other three ladies, 'fearing to let their mistress be touched by unworthy hands, forced themselves' to wrap her body in a sheet before they carried her remains into the nearby chapel and placed them in a chest of elm.[29] Similarly, at Katherine Howard's execution in 1542, Chapuys acknowledged briefly the presence of her women. After the queen was beheaded, 'her body had been covered with a black cloak', and 'her ladies took it away'. In the days after, Chapuys noted that there was no mourning period, as Henry was 'in better spirits', even 'joyful'. With the ladies at court, the king participated in 'much feasting and banqueting', and 'made them great and hearty cheer'.[30] Would any of these women have dared to put on mourning apparel, or have shown themselves to be grieving their late mistress in the presence of the jovial king?

While some servants mourned publicly, others did so more privately. Many of the Tudors were honoured and memorialised by their servants in their retelling of anecdotes from their years spent together at court. George Wyatt, the grandson of poet and courtier Sir Thomas Wyatt, wrote his biography of Anne with the testimony of Anne Gainsford, the queen's maid-of-honour, and also, as Wyatt described her, 'a lady, that first attended on her both before and after she was queen, with whose house and mine there was then kindred and strict alliance'.[31] The martyrologist John Foxe attributed his account of the queen to 'the chief and principal of her waiting maids about her', and 'especially the Duchess of Richmond', Mary Howard, Anne's cousin and lady-in-waiting, as well as her silkwoman, Joan Wilkinson.[32] In around 1564, William Latymer, Anne's chaplain, related all as he 'did hear, see and certainly know' of his former mistress. To substantiate his account, Latymer claimed to have spoken with those 'who did attend her highness in diverse kinds of service', namely Thomas, Lord Burgh, her lord chamberlain, Sir James Boleyn, her chancellor, Sir Edward Baynton, her vice-chamberlain, and John Uvedale, her secretary.[33] Clearly Anne's servants reminisced about her, and kept her memory alive by sharing what they could remember of their mistress. Latymer would recall, nearly thirty years after her death, that 'we that did attend her majesty must needs justly lament the sudden departing of so good a princess', so much so that their 'hearts might seem for sorrow to pine and melt away'.[34]

The Tudors took care to provide generously for their households in their last wills, rewarding their loyal and enduring service. Henry VIII's will provided to the gentlemen of his Privy Chamber, Sir Thomas Cawarden, Sir Philip Hoby, Sir Peter Mewtas, Sir Maurice Berkeley and others, £200 or 200 marks (£133 6s. 8d.) each; Henry, Earl of Arundel, the king's lord chamberlain, Sir Anthony Wingfield, vice-chamberlain, and John Gates, gentleman usher of the Privy Chamber, all received £200 too; his physicians Dr George Owen and Dr Thomas Wendy, received £100 each, as did grooms of the Privy Chamber William Saintbeck, Richard Cooke and Davy Vincent; Edmund Harman, the king's barber, was granted 200 marks, and to the staff who handled the king's robes, Richard Cecil, yeoman, 100 marks, Thomas Sternhold, groom, 100 marks, and John Rowland, page, £50. In his will, Henry acknowledged that his bequests were made for the 'special love and favour' he held for them. He took care to remember those who were less prominent, instructing the executors to 'give order for the payment of such legacies as they shall think meet to such our ordinary servants as unto whom we have not appointed any legacy by this our present testament'.[35] Days before her death in 1536, Catherine of Aragon dictated her last will in the form of a letter to the king. English law forbade a wife from drafting a will while her husband was still alive, so Catherine wrote a list of requests for Henry, chief among them that she may be granted various goods, gold and silver, and money due to her, 'to the intent', as she wrote, 'that I may pay my debts and recompense my servants for the good services they have done unto me'. Chapuys recorded that the late queen 'by way of request caused her physician to write a little bill, which she commanded to be sent to me immediately, and which was signed by her hand, directing some little reward to be made to certain servants who had remained with her'. Cromwell assured the ambassador that her servants would be treated 'honourably and magnificently'.[36] Francisco Felipez, her sewer, was to be granted £40, and, as Catherine urged, 'all that I owe him', Isabel de Vargas, £20, and Mary Victoria, the wife of her physician, £40. Elizabeth Darrell was to receive £200, Blanche Twyford, £100, Margery Otwell and Dorothy Wheler, £40, Dr Miguel de la Sá and John Sotha, a year's wages each, and Philip Greenacre, Anthony Rocke and Bastian Hennyocke, £20, all of whom were discharged from her service for the loyalty they had shown to their mistress when they refused to swear a new oath to her as Princess Dowager.[37] Anne of Cleves urged her executors 'to be good lords and masters to all our poor servants', to each of whom she left a year's wages, as well as, among others, £100 'to every one of the gentlewomen of our Privy Chamber, for their great pains taken with us'.[38] Katherine Howard, upon learning of her fate, pleaded with Henry 'to bestow some of her clothes on those maid-servants who had been with her from the time of her marriage, since she had nothing else left to recompense them as they deserved'.[39]

When a servant died, their loss could be grieved not only by their royal master or mistress, but the wider court too. When Andrew Ammonius, Henry VIII's secretary 'of the Latin tongue' died in 1517 of the sweating sickness, the Bishop of Worcester wrote to Wolsey lamenting the passing of 'the King's faithful servant', whom he described as having 'no fellow'.[40] In 1539, Margaret Coffin, gentlewoman to the late Jane Seymour, wrote to Thomas Cromwell upon the death of her husband, Sir William Coffin, who had served both in the king's Privy Chamber and as the late queen's master of the horse, 'to advertise the king's highness of his departing'. Margaret reveals that her husband died of 'the great sickness and full of God's marks on all his body'. 'As a poor widow full of heaviness and without comfort', Margaret petitioned Cromwell to 'beseech his grace to be a good and gracious Lord to me in all my rightful causes, for I know not what case I and my servants stand in'.[41] In that same year, Sir John Russell wrote of Sir Piers Edgecombe, who began his career as a knight of the body to Henry VII, and served Henry VIII dutifully through the rest of his life. 'Though his body be participate from this life and be clearly dead,' Russell reflected, 'yet remains his good name, and still stands alive in the hearts and mouths of the people'. Russell regarded Edgecombe's son as 'a follower of his father in all sobriety and worshipful demeanour', and recommended that Cromwell 'advance and prefer him unto the king's service, for well assured I am that he is a man, what for his ability and approved honesty, very meet to do his grace service'.[42] He wrote also on behalf of Edgecombe's widow, Catherine St. John, 'now left alone', believing 'that widows shall not achieve otherwise than favour at your good lordship's hands'.[43] It was likely Cromwell who ensured that, within a few weeks, Lady Edgecombe was appointed to attend upon Anne of Cleves in the new queen's Privy Chamber.[44]

If they outlived their servants, the Tudors sometimes paid the expenses for their burial. Princess Mary, for instance, laid out 13s. 6d. for William ap Richard and his wife, who died prematurely of the plague in 1537 while in her service.[45] An account for the funeral of Margaret Neville, Katherine Parr's chamberer who died in 1546, reveals that her mistress covered the costs incurred, from dressing and conveying the hearse with standards and candles, to providing mourning clothes for her gentlewoman's own servants and subsidising their travel from Greenwich to St Paul's in London, where she was to be buried. The queen charged her groom, William Savage, with taking care of the arrangements for the funeral, ensuring that her chamberer was, in death, shown due honour and ceremony.[46] Elizabeth I laid out £640 2s. 11d. for Katherine, Lady Knollys' funeral. It was noted that the queen suffered from 'natural passions of grief, which she conceived for the death of her kinswoman, and good servant the Lady Knollys'. 'By that occasion', this report continued, 'her Highness fell for a while, from a Prince wanting nothing in this world, to private mourning, in which solitary estate being forgetful of her own health, she took cold, wherewith she was much troubled'.[47] Her epitaph acknowledged that she was 'in favour with our noble Queen, above the common sort'.[48]

Servants were remembered for the duties they fulfilled on behalf of the Tudors, and their devotion to the crown. Sir William Sidney, who died in 1554, served Prince Edward as his lord chamberlain from 1538. His epitaph at Penshurst, Kent, began proudly, 'here lies Sir William Sidney, knight and banneret, sometime Chamberlain and after Steward to the most mighty and famous prince King Edward VI, in the time of his being Prince'. On the tower at the entrance of his house, it was inscribed that Sidney was Edward's 'trusty and well-beloved servant' who attended him 'from the time of his birth unto his coronation'.[49] Funerary monuments acknowledged the long service that men and women performed on behalf of the crown. An effigy of Blanche Parry, who died in 1590, dressed all in black and kneeling on a cushion, was carefully carved and painted in St Margaret's chapel, aside Westminster Abbey, bearing the inscription, 'Gentlewoman of Queen Elizabeth's most honourable Bedchamber and keeper of her Majesty's jewels whom she faithfully served from her Highness' birth'.[50] Likewise, her epitaph emphasised the utmost trust which Elizabeth had confided in her, and reflected on what it meant for Parry to serve her mistress:

> I lived always as handmaid to a queen
> In chamber chief my time did overpass
> Uncareful of my wealth there was I seen
> Whilst I abode the running of my glass.
> Not doubting want whilst that my mistress lived
> In woman's state whose cradle saw I rocked.
> Her servant then as when she her crown achieved
> And so remained til death my door had knocked.
> Preferring still the causes of each wight
> As far as I durst move her grace's ear
> For to reward desserts by course of right
> As needs resit of service done each were
> So that my time I thus did pass away
> A maid in Court and never no man's wife
> Sworn of queen Elizabeth's bed chamber always
> With maiden queen a maid did end my life.[51]

The last wills and testaments which have survived reveal that both men and women amassed great fortunes, fostered meaningful relationships, forged useful networks, and garnered much prestige from serving the Tudors. Sir William Compton accumulated significant wealth and estate through his career serving Henry VIII, 'of whom', Compton wrote in his will, 'I have had all my preferment'.[52] An inventory taken of Compton's goods after his death in 1528 reveals that he had £2342 13s. 5½d.

in ready money alone, and jewels and plate exceeding £1000 in value (though it would appear that some of these moveables actually belonged to the king).[53] What is striking is that many servants gave money and other items to those in the household alongside whom they had lived for many years. Blanche Parry left a total of £2708, 6s. 8d.,[54] with bequests of 'one diamond set in gold with a broad hoop' to Dorothy, Lady Stafford, 'one ring with a pointed diamond and a chain of knobs enamelled work' to Frances, Lady Cobham, £100 to Frances, Lady Burgh, £5 to Anthony Marten, the queen's sewer, a ring worth £3 to Hugh Morgan, the queen's apothecary, and twenty shillings to each of the pages.[55] An earlier draft of her will left 'to every of the ladies and gentlewomen of the Privy Chamber and the grooms of the same and every of the maids-of-honour that shall be at the court when God shall call me out of this life, rings made like hoops with death's head of the value of 20 shillings apiece'.[56] Sir Thomas Speke, of Edward VI's Privy Chamber, who died prematurely of the 'sweating sickness' in 1551, left his fellow Sir Thomas Wroth his 'sore goshawk'.[57] When Roger North, Elizabeth I's treasurer of the household, died in 1600, he too made bequests to the queen's servants: his 'fairest cup' and £20 was given to Anne, Countess of Warwick, 'a convenient fair cup' to Mary, Lady Scudamore, and £10 each to Thomas Cornwallis, groom porter, and Ferdinando Heyborne, groom of the Privy Chamber.[58] Henry Whittell, Elizabeth's yeoman who died in 1591, gave 40s., as he wrote it, 'to my watch fellows'.[59] John Greenhill, Edward VI's yeoman, would not have been the only attendant 'above-stairs' to have struck up a friendship with the household 'below-stairs', leaving in 1549 to Cox and Poleford, of the king's pantry, a ring of gold each worth 13s. 4d., and to Wallace, his 'entire friend', £6 13s. 4d.[60] Sir Robert Rochester, Mary I's comptroller who died in 1557, wrote in his will with affection for the queen's ladies and gentlewomen, 'mine old fellows which served her Grace before she came to this estate and being yet attending in her Majesty's service', giving each of them 'one ring of fine gold', which, as he stated, 'I require them to wear as a token of my goodwill borne to them and to put them in remembrance to pray Christ to have mercy upon my soul'.[61]

Servants sometimes left money or gifts to their royal master or mistress, and occasionally, a last request for them to fulfil. 'As a poor witness of mine humble heart, duty and service', Sir Robert Rochester gave Mary £100 in angels, asking that the queen to whom I have borne my faithful and true service to the uttermost of my small power according to my most bounden duty in this my transitory life, that it would please her Majesty after my decease to give her royal assistance unto such as I shall put in trust that the same my said will may be performed and take place according to my true meaning.[62]

Philip van Wilder, gentleman of Edward VI's Privy Chamber, his lutenist, died in the beginning of 1553. An elegy printed a few years later recognised his musical talent:

> Bewail with me all ye that have professed
> Of music the art by touch of cord or wind:
> Lay down your lutes and let your gitterns rest.
> Phillips is dead who's like you can not find.
> Of music much exceeding all the rest,
> Muses therefore of force now must you wrest
> Your pleasant notes into another sound,
> The string is broke, the lute is dispossessed,
> The hand is cold, the body in the ground.
> The lowering lute laments now therefore,
> Phillips her friend that can her touch no more.[63]

Before he died, Wilder requested that Edward ensure that his son, Henry, 'shall best proceed in the use, exercise and knowledge of music, playing of instruments according as I intend to have brought him up in the same if God had spared me longer life to the intent he might be able to serve the King's Majesty therein hereafter as I have done'. 'If it shall not please the King's Majesty to appoint the government and tuition of my son', Wilder entrusted the task to his 'special and dear beloved' fellow in the Privy Chamber, Sir Philip Hoby, 'so as shall be thought meet to him'.[64] It was not unusual for servants to name their fellows in the household as the executors or overseers of their will. Nicholas Fortescue, Henry VIII's groom porter, who died in 1549, chose William Fitzwilliam, Edward VI's gentleman usher and Fortescue's 'trusty and beloved friend', as his executor, 'heartily desiring him to see this my last will and testament fulfilled', and 'for his pains therein', gave him a gelding worth 5 marks.[65] Richard Tarleton, Elizabeth I's groom, named his 'loving and trusty' friend, and fellow in the Chamber, William Johnson, as one of two men granted custody of his son Phillip and his inheritance until he came of age.[66]

Beyond the confines of the Tudor court, servants had their own families, friends and clientele, belonged to local communities and parishes – many even had their own households. Thomas, Earl of Rutland, who attended Henry VIII as his cupbearer and three of his queens as lord chamberlain, served alongside his wife, Eleanor, Countess of Rutland, Lady of the Privy Chamber to Anne Boleyn, Jane Seymour, Anne of Cleves and Katherine Howard. Their accounts from 1528 to 1543 illustrate how they negotiated their lives at home, chiefly Belvoir Castle, with their careers at court. They kept a stable of horses and hired boats as they travelled from their manors in Belvoir, Enfield and Holywell to royal palaces in Greenwich, Westminster, and wherever else the court resided. In 1537, the Earl employed a local joiner to make a 'trusty bedstead for my Lord to carry to the Court', gilding its frame and posts, adorning it with silk and sarsenet curtains, and paying for the carriage of the bed to the water side and thereafter to his lodging at Whitehall, totalling 18*s.* 4*d.* There are several payments to merchants, silkwomen and embroiderers for satin, velvet and other materials to make up their new apparel for accompanying the king to Calais in 1532, and the blue livery coats of their own servants 'at the time of the insurrection', the Pilgrimage of Grace in 1536, ensuring that they were properly attired when they marched alongside the Earl to Doncaster. They celebrated births, christenings, marriages and anniversaries both within the family and in their wider networks at court. To prepare their nine-year old son, Henry, for his wedding to Margaret, Lady Neville, the Earl called upon the king's barber and paid him 20*d.* for 'rounding', 'washing' and 'trimming' the boy's head on the big day. He laid out a further 40*s.* to the king's minstrels to teach his son how to dance, and 8*d.* 'for making clean the house of Holywell after the marriage'. Both the Earl and the Countess frequently laid out small sums for their fellows in the king's and queen's households. From Anne Boleyn's household, 7*s.* 6*d.* was rewarded to the chamberer, Anne Joscelyn, 22*s.* 6*d.* to the yeoman Thomas Lewis for bringing a New Year's gift, and to unnamed servants 10*s.* 'for bringing a letter' and 5*s.* for 'a kirtle from her Grace'. Amidst these entries were others for maintaining their kinsmen and women, paying the wages of their own servants, and rewarding local townsfolk who brought them cherries, strawberries, a boar, a crane and a peacock. They frequently made offerings to religious houses, and on one occasion, the Earl gave 40*s.* to the friars at Boston to say three hundred masses 'for the soul of' his jousting buddy at court, Sir Henry Guildford. The Countess was a generous patron: she gave 11*d.* to a man 'for making of a glass window' for a church in Enfield, and 13*s.* 4*d.* to a prioress 'for finding of a lamp' at a priory in Holywell. They both purchased necessaries, like gallons of claret wine, meat for their horses, or a pan 'to boil conserves'.[67] Shortly after the Earl died in 1543, the executors of his will ensured that the debts incurred for his funeral and burial, like black cloth for his attendants to wear, alms to be distributed to the poor, the cering of his corpse, the construction of a hearse, and the making of an alabaster tomb, were all paid off. Thomas Wendy, the king's physician, was paid £6 3*s*. 10*d*. for his 'pains' during the Earl's sickness, while 8*s*. 8*d*. was given to one John Leek for 'riding to the Court to the King's Majesty', Henry VIII, to inform him of the Earl's death.[68] Some servants had rather extraordinary careers, and yet, most of them also led quite ordinary lives, which, it is evident, were sustained by their connection with the Tudor dynasty.

SELECT BIBLIOGRAPHY

Primary sources

APC	Dasent, John Roche (ed.), *Acts of the Privy Council of England*, vol. 1, 1542-1547 (London, 1890)
AR	Grose, Francis, Astle, Thomas, and Jefferey, Edwards (eds), *The Antiquarian repertory*, 4 vols. (London, 1808)
Bacon	*The Letters of Lady Anne Bacon*, Royal Historical Society, Camden Fifth Series, 44 (2013), pp. 51-288.
BB	Myers, A. R., (ed.), *The household of Edward IV, the Black Book and the Ordinance of 1478* (Manchester, 1959)
BL	British Library, London
Bodleian	Bodleian Library, Oxford
Cavendish	Cavendish, George, *The Life of Cardinal Wolsey*, ed. by Singer, Samuel Weller (London 1827)
CEVI	W. K. Jordan (ed.), *Chronicle of Edward VI* (London, 1966)
CPR	Calendar of the Patent Rolls
CSP Dom	Green, Mary Anne Everett and Lemon, Robert (eds), Calendar of State Papers, Domestic, Edward VI, Philip and Mary, Elizabeth, 9 vols. (1856–72).
CSP Scot	Bain, Joseph (ed.), *Calendar of the state papers relating to Scotland and Mary, Queen of Scots, 1547-1603*, 13 vols. (1898-1969).
CSP Sp	Gayangos, Pascual de, et al. (eds), *Calendar of State Papers, Spanish*, 13 vols. (1888-1954)
CSP Ven	Brown, Rawdon, et al. (eds), *Calendar of State Papers, Venetian*, 38 vols. (1867-1947)
Ellis	Ellis, Henry (ed.), *Original Letters illustrative of English History*, 2 vols. (London, 1825)
EH	Bentley, Samuel (ed.), *Excerpta Historica, or, Illustrations of English History* (London, 1831)

Foxe	Foxe, John, 'Actes and Monuments', in Cattley, Stephen Reed (ed.), *The Acts and Monuments of John Foxe: A New and Complete Edition*, 8 vols. (London, 1837-41)
Hatton	Harris, Sir Nicolas (ed.), *Memoirs of the life and times of Sir Christopher Hatton* (1847)
Haynes	Haynes, Samuel (ed.) *A Collection of State Papers : relating to Affairs In the Reigns of King Henry VIII, King Edward VI, Queen Mary and Queen Elizabeth : From the year 1542 to 1570* (London, 1740)
HC	Hall, Edward, *Hall's Chronicle: containing the history of England, during the reign of Henry the Fourth, and the succeeding monarchs, to the end of the reign of Henry the Eighth*, 2 vols. (1809)
HMC Bath	Historical Manuscripts Commission, *Calendar of the Manuscripts of the Marquis of Bath preserved at Longleat, Wiltshire*, 5 vols. (Dublin, 1907)
HMC Rutland	Historical Manuscripts Commission, *The Manuscripts of His Grace, The Duke of Rutland, Preserved at Belvoir Castle*, 4 vols. (London, 1888-1905)
HMC Salisbury	Historical Manuscripts Commission, *Calendar of the Manuscripts of the Marquis of Salisbury, Preserved at Hatfield House, Hertfordshire*, 14 vols. (London, 1883-1923)
HO	*A collection of ordinances and regulations for the government of the royal household, made in divers reigns : from King Edward III to King William and Queen Mary, also receipts in ancient cookery* (London, 1790)
Inventories	Nichols, J. G. (ed.), *Inventories of the wardrobes, plate, chapel stuff, etc. of Henry Fitzroy, Duke of Richmond, and of the wardrobe stuff at Baynard's Castle of Katharine, Princess Dowager* (London, 1855)
Latymer	Latymer, William, 'A briefe treatise or cronickille of the moste vertuous ladye Anne Bulleyne late quene of England', in Bodleian MS Don., C, 42, ff. 21r-33v transcribed in Dowling, Maria, 'William Latymer's Chronickille of Anne Bulleyne', *Camden Fourth Series*, 39 (1990), pp. 23-65.
Leland	John Leland, *De rebus Britannicis collectanea,* ed. Thomas Hearne, 6 vols. (London, 1774)

Lisle	Byrne, Muriel St. Clare (ed.), *The Lisle Letters*, 6 vols. (London, 1981)
LP	Brewer, J. S., et al. (eds), *Letters and Papers, Foreign and Domestic, of the Reign of Henry VIII, 1509-47*, 21 vols. and addenda (1920)
LP, Hen VII	Gairdner, James (ed.), *Letters and Papers Illustrative of the Reigns of Richard III and Henry VII*, 2 vols (London, 1861)
LPL	Lambeth Palace Library, London
LR	Nichols, J. G. (ed.) *The literary remains of King Edward VI*, 2 vols. (1857)
Manning	Manning, C. R. (ed.), 'State Papers relating to the custody of the Princess Elizabeth at Woodstock, in 1554', *Journal of the Norfolk and Norwich Archaeological Society*, IV (1855)
Materials	Campbell, William (ed.), *Materials for a History of the Reign of Henry VII*, 2 vols. (London, 1873)
Memorial	'A Memoriall of such things as be requisite' in 'Two papers relating to the interview between Henry the Eighth of England and Francis the First of France', ed. John Caley, *Archaeologia*, 21 (1827), pp. 176–91.
Mueller	Mueller, Janel (ed.), *Katherine Parr: Complete Works and Correspondence* (London, 2011)
ODNB	Oxford Dictionary of National Biography
PCP	Nicolas, Sir Nicholas Harris (ed.), *Privy Council of England, Proceedings and Ordinances (1386-1542)*, 7 vols. (1834-1837)
PPE, Hen	Nicolas, Sir Nicholas Harris (ed.), *The Privy Purse Expenses of King Henry VIII from Nov. 1529 to Dec. 1532* (London, 1827)
PPE, Mary	Madden, Frederick, *Privy purse expenses of the Princess Mary, daughter of King Henry the Eighth, afterwards Queen Mary* (London, 1831)
SOR	A. Luders et al. (eds), *The Statutes of the Realm: Printed by command of his Majesty King George the Third in pursuance of an address of The House of Commons of Great Britain, from Original Records and Authentic Manuscripts*, 10 vols. (1831)

SP, Hen VIII	*State Papers Published Under The Authority His Majesty's Commission, King Henry the Eighth*, 10 vols. (1830-49)
Strype	Strype, John, *Ecclesiastical Memorials relating chiefly to religion, and the reformation of it, and the emergences of the Church of England, under King Henry VIII, King Edward VI and Queen Mary I*, 3 vols. (Oxford, 1822)
TEC	Colthorpe, Marion E. (ed.) *The Elizabethan Court Day by Day*, Folger Shakespeare Library
TGC	Fabyan, Robert, Thomas, and Thornley, I. D. (eds), *The Great Chronicle of London* (London, 1938)
TNA	The National Archives, Kew
TT	Pollard, A. F. (ed.), *Tudor Tracts, 1532-1588* (New York, 1903)
WC	Wriothesley, Charles, *A Chronicle of England during the Reigns of the Tudors, From A.D 1485 to 1559*, ed. William Douglas Hamilton, 2 vols. (1838)
Wingfield	The *Vita Mariae Angliae Reginae* of Robert Wingfield of Brantham, ed. D. MacCulloch, *Camden Miscellany*, 28 (1984)
Wood	Wood, Mary Anne Everett (ed.), *Letters of Royal and Illustrious Ladies of Great Britain, from the commencement of the twelfth century to the close of the reign of Queen Mary*, 3 vols. (London, 1846)
Wyatt	Wyatt, George, 'Life of The Virtuous Christian and Renowned Queen Anne Boleigne' in 'Appendix' Samuel Weller Singer (ed.), *The Life of Cardinal Wolsey* (London, 1827)

Secondary sources

Bernard, G. W., 'The rise of Sir William Compton, early Tudor courtier', *English Historical Review*, 96, 381 (1981), pp. 754-777.

Betteridge, Thomas, and Lipscomb, Suzannah (eds), *Henry VIII and his Court: Art, Politics and Performance* (London, 2013)

Braddock, Robert Cook, 'The Royal Household, 1540-1560: A Study of Officeholding in Tudor England' (Northwestern University, Unpublished Ph.D. thesis, 1971)

Clark, Nicola, *The Waiting Game: The Untold Story of the Women Who Served the Tudor Queens* (London, 2024)

Culling, Elizabeth Ann, 'The Impact of the Reformation on the Tudor Royal Household to 1553' (University of Durham, Unpublished Ph.D. thesis, 1986)

Doran, Susan, *Elizabeth I and her Circle* (Oxford, 2015)

Gunn, Steven, *Henry VII's New Men and the Making of Tudor England* (Oxford, 2016)

Gunn, Steven, 'The Courtiers of Henry VII', *English Historical Review*, 108 (1993), pp. 23-49.

Harris, Barbara J, 'The View from My Lady's Chamber: New Perspectives on the Early Tudor Monarchy', *Huntingdon Library Quarterly*, 60, 3 (1997), pp. 215-247.

Hayward, Maria, *Dress at the Court of Henry VIII* (Abington, 2007)

Hoak, Dale, 'The King's Privy Chamber, 1547-1553', in Delloyd J. Guth and John McKenna (eds), *Tudor Rule and Tudor Revolution, Essays for G.R. Elton from his American Friends* (Cambridge, 1982), pp. 87-108.

Howey, Catherine Louise, 'Busy Bodies: Women, Power and Politics at the Court of Elizabeth I, 1558-1603' (Rutgers, The State University of New Jersey, Unpublished Ph.D. thesis, 2007)

Kisby, Fiona, '"When the King Goeth a Procession": Chapel Ceremonies and Services, the Ritual Year, and Religious Reforms at the Early Tudor Court, 1485-1547', *Journal of British Studies*, 40, 1 (2001), pp. 51-56.

Lipscomb, Suzannah, *The King is Dead: The Last Will and Testament of Henry VIII* (London, 2015)

Loades, David, *The Tudor Court* (Bangor, 1992).

McIntosh, J. L., 'Sovereign Princesses: Mary and Elizabeth Tudor as Heads of Princely Households and the Accomplishment of the Female Succession in Tudor England, 1516-1558' (John Hopkins University, Unpublished Ph.D thesis, 2002)

Mears, Natalie, 'Courts, Courtiers, and Culture in Tudor England', *Historical Journal*, 46 (2003), pp. 703-722.

Mears, Natalie, 'Politics in the Elizabethan Privy Chamber: Lady Mary Sidney and Kat Ashley', in Daybell, James (ed.), *Women and Politics in Early Modern England, 1450-1700* (Hampshire, 2004), pp. 67-82.

Merton, Charlotte Isabelle, 'The Women Who Served Queen Mary and Queen Elizabeth: Ladies, Gentlewomen and Maids of the Privy Chamber, 1553-1603' (University of Cambridge, Unpublished Ph.D. thesis, 1990)

Murphy, John, 'The illusion of decline: the Privy Chamber, 1547-1558' in Starkey, David (ed.), *The English Court: from the Wars of the Roses to the Civil War* (Essex, 2002), pp. 119-146.

Richardson, Glenn, "As presence did present them': Personal Gift-giving at the Field of Cloth of Gold', in Betteridge and Lipscomb (eds), *Henry VIII and his Court*, pp. 47-64.

Russell, Gareth, *Young and Damned and Fair: The Life and Tragedy of Catherine Howard at the Court of Henry VIII* (London, 2017)

Samman, Neil, 'The Henrician Court during Cardinal Wolsey's Ascendancy, c. 1514-1529 (University of Wales, Unpublished Ph.D. thesis, 1988)

Sil, Narasingha Prosad, *Tudor Placemen and Statesmen: Select Case Studies* (New Jersey, 2001)

Starkey, David (ed.), *The English Court: from the Wars of the Roses to the Civil War* (Essex, 2002)

Starkey, David, 'The King's Privy Chamber, 1485-1547' (University of Cambridge, Unpublished Ph.D. thesis, 1973)

Thurley, Simon, *The Royal Palaces of Tudor England: Architecture and Court Life, 1460-1547* (London, 1993)

Weir, Alison, *Henry VIII: King and Court* (London, 2008)

Whitelock, Anna, *Elizabeth's Bedfellows: An Intimate History of the Queen's Court* (London, 2013)

Whitelock, Anna, and MacCullouch, Diarmaid, 'Princess Mary's Household and The Succession Crisis, July 1553, *The Historical Journal*, 50, 2 (2007), pp. 265-287.

NOTES AND REFERENCES

All institutions and departments of the English royal household (Chamber, Privy Chamber, Household, Wardrobe, etc.) are capitalised, whereas physical spaces (chamber, the king or queen's chambers, Presence chamber, Privy chamber, court, etc.) are not.

In Tudor England, money was calculated in pounds, shillings and pence. One pound ('li' or £) was twenty shillings. One shilling (*s.*) was twelve pennies. One penny (*d.*) was two halfpennies (ob).

Chapter 1
'The accustomed good order': Offices and Ordinances

[1] G. R. Elton, 'Tudor Government: The Points of Contact. III. The Court', *Transactions of the Royal Historical Society*, 26 (1976), pp. 211-228 (p. 217).
[2] *HO*, p. 144.
[3] *AR*, II, pp. 186-193. *HO*, pp. 38, 340-342. BL Add MS, 71009, f. 10v-11r.
[4] *HO*, pp. 144, 152-153. *AR*, II, pp. 199-201.
[5] *HO*, pp. 41, 155. *AR*, II, pp. 203-205; IV, pp. 648-649, 651.
[6] *HO*, p. 147.
[7] *HO*, p. 41.
[8] *HO*, pp. 48-49. *AR*, II, pp. 205-206.
[9] *HO*, p. 156.
[10] *HO*, pp. 118, 156. *AR*, IV, p. 649.
[11] *BB*, pp. 111, 129, 201.
[12] *HO*, p. 158.
[13] TNA SP 1/47, f. 56 (*LP* IV 4005).
[14] My italics. BL Add MS, 71009, f. 10r-17v. *AR*, IV, pp. 651-652.
[15] *BB*, pp. 92-93.
[16] *AR*, IV, pp. 651-652.
[17] *LP* IV 1939 [7].
[18] *HO*, pp. 45, 341. *AR*, II, pp. 185-186.
[19] *HO*, p. 347.
[20] BL Add MS, 4712, f. 15r. (*AR*, vol. 1, p. 305).
[21] BL Harleian MS, 41, f. 10 (*LP* VI 601).
[22] Leland, IV, p. 226.
[23] TNA SP 1/153 f. 85 (*LP* XIV, ii., 149). TNA SP 1/153 f. 88 (*LP* XIV, ii., 153).
[24] *HO*, p. 155.
[25] *AR*, IV, p. 652.
[26] TNA SP 1/138, f. 224. *LP* XIII, ii, 804 [3].
[27] *LP* V 756.
[28] *LP* XVI 867, 962, 1137.
[29] TNA E101/422/15.
[30] TNA SP 1/167, ff. 142-143 (LP XVI 1339).
[31] TNA E101/424/12, f. 4, TNA E315/161, ff. 66, 111, 160, 192, 204.
[32] BL Add MS, 45716A, ff. 22v-26r. *HO*, pp. 138-144. TNA SP 1/37, f. 62.
[33] *HO*, p. 137.
[34] *HO*, p. 161.
[35] *LP* IV 1572.
[36] *HO*, pp. 40, 118.
[37] *HO*, pp. 118, 156.
[38] *HO*, p. 156.
[39] *HO*, p. 156.
[40] *HO*, p. 122.
[41] *HO*, p. 127.
[42] *HO*, pp. 215-6.
[43] *HO*, p. 146.
[44] *AR*, IV pp. 648-649.
[45] Thomas Wilson, *The State of England Anno Dom. 1600*, ed. E. J. Fisher (London, 1936), p. 29.
[46] Gottfried von Bulow (trans.), 'Journey through England and Scotland made by Lupold von Wedel in the Years 1584 and 1585', *TRHS*, 9 (London, 1895), pp. 223–70 (pp. 263-264).
[47] Paul Hentzner, *Travels in England, during the Reign of Queen Elizabeth*, ed. and trans. Horace, late earl of Orford (London, 1797), pp. 36-7. *AR*, IV, p. 652.
[48] *LR*, I, p. xxix.
[49] *HO*, p. 155.
[50] *HO*, p. 158.
[51] *LP* IV 4404, 4409.
[52] *LP* IV 4440.
[53] CEVI, p. 71.
[54] TEC, 1573, p. 46.
[55] TEC, 1593, p. 39.
[56] TNA SP 12/159, f. 38v.
[57] *HO*, pp. 42-3.

⁵⁸ BL Sloane MS, 1047, f. 44.
⁵⁹ BL Cotton MS, Otho, C, X, f. 206 (*LP* VII 786).
⁶⁰ BL Sloane MS, 5017, in Leslie G. Matthews, 'Royal Apothecaries of the Tudor Period', *Medical History*, 8, 2 (1964), pp. 170-180 (p. 174).
⁶¹ TEC, 1572, p. 12.
⁶² David Starkey, 'The King's Privy Chamber, 1485-1547' (University of Cambridge, Unpublished Ph.D. thesis, 1973), pp. 29-35.
⁶³ TNA E36/210, ff. 14, 32, 35, 39, 40.
⁶⁴ BL Royal MS, Appendix, 68, in Anna Whitelock, *Elizabeth's Bedfellows: An Intimate History of the Queen's Court* (London, 2013), p. 269.
⁶⁵ TNA, C 115/91 f.19. Janet Arnold (ed.), *Lost from Her Majesties Back*, Costume Society Extra Series 7 (1980), pp. 30-31.
⁶⁶ CSP Sp, XVI, p. 282.
⁶⁷ TNA SP 12/275, f. 138.
⁶⁸ *HO*, p. 145.
⁶⁹ TNA SP 12/8, ff. 51r-54v.
⁷⁰ CPR, Edward VI, V, 85.
⁷¹ CPR, Edward VI, V, 185.
⁷² TEC, 1587, p. 34.
⁷³ BL Harleian MS, 6850, f. 91.
⁷⁴ *HO*, p. 146.
⁷⁵ *HO*, p. 239.
⁷⁶ *HO*, p. 230.
⁷⁷ BL Lansdowne MS, 21, f. 141r.
⁷⁸ BL Add MS, 34319, f. 3r.
⁷⁹ TNA SP 1/23, f. 63 (*LP* III 1597).
⁸⁰ TNA SP 1/47, f. 54 (*LP* IV 4005).
⁸¹ *LP* V 927. Starkey, 'Privy Chamber', pp. 188-194.
⁸² CEVI, p. 26.
⁸³ *HO*, pp. 145, 160.
⁸⁴ *HO*, p. 149. *PCP*, VII, 51 (*LP* XVI 127).
⁸⁵ TEC, 1582.
⁸⁶ *LP* II 1815. *LP* II 1861.
⁸⁷ *LP* II 1832.
⁸⁸ *LP* II 1836. *LP* II 1887.
⁸⁹ *LP* II 1941. *LP* II 1959.
⁹⁰ TNA SP 1/15, f. 79 (*LP* II 3100).
⁹¹ Bacon, pp. 118, 153, 233.
⁹² *HO*, p. 139.
⁹³ Latymer, f. 26r.
⁹⁴ 'Papers Relating to Mary, Queen of Scots, Mostly Addressed to or Written by Sir Francis Knollys', Philobilon Society Miscellanies, 14 (1872), pp. 60-67.
⁹⁵ BL Harleian MS, 6807, ff. 10-12.
⁹⁶ *LP* IV 4584.
⁹⁷ CPR, Edward VI, pp. 322, 381.
⁹⁸ APC, V, p. 48.
⁹⁹ APC, XXI, p. 53.
¹⁰⁰ *HO*, p. 155.
¹⁰¹ Sir John Harington, *Nugae Antiquae* (1792) vol. 2, pp. 232-235.
¹⁰² BL Harleian MS, 6807, f. 11.
¹⁰³ HMC Rutland, I, pp. 275-6.
¹⁰⁴ *HO*, pp. 139, 147, 229-230. BL Harleian MS, 6807, f. 12.
¹⁰⁵ *PCP*, VII, p. 39.
¹⁰⁶ *PCP*, VII, pp. 51-52.
¹⁰⁷ *HO*, p. 137.
¹⁰⁸ BL Lansdowne MS, 21, f. 142r.
¹⁰⁹ Manning, pp. 162, 165.
¹¹⁰ HMC, Rutland, I, 107.
¹¹¹ Whitelock, *Bedfellows*, p. 153.
¹¹² *LR*, I, p. lxxiv. Gareth Russell, *The Palace: From the Tudors to the Windsors, 500 Years of British History at Hampton Court* (Glasgow, 2023), p. 112.
¹¹³ *HO*, pp. 109, 148.

Chapter 2
'The nearer I were to you the gladder I would be':
Appointments and Composition

¹¹⁴ APC, II, p. 399. HMC Rutland, I, p. 55.
¹ CSP Sp, IV, ii., 1158.
² TNA SP 1/133, f. 240 (*LP* XIII, i., 1290).
³ *HO*, p. 127.
⁴ SP Hen VIII, vol. 1, p. 764. *LR*, II, p. 209.
⁵ TNA LC 9/50, f. 212.
⁶ *Lisle*, III, 713, pp. 395-6.
⁷ WC, vol. 1, pp. 43-44.
⁸ *Lisle*, VI, 1636, p. 12. WC, vol. 1, pp. 109-111. HC, pp. 832-838.
⁹ TNA SP 11/6, f. 3r.
¹⁰ CSP Ven, VI, 884.
¹¹ TEC, 1597, p. 6.
¹² *Lisle*, III, p. 25.
¹³ Sir Robert Naunton, *Fragmenta Regalia*, ed. Edward Arber (London, 1870), p. 31.
¹⁴ HMC Rutland, I, pp. 304-5.
¹⁵ *HO*, p. 144.
¹⁶ CSP Dom, III, pp. 238-240.
¹⁷ Haynes, p. 89.
¹⁸ TEC, 1598, p. 11.
¹⁹ TNA SP 1/39, f. 55.
²⁰ CSP Sp, I, 268.
²¹ *LP* XV 229.

[22] *HC*, p. 703.
[23] David Loades, *The Tudor Court* (Bangor, 1992), pp. 212-3.
[24] BL Stowe MS, 560, f. 24v, in Charlotte Isabelle Merton, 'The Women Who Served Queen Mary and Queen Elizabeth: Ladies, Gentlewomen and Maids of the Privy Chamber, 1553-1603' (University of Cambridge, Unpublished Ph.D. thesis, 1990), p. 67.
[25] CSP Sp, I, 260.
[26] *LP*Hen VII, I, p. 232.
[27] *HO*, pp. 31-32; *BB*, pp. 105-6.
[28] *HO*, p. 146; *BB*, pp. 105-6.
[29] TNA SP 1/235, f. 235 (*LP* Addenda I, i., 553).
[30] TNA SP 1/161, f. 85 (*LP*XV 875).
[31] TNA SP 12/1, f. 8. J. E. Neale (ed.), 'Sir Nicholas Throckmorton's Advice to Queen Elizabeth on Her Accession to the Throne', *The English Historical Review*, 65, 254 (1950), pp. 91-8.
[32] TNA SP 70/37, f. 101.
[33] TNA SP 70/16, f. 47.
[34] TNA SP 70/41, f. 16.
[35] William Tighe, 'Familia reginae: the Privy Court', in Susan Doran and Norman Jones (eds), *The Elizabethan World* (Abington, 2011), pp. 81-4 (p. 82).
[36] BL Cotton MS, Vespasian, F, XIII, f. 210 (*LP*IV 3479).
[37] TNA SP 1/241, f. 285 (*LP* Addenda, I, ii., 1297).
[38] *LP*XIII, ii., 1183.
[39] *LR*, I, p. xxxiv.
[40] *Lisle*, V, 1593, pp. 701-703.
[41] CSP Dom, IV, p. 429.
[42] TNA SP 12/242, f. 120.
[43] D. J. H. Clifford (ed.), *The Diaries of Lady Anne Clifford* (Gloucestershire, 1990), p. 21.
[44] TNA SP 1/68, f. 137 (*LP*V 652).
[45] TNA SP 1/81, f. 95 (*LP*VI 1642).
[46] *Lisle*, IV, 887, pp.150-152 (*LP*XII, ii., 271).
[47] Violet A. Wilson, *Queen Elizabeth's Maids of Honour and Ladies of the Privy Chamber* (New York, 1922), p. 41.
[48] BL Cotton MS, Caligula, E, IV, f. 55. (*LP* XIX, ii., 201).
[49] *Lisle*, V, 1574, pp. 681-2 (*LP*XIV, ii., 436); *Lisle*, VI, 1649, p. 25 (*LP*XV 215).
[50] *Lisle*, VI, 1653, pp.33-34 (*LP*XV 229).
[51] *LP*XV 22; *LP*XV 23; *LP*XV 33.
[52] *LP*X 1186.
[53] *HO*, p. 146.
[54] TNA SP 1/50 f. 214 (*LP*IV 4889). TNA SP 1/50, f. 215 (*LP*IV 4890).
[55] *LP*X 181.
[56] Manning, pp. 177, 179, 184, 189-9, 198-9.
[57] TEC, 1589, pp. 32-33.
[58] HMC Salisbury, XII, p. 679.
[59] TEC, 1601, p. 54.
[60] *Lisle*, IV, 865, p. 117; *Lisle*, IV, 864, pp. 111-112; *Lisle*, IV, 891, pp. 156-7.
[61] *Lisle*, IV, 874, pp. 136-8 (*LP*XII, i., 1069).
[62] Joseph Stephenson (ed.), *Calendar of State Papers, Foreign, Elizabeth I*, 28 vols. (1863), 1560-61, p. 215.
[63] *LP*XVI 1192. *PCP*, VII, p. 246.
[64] *LR*, II, p. 245.
[65] CSP Sp, X, p. 14.
[66] CSP Sp, Supplement to I and II, 8 (*LP*I 474).
[67] CSP Ven, III, 1053.
[68] TNA SP 1/84 f. 51 (*LP*VII 684).
[69] Manning, pp. 169-70.
[70] William Turnbull (ed.), *Calendar of State Papers, Foreign, Mary I, 1553-1558* (London, 1861), 523, 524.
[71] *ACP*, V, p. 354.
[72] *LP*IV 2885.
[73] *LP*IV 2861.
[74] BL Cotton MS, Caligula, D, VII, f. 121 (*LP*III 246).
[75] *HC*, p. 598.
[76] Starkey, 'Privy Chamber', pp. 108-14.
[77] Sebastian Giustinian, *Four Years at the Court of Henry VIII*, ed. and trans. by Rawdon Lubbock Brown, 2 vols. (London, 1854), II, p. 271.
[78] Greg Walker, 'The 'Expulsion of the Minions' of 1519 Reconsidered', *The Historical Journal*, 32, 1 (1989), pp. 1-16.
[79] CSP Sp, XI, p. 324.
[80] TEC, 1559, p. 65; TEC, 1561, p. 2. TNA SP 12/16, f. 5.
[81] *LP*XVI 314.
[82] *LP*XVI 523.
[83] William Jerdan (ed.), *Rutland papers: Original documents illustrative of the courts and times of Henry VII. and Henry VIII. Selected from the private archives of His Grace the Duke of Rutland* (London, 1842), p. 26.
[84] *HC*, p. 707.
[85] TNA SP 1/47, f. 127 (*LP*IV 4096).
[86] TNA SP 1/47, f. 127 (*LP*IV 4096).

[87] TNA SP 1/72, f. 20 (*LP* V 1529).
[88] *LP* XI 164.
[89] TNA SP 1/106, f. 219 (*LP* XI 502).
[90] BL Cotton MS, Titus, B, I, f. 390 (*LP* XII, ii., 976).
[91] TNA SP 1/106, f. 231 (*LP* XI 516).
[92] TNA SP 1/143, f. 186 (*LP* XIV, i., 397).
[93] *LP* XII, i., 1103 [36].
[94] WC, vol. 1, pp. 36-37.
[95] Lisle, III, 698, pp. 365-6 (*LP* X 919). Lisle, IV, 846, pp. 47-8 (*LP* X 920).
[96] *LP* X 1036.
[97] Lisle, IV, 846a.
[98] Lisle, III, 698, pp. 365-6 (*LP* X 919); Lisle, IV, 846, pp. 47-8 (*LP* X 920).
[99] *LP* Addenda II 1593, 1594.
[100] TNA SP 1/127, f. 49 (*LP* XII, ii., 1209); Lisle, V, 1249, pp. 250-1 (*LP* XIII, ii., 591).
[101] TNA SP 3/1, f. 83 (*LP* XIV, ii., 284).

Chapter 3
'I was made of the pliable willow, not of the stubborn oak':
Oaths, Loyalty and Allegiance

[1] *AR*, IV, pp. 652-653. BL Cotton MS, Vespasian, C, XIV, f. 438v.
[2] Thea Cervone, *Sworn Bond in Tudor England: Oaths, Vows and Covenants in Civil Life and Literature* (London, 2011), p. 6.
[3] *LP* XII, ii., 704; *LP* XII, ii., 711.
[4] BL Add MS, 34563, f. 2, in R. C. Braddock, 'The Royal Household, 1540-1560: A Study of Officeholding in Tudor England' (Northwestern University, Unpublished PhD thesis, 1971), p. 119.
[5] TEC, 1601, pp. 29, 32.
[6] Hatton, pp. 300-301.
[7] A. E. Newdigate (ed.), *Gossip from a muniment-room: being passages in the lives of Anne and Mary Fytton, 1574–1618* (London, 1897), p. 34.
[8] TNA STAC 2/2, f. 134.
[9] BL Cotton MS, Vespasian, C, XIV, ff. 144r-144v. BL Add MS, 71009, ff. 60-61.
[10] *HC*, pp. 599-600.
[11] TNA SP 1/99, f. 8 (*LP* IX 787).
[12] BL Cotton MS, Otho, C, X, f. 213 (*LP* VI 1253).
[13] My italics. TNA SP 1/196, f. 32.
[14] BL Cotton MS, Otho, C, X, f. 199 (*LP* VI 760); CSP Sp, IV, ii., 1061 (*LP* VI 351).
[15] CSP Sp, IV, ii., 808 (*LP* V 478).
[16] BL Cotton MS, Otho, C, X, f. 199 (*LP* VI 760); CSP Sp, IV, ii., 1165 (*LP* VI 1571). BL Cotton MS, Otho, C, X, f. 177 (*LP* VI 352).
[17] BL Cotton MS, Otho, C, X, f. 213 (*LP* VI 1253).
[18] TNA SP 1/79, f. 158 (*LP* VI 1252). BL Cotton MS, Otho, C, X, f. 210 (*LP* VI 1541).
[19] TNA SP 1/79, f. 158 (*LP* VI 1252). BL Cotton MS, Otho, C, X, f. 177 (*LP* VI 352).
[20] TNA SP 1/79, f. 158 (*LP* VI 1252).
[21] TNA SP 1/79 f. 158 (*LP* VI 1252).
[22] TNA SP 1/81, f. 3 (*LP* VI 1543).
[23] BL Cotton MS, Otho, C, X, f. 210 (*LP* VI 1541). TNA SP 1/81, f. 1 (*LP* VI 1542).
[24] CSP Sp, V, i., 60 (*LP* VII 726).
[25] CSP Sp, V, i., 68 (*LP* VII 871).
[26] CSP Sp, IV, ii., 619 (*LP* V 700).
[27] CSP Sp, IV, i, 509 (*LP* V 6738); CSP Sp, IV, ii., 720 (*LP* V 238); *LP* VI 585.
[28] CSP Sp, V, i., 75 (*LP* VII 1013).
[29] TNA SP 1/99, f. 163 (*LP* IX 1040).
[30] TNA SP 1/99, f. 163 (*LP* IX 1040).
[31] BL Cotton MS, Otho, C, X, f. 215 (*LP* X 28).
[32] TNA SP 1/81, f. 3 (*LP* VI 1543).
[33] BL Cotton MS, Otho, C, X, f. 210 (*LP* VI 1541); CSP Sp, IV, ii., 1165 (*LP* VI 1571); *HC*, pp. 807-8.
[34] CSP Sp, V, i., 4 (*LP* VII 83).
[35] CSP Sp, IV, ii., 1165 (*LP* VI 1571); CSP Sp, V, i., 75 (*LP* VII 1013).
[36] BL Cotton MS, Otho, C, X, f. 206 (*LP* VII 786).
[37] BL Add MS, 28588, f. 87 (*LP* IX 983).
[38] TNA SP 1/79 f. 103 (*LP* VI 1186).
[39] CSP Sp, V, i., 57.
[40] CSP Sp, V, i., 45, 57.
[41] *LP* VII 214.
[42] LP VII 1437. LP XI 7.
[43] TNA SP 1/85, f. 82 (*LP* VII 1035). *LP* VII 1036.
[44] J. L. McIntosh, 'Sovereign Princesses: Mary and Elizabeth Tudor as Heads of Princely Households and the Accomplishment of the Female Succession in Tudor England, 1516-1558' (John Hopkins University, Unpublished Ph.D thesis, 2002), p. 25.
[45] Anna Whitelock and Diarmaid MacCullouch, 'Princess Mary's Household and The Succession Crisis, July 1553, *The Historical Journal*, 50, 2 (2007), pp. 265-287 (pp. 268-9, 275).
[46] Wingfield, pp. 251-3.

[47] Wingfield, pp. 253, 256-7.
[48] Wingfield, pp. 253-254, 269.
[49] WC, vol. II, p. 99. *LR*, II, p. 573.
[50] *LP* XI 556.
[51] TNA SP 1/112 f. 197 (*LP* XI 1306).
[52] *LP* XI 828.
[53] *LP* XI 567, 673.
[54] *LP* XI 569.
[55] *LP* XI 665.
[56] *LP* XI 568.
[57] *LP* XI 728, 764, 853.
[58] *LP* XI 828, 854.
[59] *LP* XI 853.
[60] *LP* XI 539, 705, 853.
[61] *LP* XI 971.
[62] *LP* XI 536, 567, 968.
[63] TNA SP 1/108 f. 221 (*LP* XI 820).
[64] TNA SP 1/108 f. 188 (*LP* XI 789).
[65] TNA SP 1/110 f. 25 (*LP* XI 921).
[66] *LP* XI 985, 986, 1009.
[67] *LP* XI 1064.
[68] *LP* XI 1174, 117
[69] TNA SP 1/115 f. 13 (*LP* XII, i., 200). *LP* XII, i., 160, 174.
[70] TNA SP 1/115 f. 57 (*LP* XII, i., 228).
[71] TNA SP 1/121 f. 61 (*LP* XII, ii., 43).
[72] Naunton, *Fragmenta Regalia*, p. 25.

Chapter 4
'If you serve us heartily, you shall not be forgotten':
Wages, Perquisites and Advancement

[1] TNA E101/422/15; TNA E101/422/16.
[2] BL Add MS, 45716A, f. 13v.
[3] BL Lansdowne MS, 3, f. 192. BL Lansdowne MS, 34, f. 76.
[4] Braddock, 'Household', p. 57.
[5] BL Lansdowne MS, 34, ff. 95-6. R. C. Braddock, 'The Rewards of Office-holding in Tudor England', *The Journal of British Studies* (1975), pp. 29-47 (p. 44).
[6] *HO*, p. 199.
[7] *HO*, pp. 155-156.
[8] SP Hen VIII, vol. 1, p. xiii.
[9] BL Cotton MS, Vespasian, F, XII, f. 179, in Whitelock, *Bedfellows*, p. 156.
[10] BL Cotton MS, Titus, B, II, f. 302, in Whitelock, *Bedfellows*, p. 155.
[11] TEC, 1574, p. 4.
[12] TEC, 1578, p. 57.
[13] CSP Dom, I, p. 648.
[14] CSP Dom, II, p. 30.
[15] TEC, 1580, p. 25.
[16] TEC, 1594, p. 15.
[17] Merton, 'Privy Chamber', p. 17.
[18] BL Add MS, 45716A, f. 3v.
[19] *HO*, p. 153.
[20] Merton, 'Privy Chamber', p. 17. *HO*, p. 164.
[21] BL Add MS, 71009, f. 10r.
[22] APC, XIII, p. 286.
[23] TNA SP 12/183, f. 202 (CSP Dom, II, p. 281).
[24] *LP* XII, ii., 437. *LP* XII ii., 438.
[25] *LP* V 978 [10].
[26] CPR, Edward VI, III, p. 222.
[27] CPR, Philip and Mary, I, p. 193; III, p. 519.
[28] BL Arundel MS, 97, f. 100r.
[29] CSP Dom, IV, p. 292.
[30] CSP Dom, V, p. 256.
[31] TNA E404/86/3/33; E404/86/1/28, in Steven Gunn, 'The Courtiers of Henry VII', *English Historical Review*, 108 (1993), pp. 23-49 (p. 26).
[32] TNA E36/210, ff. 54, 70.
[33] Latymer, f. 32v.
[34] TNA SP 1/103, f. 318r (*LP* X 912); TNA SP 1/104, f. 262r (*LP* X 1257); BL Royal MS, 7, C, XVI, f. 76 (*LP* XI 117).
[35] TNA SP 1/129, f. 174 (*LP* XIII, i., 450).
[36] TNA SP 1/129, f. 174 (*LP* XIII, i., 450).
[37] TNA SP 3/8 f. 11 (*LP* X 33).
[38] TNA SP 1/107 f. 131 (*LP* XI 639).
[39] TNA SP 1/154, f. 5 (*LP* XIV, ii., 297).
[40] TNA E404/86/3/14. in Gunn, 'Courtiers', p. 44.
[41] Strype, I, ii., pp. 8-12.
[42] *LP* IX 1135.
[43] My italics. *Lisle*, IV, 887. *Lisle*, IV, 894.
[44] Historical Manuscripts Commission, *Report on the manuscripts of Lord De l'Isle and Dudley preserved at Penhurst Place* (London, 1925), vol. 1, p. 426.
[45] CSP Dom, III, p. 513.
[46] TNA E101/422/15.
[47] BL Royal MS, 7, C, XVI, ff. 18-32 (*LP* XII, ii., 973). BL Stowe MS 559, ff. 55r-68r (*LP* XVI 1389).
[48] TNA E36/210, ff. 31, 35, 39.
[49] TNA E101/422/15.
[50] TNA SP 1/9, f. 123 (*LP* I 5582).
[51] *LP* II 3851.
[52] TNA SP 1/232, f. 148 (*LP* Addenda I, i., 251).
[53] Wood, I, pp. 260-261 (*LP* IV 1032).

[54] BL Cotton MS, Galba, B, VIII, f. 150 (*LP* IV 882).
[55] *Lisle*, IV, 870, pp. 125-6 (*LP* XII, i., 586).
[56] CPR, Philip and Mary, III, p. 270.
[57] TNA E101/417/3, f. 33. TNA E101/418/5, f. 27. *LP* III 3495 [10].
[58] TEC, 1591, p. 40.
[59] *LP* XXI, i., 1165 [91].
[60] Catherine Louise Howey, 'Busy Bodies: Women, Power and Politics at the Court of Elizabeth I, 1558-1603' (Rutgers, The State University of New Jersey, Unpublished Ph.D. thesis, 2007), p. 44.
[61] CPR, Philip and Mary, I, p. 225.
[62] *LP* XXI, ii., 648 (50).
[63] *ACP*, II, pp.471-472.
[64] Materials, I, pp. 26, 43-44, 65, 93, 99.
[65] Materials, I, p. 410.
[66] *LP* IV 6248 [22]. *LP* XIV, i., 181 [2]. *LP* XIV, i., 681 [49].
[67] *LP* X 778.
[68] *LP* I 60, 61.
[69] *LP* I 619.
[70] *LP* I 131.
[71] TNA SP 1/85, f. 72 (*LP* VII 1010). G. W. Bernard, 'The rise of Sir William Compton, early Tudor courtier', *English Historical Review*, 96, 381 (1981), pp. 754-777.
[72] TNA SP 1/48 f. 230 (*LP* IV 4438).
[73] TNA SP 1/49 f. 78 (*LP* IV 4470).
[74] TNA SP 1/49 f. 124 (*LP* IV 4536).
[75] TNA SP 1/49 f. 53v (*LP* IV 4449).
[76] TNA SP/1/49, f. 124 (*LP* IV 4536).
[77] *LP* XXI, i., p. 71.
[78] *LP* XXI, ii., p. 328.
[79] *LP* XV 1027 [24].
[80] *LP* XII, i, 1104 [2].
[81] *LP* XII, i., 1330 [3].
[82] Calendar of Charter Rolls, Preserved in the Public Record Office, Volume VI: 5 Henry VI – 8 Henry VIII, 1427-1516, pp. 270, 275.
[83] *LP* XXI, ii., 332.
[84] *LP* XII, ii., 617 [10].
[85] CPR, Philip and Mary, II, p. 53.
[86] HMC Salisbury, III, p. 323.
[87] APC, XXV, p. 80.
[88] *LP* I 146.
[89] *LP* II 1624.
[90] *LP* I 1447.
[91] *LP* I 1834.
[92] APC, XXXI, pp. 333-4.
[93] CSP Dom, VI, p. 46.
[94] CSP Dom, VI, p. 210.
[95] CSP Dom, VI, p. 108.
[96] CSP Dom, VI, p. 278.
[97] APC, XXXI, p. 55.
[98] APC, XXXII, pp. 132-33.
[99] *LP* II 172, *LP* II 173.
[100] TNA SP 1/93, f. 189 (*LP* VIII 981).
[101] *Inventories*, pp. xxxiv-xxxv.
[102] *Inventories*, pp. xxxv-xxxvi.
[103] *Inventories*, p. lii.
[104] BL Cotton MS, Vespasian, F, III, f. 38 (*LP* XIX, i., 967).
[105] *HC*, pp. 599-600.
[106] TNA SP 1/41, f. 175 (*LP* IV 3069).
[107] Wood, I, pp. 260-261 (*LP* IV 1032).
[108] Latymer, f. 32v.
[109] HMC Salisbury, II, p. 403.
[110] CSP Dom IV, p. 44.
[111] TNA SP 1/48, f. 230 (*LP* IV 4438).
[112] TNA SP 1/49, f. 73 (*LP* IV 4466).
[113] TNA SP 1/71, f. 102 (*LP* V 1427).
[114] TNA E101/417/3, f. 33.
[115] TNA SP 1/77, f. 95 (*LP* VI 727).
[116] TNA SP 12/181, f. 238.
[117] *LP* III 381.
[118] BL Cotton MS, Caligula, B, I, f. 289 (*LP* III 1024). *LP* III 381. *LP* III 1061.
[119] CSP Sp, Supplement, I, 16.
[120] CSP Sp, I, 513, 532.
[121] CSP Sp, I, 546.
[122] TNA SP 1/141, f. 178.
[123] CSP Sp, XI, p. 172.
[124] CSP Sp, XIII, 101.
[125] APC, V, p. 265.
[126] TNA SP/12/7, f. 98.
[127] APC, XXXII, pp. 142-3.
[128] APC, II, pp. 17-18.
[129] TNA SP/63/30, f. 108.
[130] CSP Dom, IV, pp. 262-3.
[131] HMC Salisbury, X, pp. 58-9.
[132] HMC Salisbury, X, pp. 80, 90-1, 122.

Chapter 5
'Apparelled according to their degrees': Livery, Majesty and Magnificence

[1] *Lisle*, IV, 887, pp.150-152 (*LP* XII, ii., 271). BL Harleian MS, 6807, f. 12r.
[2] *Lisle*, IV, 887 (*LP* XII, ii., 271).
[3] *Lisle*, IV, 895 (*LP* XII, ii., 711).
[4] *Lisle*, IV, 896 (*LP* XII, ii., 808).
[5] *Lisle*, V, 1102, pp. 36-7.
[6] *Lisle*, V, 1117, pp. 58-9.
[7] *Lisle*, V, 1126, pp. 70-2.
[8] *Lisle*, V, 1136, pp. 92-4.

⁹ *Lisle*, V, 1137, pp. 95-6.
¹⁰ BL Add MS, 71009, ff. 57v-59r.
¹¹ Ellis, II, pp. 32-33.
¹² WC, vol. 1, p. 20.
¹³ J. O. Halliwell Phillipps (ed.), *Letters of the kings of England*, 2 vols. (London, 1848), vol. 1, pp. 352-3 (*LP* X 65).
¹⁴ *LP* X 284.
¹⁵ Maria Hayward, *Dress at the Court of Henry VIII* (Abington, 2007), pp. 64-65.
¹⁶ Hayward, *Dress*, p. 65.
¹⁷ *LP* XII, ii., 106. WC, vol. 1, pp. 70-72.
¹⁸ *Lisle*, IV, 905 (*LP* XII, ii., 1157).
¹⁹ *Lisle*, IV, 908, (*LP* XII, ii., 1234).
²⁰ TNA E101/418/6, f. 8r, 20v, 22v.
²¹ *LP* V 1323.
²² TNA SP 1/174, f. 135 (*LP* XVII 1134).
²³ TNA E36/210, ff. 41, 47, 53.
²⁴ TGC, p. 254.
²⁵ A servant of King Henry VIII by Hans Holbein the Younger, 1534, in the collection of the Kunsthistorisches Museum, Vienna.
²⁶ TNA E101/418/6, f. 9r.
²⁷ APC, VI, p. 170.
²⁸ CSP Dom, III, p. 549.
²⁹ CSP Ven, IV, 923.
³⁰ CSP Sp, IV, ii., 1127.
³¹ Starkey, 'Privy Chamber', p. 185.
³² *LP* XXI, ii., 684.
³³ TNA E101/428/14, f. 8. Braddock, 'Household', pp. 12-3.
³⁴ APC, XI, pp. 451-452. CSP Dom, II, p. 300
³⁵ TNA SP 1/96, f. 199 (*LP* IX 413).
³⁶ SP Hen VIII, vol. 3, pp. 285-290.
³⁷ *LP* XI 41.
³⁸ TNA SP 15/12, f. 157 (CSP Dom, VI, pp. 565-6).
³⁹ Braddock, 'Household', pp. 116-7.
⁴⁰ TNA SP 1/97 f. 75 (*LP* IX 510).
⁴¹ TNA SP 1/104, f. 3 (*LP* X 914).
⁴² TNA SP 1/76, f. 121 (*LP* VI 559).
⁴³ TNA SP 1/78, f. 50 (*LP* VI 917). TNA SP 1/78, f. 75 (*LP* VI 934).
⁴⁴ TNA SP 1/104, f. 6 (*LP* X 914).
⁴⁵ TNA E315/161, f. 212r.
⁴⁶ TNA SP 1/195 f. 197 (*LP* XIX, ii., 724).
⁴⁷ TNA SP 1/213 f. 34 (*LP* XXI, i., 26).
⁴⁸ William Gouge, *Of Domestical Duties*, 2nd ed. (London, 1626).
⁴⁹ Sir John Hayward, *Annals of the first four years of the reign of Queen Elizabeth*, ed. John Bruce (London, 1840), p. 15.

⁵⁰ *LP* XVI 1088. Fiona Kisby, 'Kingship and The Royal Itinerary', *The Court Historian*, 4, 1 (1999), pp. 29-39 (pp. 29-32).
⁵¹ BL Cotton MS, Vitellius, B, III, f. 245r (*LP* II 4034).
⁵² TNA SP 1/16, f. 314 (*LP* II 4276).
⁵³ *LR*, I, pp. 80-1.
⁵⁴ TEC, 1567, p. 18.
⁵⁵ TEC, 1574, p. 12.
⁵⁶ *LP* III 698. HC, pp. 600-601.
⁵⁷ HC, pp. 600-601.
⁵⁸ Memorial, p. 178.
⁵⁹ TNA E 315/242/3, ffs. 22v-31r (*LP* III 852).
⁶⁰ HC, pp. 615, 618.
⁶¹ CSP Ven, III, 81.
⁶² CSP Ven, III, 50.
⁶³ CSP Ven, III, 84.
⁶⁴ *The Anglica Historia of Polydore Vergil, A. D. 1485-1537*, ed. and trans. Denys Hay, *Royal Historical Society*, Camden Series, vol. 74 (London, 1950), p. 269.
⁶⁵ CSP Ven, III, 69.

Chapter 6
'I care not to be groom of the scullery':
Access, Interaction and Intimacy

¹ Foxe, V, p. 555. HO, p. 146. BL Cotton MS, Caligula, D, VII, f. 186.
² BL Add MS, 71009, f. 19r.
³ BL Add MS, 71009, f. 20r.
⁴ Simon Thurley, *The Royal Palaces of Tudor England: Architecture and Court Life, 1460-1547* (London, 1993), pp. 135-6.
⁵ David Starkey, 'Intimacy and innovation: the rise of the Privy Chamber, 1485-1547', in David Starkey et al, eds., *The English Court from the Wars of the Roses to the English Civil War* (London, 1987), pp. 71-118.
⁶ TNA SP 1/128, f. 130 (*LP* XIII, i., 159).
⁷ *LP* XVI 1366.
⁸ *AR*, IV, p. 651. HO, pp. 154-55.
⁹ BL Royal MS, B, XL, ff. 6r-7r, in Chris Skidmore, *Edward VI: The Lost King of England* (London, 2008).
¹⁰ Naunton, *Fragmenta Regalia*, p. 17.
¹¹ HO, p. 157.
¹² BL Cotton MS, Vitellius, C, I, f. 7r, in McIntosh, 'Sovereign Princesses', pp. 132-3.
¹³ Giles Duwes, *An Introductory for to Learn to Read, to Pronounce, and to Speak*

French (1534), in McIntosh, 'Sovereign Princesses', pp. 119-127.

14 J. E. B. Mayer (ed.) *The English Works of John Fisher*, I (London, 1876), p. 296.

15 Latymer, f. 25r.

16 Latymer, ff. 24v-25r.

17 Foxe, V, pp. 62-63; Wyatt, pp. 442-3; Latymer, ff. 25r, 26v-27r, 31r-32v.

18 Latymer, f. 32v.

19 Foxe, V, pp. 62-63.

20 Wyatt, pp. 442-3.

21 Duwes, in McIntosh, 'Sovereign Princesses', pp. 119-127.

22 *HC*, p. 598.

23 David Starkey, *The Reign of Henry VIII: Personalities and Politics* (London, 2002), p. 55.

24 SP, Hen VIII, vol. 7, p. 169.

25 *HC*, pp. 798-805.

26 Mueller, pp. 169-170.

27 J. M. Rigg (ed.), *Calendar of State Papers Relating to English Affairs, Preserved Principally at Rome, in the Vatican Archives and Library*, vol. 1 (1916), p. 105.

28 Strype, I, ii., p. 456.

29 Strype, I, ii., p. 458.

30 Strype, I, ii., pp. 458-9.

31 Wyatt, pp. 429-30.

32 Mueller, pp. 177-178.

33 BL Harleian MS, 787, f. 15r, in Susan Doran, *Elizabeth I and her Circle* (Oxford, 2015), p. 199.

34 *LP*, Hen VII, II, p. xxv.

35 *LP* I 3524.

36 CSP Sp, II, 238.

37 Cavendish, p. 217.

38 *LP* X 352.

39 *LP* XV 844.

40 CSP Sp, XV, p. 515.

41 CSP Sp, XVI, p. 274.

42 TNA, C/115/M19/ 7543, in Howey, 'Busy Bodies', p. 165.

43 CSP Sp, XIV, p. 455. HMC Salisbury, VII, pp. 41–2.

44 BL Lansdowne MS, 94, f. 21, in Doran, *Circle*, p. 197.

45 Doran, *Circle*, p. 213.

46 Haynes, pp. 509-510.

47 Hatton, p. 154.

48 Hatton, p. 14.

49 Hatton, pp. 50-51.

50 APC, III, p. 431.

51 *LR*, I, p. 75.

52 *LR*, I, pp. 82-3.

53 *LR*, I, pp. 86-7.

54 *HO*, p. 156. BL Harleian MS, 2210, f. 9r. BL Add MS, 21116, ff. 3-4.

55 Cavendish, pp. 227-231.

56 *LR*, I, pp. cxv-cxvi.

57 *LR*, I, pp. cxv-cxvi.

58 *LP* XV 850. Strype, I, ii., pp. 462-3.

59 TEC, 1601, p. 18.

60 Harington, *Nugae Antiquae*, vol. 1, pp. 317-8, 234.

61 CSP Sp, XVI, p. 311.

62 TNA SP 11/7, f. 122. TNA SP 11/7, f. 71. CSP Dom, I, pp. 77-8.

63 HMC Rutland, I, pp. 310-311.

64 *LP* XXI, i., 291.

65 TNA SP 1/120, f. 200 (*LP* XI, i., 1285).

66 TNA SP 1/125, f. 93 (*LP* XII, ii., 821).

67 TNA SP 1/125, f. 98 (*LP* XII, ii., 827).

68 *LR*, I, pp. liiii-liv.

69 TNA SP 12/263, f. 105. CSP Dom, IV, p. 429.

70 CSP Sp, IX, pp. 18-21.

71 CSP Sp, XI, pp. 251-252.

72 TEC, 1592, p. 16.

73 HMC Rutland, I, pp. 275-276.

74 BL Cotton MS, Caligula, B, I, f. 184 (*LP* III 3423).

75 BL Cotton MS, Caligula, B, I, f. 250 (*LP* III 3327).

76 BL Cotton MS, Caligula, B, VI, f. 341 (*LP* III 3341).

77 BL Cotton MS, Caligula, B, I, f. 295 (*LP* III 3538).

78 *LP* III 3424, 3425.

79 BL Cotton MS, Caligula, B, I, f. 283 (*LP* III 3444).

80 BL Cotton MS, Caligula, B, II, f. 164 (*LP* IV 658).

81 BL Cotton MS, Caligula, B, II, f. 60 (*LP* IV 1170).

82 BL Cotton MS, Caligula, B, II, f. 48 (*LP* IV 1372).

83 *LP* XI 815, 1373.

84 TNA SP 1/167/157-9.

85 TNA SP 1/167 f. 14 (*LP* XVI 1134).

86 TNA SP 1/167/157-9.

87 TNA SP 1/167 f. 14.

88 *LP* XVI 1395.

89 HMC Bath, II, pp. 9-10.

90 TNA SP 1/167 f. 14. *LP* XVI 1134. TNA SP 1/167/157-9.

91 TNA SP 1/167/157-9; TNA SP/1/167/149.

92 TNA SP/167/153-4; *LP* XVI 1338.

[93] HMC Bath, II, pp.9-10; TNA SP 1/167/157-9.
[94] HMC Bath, II, pp. 9-10. TNA SP 1/167/157-9.
[95] TNA SP/1/167/159-60.
[96] TNA SP/167/153-4 (*LP* XVI 1338).
[97] TNA SP/167/153-4 (*LP* XVI 1338).
[98] *LP* XVI 1470.
[99] TNA SP 1/167, f. 144r (*LP* XVI 1339).
[100] TNA SP 1/167, f. 144r (*LP* XVI 1339). Gareth Russell, *Young and Damned and Fair: The Life and Tragedy of Catherine Howard at the Court of Henry VIII* (London, 2017), pp. 248-9.
[101] J. G. Nichols (ed.), *The Legend of Sir Nicholas Throckmorton* (London, 1874), pp. 26-7.
[102] CSP Sp, XI, p. 444.
[103] TNA SP 1/95, f. 159 (*LP* IX 172).
[104] TNA SP 1/96, f. 73 (*LP* IX 274).
[105] *LP* XV 1029 [40].
[106] TNA SP 1/154, f. 35 (*LP* XIV, ii., 371). TNA SP 1/189, f. 118 (*LP* XIX, i., 817).
[107] TNA SP 1/197, f. 185 (*LP* XX, i., 101).
[108] TNA SP 1/238, f 53 (*LP* Addenda, I, 832).
[109] Strype, I, ii., pp. 256-8.
[110] Alexander Samson, *Mary and Philip: The marriage of Tudor England and Habsburg Spain* (Manchester, 2020), pp. 70-1.
[111] TNA SP 11/1/20, p. 7, in Samson, *Mary and Philip*, pp. 70, 205-6.
[112] CSP Sp, XIII, p. 50.
[113] Samson, *Mary and Philip*, p. 106. TNA SP 11/4, f. 21.

Chapter 7
'Now here comes in the cogging of this place': Government, Politics and Patronage

[1] TNA SP 1/4, f. 78 (*LP* I 1960). SP, Hen VIII, vol. 1, pp. 297-298 (*LP* IV 4409).
[2] TNA SP 1/153 f. 88 (*LP* XIV, ii., 153).
[3] TNA SP 1/153 f. 85 (*LP* XIV, ii., 149).
[4] TNA SP 1/153 f. 93 (*LP* XIV, ii., 163).
[5] Robert Beale, 'A Treatise of the Office of ... Principall Secretarie', in Conyers Read, *Mr Secretary Walsingham and the Policy of Queen Elizabeth*, 3 vols. (Cambridge, 1925), vol. 1, pp. 423-43.
[6] Doran, *Circle*, p. 203.
[7] *LR*, I, p. cvi-cxvii.
[8] BL Cotton MS, Titus, B, II, 161, f. 344, in Merton 'Privy Chamber', p. 171.
[9] CSP Sp, XI, p. 397.
[10] HMC Salisbury, I, p. 153.
[11] CSP Sp, XI, p. 397.
[12] CSP Sp, XI, pp. 309-311.
[13] CSP Sp, XI, p. 329.
[14] D. M. Loades (ed.), *The Papers of George Wyatt, Esquire, Of Boxley Abbey in the County of Kent*, Camden Fourth Series, V (London, 1968), p. 203.
[15] CSP Sp, XI, p. 444.
[16] CSP Sp, XIV, p. 21.
[17] CSP Rome, I, p. 105.
[18] Natalie Mears, 'Politics in the Elizabethan Privy Chamber: Lady Mary Sidney and Kat Ashley', in James Daybell (ed.), *Women and Politics in Early Modern England, 1450-1700* (Hampshire, 2004), pp. 67-82.
[19] CSP Scot, IV, p. 36.
[20] Cavendish, p. 156.
[21] HC, p. 622.
[22] *PCP*, VII, pp. 147-8 (*LP* XVI 583).
[23] TNA SP 1/227, f. 82 (*LP* XXI, ii., 548).
[24] TNA SP 1/144 f. 155 (*LP* XIV, i., 581).
[25] *LP* XXI, i., 1350.
[26] CSP Dom, II, p. 345.
[27] CSP Dom, IV, p. 264.
[28] BL Cotton MS, Titus, B, I, f. 192r (*LP* III 576 [3]).
[29] TNA E36/130, ff. 165-131 (*LP* III 578).
[30] S. J. Gunn, *Early Tudor Government, 1485-1558* (Hampshire, 1995), pp. 29, 36. E. W. Ives, 'Court and County Palatine in the Reign of Henry VIII: The Career of William Brereton of Malpas', *Transactions of the Historic Society of Lancashire and Cheshire*, 123 (1971), pp. 1-38.
[31] Gunn, 'Courtiers', p. 29.
[32] CPR, Edward VI, IV, p. 234.
[33] Materials, II, pp. 227-228, 237.
[34] *LP* XII, ii., 1224.
[35] TNA SP 1/83, f. 185 (*LP* VII 600). *LP* VII 641. TNA SP 1/89, f. 50 (LP VIII 81), *LP* VIII 94. *LP* VII Appendix 22. TNA SP 1/83, f. 185 (*LP* VII 600).
[36] APC XXIV, p. 323.
[37] TNA SP 10/6, ff. 35r, 70r.
[38] D. E. Hoak, *The King's Council in the Reign of Edward VI* (Cambridge, 1976) p. 123.
[39] *LR*, II, p. ccxxvii.
[40] CSP Sp, X, p. 249.
[41] William Jerdan (ed.), *Rutland papers: Original documents illustrative of the courts and times of Henry VII. and Henry VIII. Selected*

from *the private archives of His Grace the Duke of Rutland* (London, 1842), pp. 25-26.
   [42] Ellis, I, pp. 116-7; *LP* I 3356; BL Cotton MS, Caligula, D, VI, f. 257.
   [43] *LP* I 3381.
   [44] BL Cotton MS, Caligula, D, VI, f. 205r (*LP* I 3416).
   [45] *LP* I 3440.
   [46] TGC, p. 258. Gunn, 'Courtiers', pp. 29-30.
   [47] *LP* III 2356 (20).
   [48] Foxe, VIII, p. 594.
   [49] CPR Elizabeth I, V, p. 173.
   [50] LPL MS, 2004, f. 4, in Merton, 'Privy Chamber', p. 180.
   [51] *LP* XIX, i., 610 [51].
   [52] *LP* XIX, i., 1035 [40].
   [53] TNA SP 1/39, ff. 96-7 (*LP* IV 2431). TNA SP 1/59, f. 141. E. W. Ives, 'Patronage at the Court of Henry VIII: The Case of Sir Ralph Egerton of Ridley', *Bulletin of the John Rylands Library*, 52 (1969-70), pp. 346-74.
   [54] *HO*, p. 157.
   [55] *PCP*, VII, pp. 51-52.
   [56] HMC Salisbury, X, p. 125.
   [57] TNA SP 12/206, f. 80.
   [58] TNA SP 12/208, f. 17.
   [59] Rowland Vaughan, *Most approved and long experienced Waterworkes* (London, 1610).
   [60] CSP Rome, I, p. 105.
   [61] CSP Sp, XI, p. 180.
   [62] CSP Sp, 1553, p. 189.
   [63] *Lisle*, III, 658, pp. 300-1 (*LP* X 499).
   [64] TNA SP 1/85, f. 43 (*LP* VII 964).
   [65] TEC, 1580, p. 26.
   [66] TEC, 1593, p. 35.
   [67] Howey, 'Busy Bodies', pp. 51-52.
   [68] Arthur Collins (ed.), *Letters and Memorials of State*, 2 vols. (London, 1746), II, pp. 81, 97.
   [69] Collins (ed.), *Letters and Memorials*, II, p. 87.
   [70] *LP* X 919.
   [71] *LP* XIII, ii., 591.
   [72] *LP* X 865, 952, 1074.
   [73] *LP* X 994.
   [74] *LP* X 1100. *LP* Addenda, I, 1077.
   [75] *Lisle*, III, 753.
   [76] TNA SP 1/105, f. 12 (*LP* XI 31).
   [77] TNA SP 3/4 f. 99 (*LP* XII, i., 1068)
   [78] TNA SP 3/10, f. 133 (*LP* VII 986).
   [79] LP VII 304.
   [80] *LP* VII 95.

   [81] Barbara J. Harris, 'The View from My Lady's Chamber: New Perspectives on the Early Tudor Monarchy', *Huntingdon Library Quarterly*, 60, 3 (1997), pp. 215-247.
   [82] *Lisle*, IV, 896, pp. 167-8 (*LP* XII, ii., 808).
   [83] *Lisle*, IV, 868a, pp. 121-3.
   [84] *Lisle*, IV, 875, pp. 138-9.
   [85] *Lisle*, IV, 855a, pp. 71-2.
   [86] *Lisle*, IV, 887, pp. 150-152 (*LP* XII, ii., 271). *Lisle*, IV, 878, p. 141.
   [87] *Lisle*, IV, 887, pp. 150-152 (*LP* XII, ii., 271).
   [88] *Lisle*, IV, 850ii, pp. 109-110.
   [89] *Lisle*, V, 1620, pp. 730-1 (*LP* XIV, ii., 718).
   [90] *Lisle*, V, 1620, pp. 730-1 (*LP* XIV, ii., 718).
   [91] *Lisle*, V, 1620, pp. 730-1 (*LP* XIV, ii., 718).
   [92] *Lisle*, VI, 1653, p. 33-4 (*LP* XV 229).
   [93] *Lisle*, VI, 1653, p. 33-4 (*LP* XV 229).
   [94] *LR*, I, p. cxvii-cxviii.
   [95] CSP Dom, VII, pp. xiii-xiv, 3-4.
   [96] TNA SP 12/171, f. 43.
   [97] Historical Manuscripts Commission, *Report on the manuscripts of Allan George Finch, Esq., of Burley-on-the-Hill, Rutland* (London, 1913), I, pp. 24-5.
   [98] HMC Salisbury, IX, p. 76.
   [99] HMC Salisbury, X, p. 308.
   [100] HMC Salisbury, V, pp. 30-1.
   [101] LPL Talbot MS, 3199, f. 441.
   [102] LPL Shrewsbury MS, 707, f. 221.
   [103] TNA SP 12/176/1, f. 10.
   [104] TEC, 1595, p. 44.
   [105] TNA SP 1/244, f. 15 (*LP* Addenda I, ii., 1553).
   [106] CSP Ven, VI, pp. 1083-4.
   [107] LPL Bacon MS, 652, f. 312-3.
   [108] LPL Bacon MS, 652, f. 312-3.
   [109] SOR, II, p. 533.
   [110] TNA SP 1/74, f. 134 (*LP* VI 133).
   [111] CSP Dom, VII, pp. 41-42.
   [112] CSP Foreign, Elizabeth I, 1566-8, p. 130.
   [113] BL Lansdowne MS, 34, f. 91.

Chapter 8
'I pray you pray for me your loving master': Religion, Faith and Reform

   [1] *HO*, pp. 188-189. Fiona Kisby, '"When the King Goeth a Procession": Chapel Ceremonies and Services, the Ritual Year, and

Religious Reforms at the Early Tudor Court, 1485-1547', *Journal of British Studies*, 40, 1 (2001), pp. 51-56.

[2] *LP* V 614.
[3] *LP* VI 351.
[4] CSP Sp, IV, ii., 1061.
[5] Merton, 'Privy Chamber', p. 107. TEC, 1560, p. 16.
[6] Joseph Stevenson (ed.) *The Life of Jane Dormer, Duchess of Feria by Henry Clifford, Transcribed from the Ancient Manuscript in the possession of Lord Dormer* (London 1887), pp. 64-65.
[7] *HO*, p. 35.
[8] *HO*, pp. 160-161.
[9] *HO*, pp. 160-1.
[10] *AR*, IV, pp. 648-649.
[11] BL Harleian MS, 6807, ff. 10r, 18r.
[12] TEC, 1598, p. 29.
[13] Robert Carey, *The Memoirs of Robert Carey, Earl of Monmouth* (London, 1808), p. 117.
[14] TEC, 1603, p. 10.
[15] Sir John Harington, *Nugae Antiquae* (1792), vol. 2, p. 215.
[16] G. W. Bernard, 'Reflecting on the King's Reformation', in Thomas Betteridge and Suzannah Lipscomb (eds), *Henry VIII and his Court: Art, Politics and Performance* (London, 2013), pp. 9-26 (p. 22).
[17] BL Add MS, 17012, ff. 20-21, 192. Calum Cockburn, 'A Tudor autograph book' https://blogs.bl.uk/digitisedmanuscripts/2023/03/a-tudor-autograph-book, 2023.
[18] TNA E315/161, f. 46.
[19] Mueller, p. 159.
[20] BL Lansdowne MS, 97, f. 43. Mueller, pp. 75-78 (*LP* XVIII, ii., 531).
[21] Mueller, pp. 122-125; BL Harleian MS, 5087, 27, f. 11r.
[22] Latymer, f. 22r-22v.
[23] Latymer, f. 25r.
[24] Latymer, f. 23v, 32v.
[25] Foxe, V, pp. 62-63.
[26] G. W. Bernard, 'Anne Boleyn's religion', *Historical Journal*, 36 (1993), pp. 1-20 (pp. 3-4).
[27] Nicholas Harpsfield, *A Treatise on the Pretended Divorce Between Henry VIII. and Catharine of Aragon*, ed. by Nicholas Pocock, (London, 1878), p. 200.
[28] Nicholas Sander, *The Rise and Growth of the Anglican Schism*, ed. by David Lewis (London, 1877), p. 7.
[29] TNA SP 1/78, f. 104 (*LP* VI 965). TNA SP 1/78, f. 105 (*LP* VI 966).
[30] *LP* VII 14.
[31] Elizabeth Ann Culling, 'The Impact of the Reformation on the Tudor Royal Household to 1553' (University of Durham, Unpublished Ph.D. thesis, 1986), p. 262.
[32] CSP Sp, V, ii., 17.
[33] Carolyn Forché and Duncan Wu (eds), *Poetry of Witness: The Tradition in English, 1500-2001* (London 2014), p. 71.
[34] *LP* IV 5416.
[35] Strype, I, i., pp. 171-3. Wyatt, pp. 438-40. Nichols, *Narratives*, pp. 52-7.
[36] TNA SP 1/103, f. 259 (*LP* X 827).
[37] Freeman, 'Anne Boleyn', pp. 804-5.
[38] TNA SP 1/109 f. 198 (*LP* XI 879).
[39] TNA SP 1/106, f. 291 (*LP* XI 567).
[40] TNA SP 1/109 f. 198 (*LP* XI 879).
[41] TNA SP 1/120 f. 136 (*LP* XII, i., 1225).
[42] *LP* XI 860. *LP* XI 1250.
[43] Foxe, V, pp. 494-5.
[44] Foxe, V, p. 495.
[45] *LP* XVIII, ii., 241 [6]. *LP* XVIII, i., 287, 292, 310. CSP Sp, VI, ii., 120.
[46] *LP* XXI, i., 1383 [72].
[47] Foxe, V, p. 564.
[48] Foxe, V, p. 654.
[49] WC, vol. 1, p. 118.
[50] APC, I, p. 400.
[51] TNA SP 1/163, f 38 (*LP* XVI 101).
[52] Foxe, V, pp. 550-552.
[53] CSP Sp, X, pp. 176-177.
[54] *APC*, I, pp. 400-408; *LP* XXI, i., 759.
[55] *LP* XXI, i., 759, 769.
[56] *LP* XXI, ii., 756; CSP Sp, VIII, 386. Foxe, V, pp. 553-561.
[57] Culling, 'Reformation', p. 171.
[58] Foxe, V, p. 557.
[59] *LP* XXI, ii, 756. *LP* XXI, i, 1181.
[60] Foxe, V, p. 547.
[61] Foxe, V, p. 547. *LP* XXI, i., 1181.
[62] TNA E315/161/46.
[63] Foxe, V, p. 554.
[64] Foxe, V, p. 554.
[65] Foxe, V, p. 557.
[66] Foxe, V, pp. 556-8.
[67] Freeman, 'Katherine Parr', pp. 238-245.
[68] CSP Sp, IX, pp. 406-8; CSP Sp, X, pp. 5, 101.
[69] CSP Sp, X, p. 5.
[70] CSP Sp, X, p. 68.
[71] Nichols (ed.), *Machyn*, p. 20.

[72] CSP Sp, X, p. 210.
[73] LR, II, p. 316. APC, III, p. 267.
[74] LR, II, pp. 323-4.
[75] CSP Sp, X, p. 359.
[76] CSP Sp, X, p. 359.
[77] APC, II, p. 238. APC, III, pp. 333-336.
[78] CSP Sp, X, p. 359.
[79] APC, III, pp. 338-9.
[80] APC, III, p. 341.
[81] APC, III, pp. 348, 352.
[82] APC, III p. 343. CSP Sp, X, pp. 359, 362, 364.
[83] CSP Sp, IX, p. 405.
[84] Nichols (ed.), *Chronicle*, pp. 19-20.
[85] John Bayley, *The History and Antiquities of the Tower of London*, II (London, 1825), p. xlix.
[86] CSP Sp, XI, p. 418.
[87] CSP Sp, XI, p. 395.
[88] Manning, pp. 214-7.
[89] CSP Sp, XI, p. 418.
[90] Manning, pp. 166-170.
[91] Foxe, VIII, p. 581.
[92] Manning, pp. 220-221.
[93] Foxe, VIII, p. 580.
[94] M. J. Rodríguez-Salgado and Simon Adams, 'The Count of Feria's Dispatch to Philip II of 14 November 1558', *Camden Fourth Series*, 29 (1984), pp. 302-344 (p. 331).
[95] CSP Dom, I, p. 73.
[96] TT, pp. 174-5, 179.
[97] CPR, Philip and Mary, I, pp. 198-9.
[98] TT, p. 187.
[99] TT, pp. 191-192.
[100] APC, XXVI, p. 375.

Chapter 9
'Honest and moderate play':
Court Culture and Pastime

[1] *LP* III 152.
[2] *LP* III 950.
[3] TNA SP 1/47, f. 54 (*LP* IV 4005).
[4] *HO*, p. 157.
[5] *LR*, I, p. ccxxii.
[6] *LR*, I, pp. 80-1.
[7] *HC*, p. 582. *LP* II 410, 411.
[8] *LP* II 4326.
[9] CSP Sp, XIV, p. 466.
[10] *AR*, IV, p. 650.
[11] Manning, pp. 141, 152, 158.
[12] BL Cotton MS, Caligula, E, IV, f. 55. (*LP* XIX, ii., 201).
[13] Cavendish, pp. 227-228.
[14] Wyatt, pp. 442-3.
[15] BL Cotton MS, Vitellius, B, XII, f. 68 (*LP* IV 4981).
[16] William Forrest, *The history of Grisild the Second: a narrative, in verse, of the divorce of Queen Katharine of Arragon*, ed. by W. D. Macray (London, 1875), pp. 28-29.
[17] BL Harleian MS, 6807, ff. 10-12.
[18] TEC, 1598, p. 4.
[19] *HO*, p. 157.
[20] PPE, Hen VIII, pp. 32, 278.
[21] PPE, Hen VIII, pp. 113, 115.
[22] PPE, Hen VIII, p. 216.
[23] *LP* III 235.
[24] Strype, II, i., p. 388; Skidmore, *Edward VI*.
[25] TT, p. 185.
[26] TNA E101/422/15; TNA E101/422/16.
[27] TNA E36/210, ff. 56-7.
[28] TEC, 1584, p. 30.
[29] TEC, 1568, p. 45.
[30] TEC, 1583, p. 49.
[31] F. G. Emmerson, *Tudor Food and Pastimes* (London, 1964), pp. 33, 80-1.
[32] HMC Rutland, I, p. 101.
[33] TEC, 1583, p. 8.
[34] Stephen Hawes, *The Minor Poems*, ed. by Florence W. Gluck and Alice B. Morgan, Early English Text Society, Original Series, 271 (London, 1974).
[35] *LR*, I, p. 20. Andrew Ashbee, 'Groomed for Service: Musicians in the Privy Chamber at the English Court, c.1495-1558', *Early Music*, 25, 2 (1997), pp. 185-197 (p. 194).
[36] PPE, Hen VIII, pp. 11, 18.
[37] Ashbee, 'Musicians', p. 189.
[38] CSP Ven, V, p. 533.
[39] TEC, 1587, p. 53.
[40] CSP Ven, VII, p. 526.
[41] McIntosh, 'Sovereign Princesses', p. 128.
[42] Ashbee, 'Musicians', p. 195.
[43] *LP* XIX, ii., 688. PPE, Mary, pp. 48, 50, 64, 108, 113, 114, 119, 126, 130, 131, 159.
[44] The Family of Henry VIII c. 1545 © Royal Collection Trust, RCIN 405796.
[45] *LP* Hen VII, I, p. 399.
[46] Newdigate (ed.), *Gossip*, pp. 34-5.
[47] TNA SP 1/42, f. 26 (*LP* IV 3135).
[48] *HC*, pp. 513-14.
[49] *HC*, pp. 516-9.
[50] Newdigate (ed.), *Gossip*, pp. 38-39.
[51] BL Cotton MS, Vitellius, C, I, f. 10r. in McIntosh, 'Sovereign Princesses', pp. 80-1.

52 CSP Ven, IV, 682.
53 *LP* VI 212; CSP Sp, IV, ii. 1055.
54 *LP* Hen VII, I, p. 398.
55 *LP* II 3462.
56 Memorial, p. 177.
57 CSP Ven, III, 84.
58 CSP Ven, III, 84.
59 CSP Ven, III, 90.
60 *HC*, p. 614.
61 CSP Ven, III, 69.
62 E. W. Ives, *The Life and Death of Anne Boleyn: 'The Most Happy'* (Oxford, 2004), pp. 20, 68-69.
63 *HC*, pp. 594-5.
64 BL Cotton MS, Caligula, D, VI, f. 152 (*LP* I 3387).
65 *LP* VI 613.
66 TNA SP 1/76, f. 168 (*LP* VI 613).
67 Duwes, in McIntosh, 'Sovereign Princesses', pp. 128-9.
68 BL Add MS, 17492; Bradley J. Irish, 'Gender and Politics in the Henrician Court: The Douglas Howard Lyrics in the Devonshire Manuscript (BL Add 17492)', *Renaissance Quarterly*, 61, 1 (2011), pp. 79-114 (pp. 82-3).
69 Elizabeth Heale (ed.), *The Devonshire Manuscript: A Women's Book of Courtly Poetry* (Toronto, 2012), p. 7.
70 TNA E36/210, ff. 53r-55v, f. 65r. (*LP* XI 48); Irish, 'Devonshire', pp. 82-3.
71 Wyatt, pp. 426-7.
72 CSP Sp, XIV, 74.
73 CSP Sp, XIV, pp. 57-8.
74 *HC*, p. 494.
75 *LP* IV 5774
76 CSP Sp, IV, i., 572, 573, 574, 575, 577.
77 *LR*, I, pp. 68-70.
78 *LR*, I, p. 74.
79 *LR*, I, p. 73.
80 Latymer, ff. 22v-24v.
81 Lacey Baldwin Smith, *A Tudor Tragedy: The Life and Times of Catherine Howard* (London, 1962), p. 57.
82 BL Cotton MS, Otho, C, X, f. 174 (*LP* X 1134 [4]).
83 BL Cotton MS, Caligula, D, VI, f. 200 (*LP* I 3331); TNA SP 1/9, f. 114 (*LP* I 3378).
84 Lisle, IV, 887, pp. 150-152 (*LP* XII, ii., 271).
85 TEC, 1569, p. 16.
86 BL Cotton MS, Titus, B, II, 162, f. 346, in Merton, 'Privy Chamber', p. 146.
87 Doran, *Circle*, p. 210.
88 Newdigate (ed.), *Gossip*, p. 11.
89 Newdigate (ed.), *Gossip*, p. 40.
90 John Maclean (ed.), 'Letters from Sir Robert Cecil to Sir George Carew', *Camden Society*, 88 (1864), p. 65.
91 Newdigate (ed.), *Gossip*, pp. 35-52.

Chapter 10
'Expert in outward parts':
War, Security and Diplomacy

1 *HC*, p. 425.
2 *HO*, p. 118.
3 *HC*, p. 425.
4 *AR*, II, p. 258.
5 *HC*, p. 519.
6 BL Cotton MS, Titus, A, XIII, 186 (*LP* I 244).
7 *LP* XIV, ii., 572.
8 *HC*, p. 696.
9 *LR*, I, p. xxvii.
10 *LR*, I, p. xxviii.
11 CEVI, p. 26.
12 *AR*, IV, p. 650.
13 CSP Sp, XIV, p. 621.
14 Paul L. Hughes, James F. Larkin (eds), *Tudor Royal Proclamations* (London, 1969), III, p. 136.
15 TNA SP 12/247/98.
16 *LR*, I, p. xxix.
17 Charles Chadwicke Jones, *Court Fragments: Or, Recollections of Royalty, from the Death of Rufus in 1100, to that of the Cardinal York, the Last Descendant of the Stuarts in 1807*, 2 vols. (London, 1828), vol. 2, pp. 43-44.
18 TEC, 1600, p. 33.
19 CSP Sp IV, ii., 1106.
20 CSP Sp, IV, ii., 1165.
21 APC, V, p. 320.
22 CSP Dom, I, pp. 93-4.
23 Nichols, *Narratives*, p. 161.
24 Nichols (ed.), *Chronicle*, p. 49.
25 Nichols (ed.), *Chronicle*, p. 39
26 J. G. Nichols, *Narratives of the Days of the Reformation* (London, 1859), pp. 165-166.
27 J. G. Nichols (ed.), *The chronicle of Queen Jane, and of two years of Queen Mary* (London, 1850), p. 49.
28 *LP* XI 556, 562, 705.
29 *LP* XI 656, 658.
30 *LP* X 986.
31 *LP* XI 580.

[32] TNA SP 1/111 f. 95 (*LP* XI 1062).
[33] TNA SP 1/110, f. 15 (*LP* XI 918).
[34] TNA SP 1/110, f. 12 (*LP* XI 914).
[35] *LP* XI 634, 906.
[36] *LP* XIX, i., 275.
[37] TNA SP 1/212, f. 138 (*LP* XX, ii., 1052).
[38] BL Cotton MS, Caligula, D, VI, f. 93.
[39] TNA SP 1/5, fol. 28r.
[40] TNA E36/215, f. 267.
[41] TNA E101/517/23, 36. Sean Cunningham, 'Katherine of Aragon and an army for the North in 1513', https://blog.nationalarchives.gov.uk/katherine-of-aragon-and-an-army-for-the-north-in-1513, 2020.
[42] BL Cotton MS, Vespasian, F, III, ff. 33r-33v (Ellis, I, pp. 88-89).
[43] *LP* XIX, ii., 201.
[44] *LP* XIX, ii., 251.
[45] *LP* XIX, ii., 78.
[46] *LP* XIX, ii., Appendix, 10.
[47] *LP* XIX, ii., 424.
[48] *LP* XIX, ii., 416.
[49] *LP* XIX, ii., 424.
[50] *LP* XIX, ii., Appendix, 10.
[51] Starkey, 'Intimacy', in Starkey (ed.), *The English Court*, p. 86.
[52] BL Cotton Roll XIII 41. Rory MacLellan, 'Henry VIII's pastry tent', https://blogs.bl.uk/digitisedmanuscripts/2024/03/henry-viiis-pastry-tent, 2024.
[53] CSP Sp, I, 419.
[54] CSP Sp, I, 436.
[55] *LP* Hen VII, II, pp. 340-62, in Gunn, 'Courtiers', p. 40.
[56] TNA SP 1/21, f. 20 (*LP* III 936), in Starkey, 'Intimacy', in Starkey (ed.) *The English Court*, p. 84.
[57] *LP* III 987.
[58] TNA SP 1/19, f. 199.
[59] BL Cotton MS, Caligula, D, VIII, f. 16 (*LP* III 1176).
[60] TNA SP 1/21, f. 223 (*LP* III 1191). BL Cotton MS, Caligula, D, VIII, f. 24 (*LP* III 1202).
[61] *LP* III 1056.
[62] *HO*, p. 155.
[63] *LP* IV 2039.
[64] *LP* IV 2039.
[65] Dale Hoak, 'The King's Privy Chamber, 1547-1553', in Delloyd J. Guth and John McKenna (eds), *Tudor Rule and Tudor Revolution, Essays for G.R. Elton from his American Friends* (Cambridge, 1982), pp. 87-108 (pp. 103-4)
[66] Glenn Richardson, "As presence did present them': Personal Gift-giving at the Field of Cloth of Gold', in Betteridge and Lipscomb (eds), *Henry VIII and his Court*, pp. 47-64 (p. 53).
[67] TNA SP 1/47 f. 27 (*LP* IV 3987).
[68] SP Hen VIII, vol. 4, pp. 138-145.
[69] *LP* XII, i., 397. *LP* XII, ii., 55.
[70] TNA SP 49/5, f. 6 (*LP* XII, i., 540).
[71] *LP* XV 248.
[72] TEC, 1589, p. 7.
[73] HMC Salisbury, VIII, p. 16.
[74] TEC, 1589, p. 7.
[75] *LR*, I, pp. 71-2.
[76] *LR*, I, p. 76.
[77] *LR*, I, p. 72.
[78] *LR*, I, p. 91.
[79] William Turnbull (ed.), *Calendar of State Papers, Foreign, Edward VI, 1547-1553* (London, 1861), 589, 590, 592.
[80] CSP Sp, IX, p. 562.
[81] *LP* XIII, ii., 622.
[82] CSP Sp, IX, pp. 249-254.
[83] CSP Sp, X, p. 167.
[84] CSP Sp, X, p. 187.
[85] CSP Sp, X, p. 167.
[86] *HC*, p. 597.
[87] CSP Scot, II, pp. 424-5.
[88] CSP Scot, II, pp. 448-451.
[89] *LP* XV 249.
[90] TNA SP 49/6, f. 123 (*LP* XVIII, ii., 176).
[91] TNA SP 1/146, f. 241 (*LP* XIV, i., 671).
[92] *LP* II Appendix 1.
[93] *LP* III 895, 896.
[94] CSP Sp, IV, i., 160.
[95] CSP Sp, VIII, 51.
[96] CSP Sp, III, ii., 131.
[97] *LP* XI 1436.
[98] HMC Salisbury, I, p. 165, in Merton, 'Privy Chamber', p. 167.
[99] TNA SP 11/4/12, f. 25, in Merton, 'Privy Chamber', p. 167.
[100] *LP* III 869.
[101] Bodleian MS Ashmole 1116, f. 101r.
[102] Bodleian MS Ashmole 1116, f. 102v; Memorial, pp. 182-183.
[103] Memorial, p. 190; *HC*, p. 603.
[104] CSP Ven, III, 81, 83.
[105] *HC*, p. 618.
[106] Cecilia A. Hatt (ed.), *English Works of John Fisher, Bishop of Rochester: Sermons and*

Other Writings, 1520-1535 (Oxford, 2002), pp. 212-254.
[107] Barbara J. Harris, *English Aristocratic Women, 1450-1550: Marriage and Family, Property and Careers* (Oxford, 2002), p. 234.

Chapter 11
'It is hard trusting this wily world': Conspiracy, Intrigue and Treason

[1] TNA SP 3/11, f. 99 (*LP* XI 467); *LP* Addenda I 1144.
[2] TNA SP 1/138, f. 177 (*LP* XIII, ii, 804 [7]). *LP* XIII, ii., 830.
[3] Henry Ellis (ed.), *Original Letters of eminent literary men of the Sixteenth, Seventeenth, and Eighteenth Centuries* (London, 1843), p. 14.
[4] *LP* XV 954.
[5] *Lisle*, IV, 887, pp. 150-152 (*LP* XII, ii., 271); *Lisle*, IV, 895, pp. 163-5 (*LP* XII, ii., 711).
[6] HMC Rutland, I, p. 107.
[7] TEC, 1595.
[8] CSP Scot, I, 1171, p. 685.
[9] CSP Scot, I, 1170, p. 684.
[10] CSP Dom, III, pp. 436-7.
[11] CSP Dom, V, pp. 554-583. APC, XXXI, p. 161. TEC, 1601, pp. 14-5.
[12] *HO*, p. 156.
[13] TEC, 1576, p. 16.
[14] Brian A. Harrison (ed.), *A Tudor Journal: The Diary of a Priest in the Tower, 1580-1585* (London, 2000), pp. 208–9, in Whitelock, *Bedfellows*, p. 197.
[15] TNA SP 1/99, f. 7 (*LP* IX 786).
[16] *LP* VIII 595.
[17] *LP* XII, ii., 1220.
[18] TNA SP 1/131 f. 134 (*LP* XIII, i., 822).
[19] *LP*, Hen VII, I, pp. 231-240.
[20] Haynes, p. 89.
[21] APC, II, p. 240.
[22] Haynes, p. 100.
[23] TNA SP 10/6, f. 57. Haynes, pp. 96-101.
[24] CSP Dom, I, p. 82.
[25] Haynes, p. 108.
[26] Ellis, II, pp. 153-5.
[27] McIntosh, 'Sovereign Princesses', pp. 165-66.
[28] Foxe, VIII, p. 621.
[29] Manning, pp. 142-3.
[30] Manning, pp. 158, 164.
[31] Manning, p. 211.
[32] Manning, p. 177.
[33] TNA SP 1/84 f. 103 (*LP* VII 762).
[34] Hatton, pp. 256-7.
[35] Hatton, pp. 258-61.
[36] Hatton, pp. 321-324.
[37] TNA SP 11/7/57. Loades, *Tudor Court*, p. 133.
[38] LPL Talbot MS, 3206, f. 279.
[39] TNA SP 12/7 ff. 76-77, in Merton, 'Privy Chamber', p. 223.
[40] TNA SP 12/273, f. 105.
[41] TNA SP 1/117 f. 38 (*LP* XII, i., 682).
[42] Loades (ed.), *The Papers of George Wyatt*, p. 194.
[43] APC, IV, pp. 383-4. Robert C. Braddock, 'To Serve the Queen', in Alice Hunt and Anna Whitelock (eds), *Tudor Queenship: The Reigns of Mary and Elizabeth* (New York, 2010), p. 230.
[44] APC, V, p. 228.
[45] APC, V, pp. 52, 69.
[46] APC, V, p. 138.
[47] A. G. Petti (ed.), *The letters and despatches of Richard Verstegan* (1959), pp. 97-98, in Whitelock, *Bedfellows*, pp. 274-276.
[48] CSP Sp, Supp I and II, 8 (*LP* I 474).
[49] Ellis, I, pp. 88-89 (*LP* I 4365). CSP Sp, I, 603, 604.
[50] CSP Sp, Supp, I, 8.
[51] *LP* XVI 1253.
[52] Anna Whitelock, *Mary Tudor: England's First Queen* (London, 2010).
[53] TEC, 1559, p. 62.
[54] TEC, 1560, p. 50.
[55] CSP Sp, XVI, p. 246.
[56] TNA SP 1/134 f. 246 (*LP* XIII, i., 1462).
[57] TNA SP 1/135 f. 7 (*LP* XIII, ii., 13).
[58] TNA SP 1/135 f. 58 (*LP* XIII, ii., 72).
[59] APC, X, p. viii.
[60] APC, XXIII, p. 373.
[61] HMC Salisbury, X, pp. 252-253.
[62] Gunn, 'Courtiers', p. 30.
[63] *LP*, Hen VII, I, pp. 231-40.
[64] *Inventories*, p. xlvi.
[65] CSP Sp, IX, pp. 344-5. TNA SP 10/6, f. 35.
[66] CSP Sp, IX, pp. 344-5. APC, II p. 253.
[67] APC, II, p. 247.
[68] CSP Sp, IX, pp. 337-341.
[69] APC, II, pp. 236-238, 248.
[70] CSP Sp, IX, p. 332. Hastings Robinson (ed.), *Original letters relative to the English Reformation... chiefly from the archives of Zurich, Parker Society*, 2 vols. (Cambridge, 1846–7), vol. 2, p. 648.

71 APC, II, pp. 236-238, 249.
72 BL Add MS, 19398, f. 644.
73 TNA SP 1/164, f. 193 (*LP* XVI 541).
74 CSP Sp, VI, i., 155.
75 TNA SP 1/164, f. 162 (*LP* XVI 515). *LP* XVI 516.
76 SP Hen VIII, vol. VIII, p. 545.
77 TNA SP 1/164, f. 193 (*LP* XVI 541).
78 TNA SP 1/165, f. 1 (*LP* XVI 586).
79 TNA SP 1/165, f. 13 (*LP* XVI 597). *LP* XVI 594, 606.
80 SP Hen VIII, VIII, p. 546.
81 *LP* XVI 467, 482.
82 CSP Sp, VI, i., 151.
83 *LP* XVI 640, 641.
84 BL Harleian MS, 78, ff. 7, 10, in Susan Brigden, *Thomas Wyatt: The Heart's Forest* (London, 2012). *LP* XVI 488, 641.
85 CSP Sp, VI, i., 155.
86 SP, Hen VIII, VIII, p. 546.
87 *LP* XVI 650. SP Hen VIII, VIII, p. 546.
88 *HC*, p. 469.
89 TGC, p. 275.
90 CSP Ven, I, 768. Allen B. Hinds (ed.), *Calendar of State Papers and Manuscripts existing in the Archives and Collections of Milan*, vol. 1 (1912), 571.
91 SOR, II, pp. 521-522. David Grummitt, 'Household, politics and political morality in the reign of Henry VII', *Historical Research*, 82, 217 (2009), pp. 393-411 (p. 398).
92 Thomas Birch, *Memoirs of the Reign of Queen Elizabeth* (London 1754), I, p. 152; TNA SP 12/247, f. 109.
93 CSP Dom, III, pp. 447-8.
94 TEC, 1594, p. 10.
95 HMC Salisbury, IV, p. 512.
96 Bacon, p. 161.
97 TEC, 1594, pp. 3, 10.
98 BL Cotton MS, Otho, C, X, f. 213 (*LP* VI 1253).
99 BL Cotton MS, Vespasian, F, I, f. 77 (*LP* IV 3265). TNA SP 1/42, ff. 202-203 (*LP* IV 3278).
100 *LP* IV 4685, 5865.
101 Strype, I, i., p. 189; Thomas Russell (ed.), *The Works of the English Reformers: William Tyndale and John Frith*, 3 vols., vol. 1, pp. 453-4.
102 William Tyndale, *Expositions and Notes on Sundry Portions of the Holy Scriptures: Together with The Practice of Prelates*, 43 (1849), pp. 308-309.
103 *LP* IV 5255.
104 *LP* X 307.
105 CSP Sp, X, p. 126.
106 CSP Sp, X, p. 132.
107 W. K. Jordan (ed.), *The Chronicle and Political Papers of King Edward VI* (1966), p. 40
108 *LP* XVI 1023.
109 TNA SP 1/162, f. 66 (*LP* XV 991).
110 *LP* X 876.
111 BL Add MS, 25114, f. 160 (*LP* X 873); TNA SP 3/12, f. 57 (*LP* X 953); TNA SP 3/12, f. 37 (*LP* X 964).
112 *LP* X 1036.
113 CSP Sp, V, ii., 55 (*LP* X 908).
114 John Hamilton Baker (ed.), *The reports of Sir John Spelman*, vol. 1 (London, 1977), p. 71.
115 BL Add MS, 25114, f. 160 (*LP* X 873).
116 *LP* X 876.
117 Ellis, II, p. 61; BL Cotton MS, C, X, f. 209v. (*LP* X 799).
118 *LP* X 793.
119 BL Cotton MS, Otho, C, X, f. 224v.
120 BL Cotton MS, Otho, C, X, f. 224v.
121 BL Cotton MS, Otho, C, X, f. 225r (*LP* X 793).
122 BL Cotton MS, Otho, C, X, f. 222v (*LP* X 798).
123 *LP* XVI 1430. *LP* XVI 1437; *LP* XVI 1440.
124 *LP* XVI 1337.
125 *LP* XVI 1338.
126 *LP* XVI 1337; *LP* XVI 1339.
127 *LP* XVI 1395.
128 *LP* XVI 1438.

Chapter 12
'Natural passions of grief':
Death, Mourning and Memory

1 Foxe, VI, p. 352.
2 *LR*, I, p. ccliv.
3 SP, Henry VIII, I, p. 572.
4 SP, Henry VIII, VIII, p. 1.
5 *LP* X 39.
6 TNA SP 1/101, f. 21 (*LP* X 37).
7 BL Cotton MS, Otho, C, X, f. 219v (*LP* X 41).
8 CSP Ven, X, 2, 3.
9 Catherine Loomis, 'Elizabeth Southwell's Manuscript Account of the Death of Queen Elizabeth', *English Literary Renaissance*, 26/3 (1996), pp. 482-509 (pp. 486-7).
10 *LP* X 39.
11 *HC*, p. 506.

[12] Leland, V, pp. 308, 311.
[13] BL Add MS, 45716A, f. 84r-86r (LP XII, ii, 1060). *AR*, IV, pp. 656, 660.
[14] Clifford, p. 21.
[15] W. Illingworth, 'Copy of an original minute of council for preparations for the ceremonial of the funeral of Queen Catherine the divorced wife of King Henry the Eighth', *Archaeologia*, 16 (1809), p. 24 (*LP* X 39).
[16] Halliwell Phillipps (ed.), *Letters*, vol. 1, pp. 352-3 (*LP* X 65).
[17] TNA SP 1/101, f. 42 (*LP* X 57).
[18] BL Cotton MS, Otho, C, X, 219b (*LP* X 41).
[19] *HC*, p. 506.
[20] *EH*, p. 306.
[21] *AR*, IV, pp. 662-3.
[22] Thomas Penn, *Winter King: Henry VII and the Dawn of Tudor England* (New York, 2011), p. 87.
[23] *HC*, p. 507.
[24] *EH*, p. 310.
[25] CSP Dom, VI, p. 303.
[26] Mueller, pp. 183-84.
[27] *LP* X 1036.
[28] *EH*, pp. 265-266.
[29] *LP* X 1036.
[30] CSP Sp, VI, i., 232 (*LP* XVII 124).
[31] Wyatt, p. 422.
[32] Foxe, IV, pp. 62-63.
[33] Latymer, pp. 30, 43.
[34] Latymer, f. 33r.
[35] TNA E/23/4, ff. 26-27, in Suzannah Lipscomb, *The King is Dead: The Last Will and Testament of Henry VIII* (London, 2015).
[36] *LP* X 141.
[37] BL Cotton MS, Otho, C, X, f. 216 (*LP* X 40).
[38] *EH*, pp. 96-98.
[39] David Starkey, *Six Wives: The Queens of Henry VIII* (London, 2004), p. 683.
[40] *LP* I 3401. *LP* II 3657.
[41] TNA SP 1/155 f. 95 (*LP* XIV, ii., 650).
[42] TNA SP 1/154, f. 35 (*LP* XIV, ii., 371).
[43] TNA SP 1/154 f. 95 (*LP* XIV, ii., 455).
[44] TNA SP 1/155 f. 36. BL Add 45716A, f. 15v. TNA SP 1/157, f. 14.
[45] PPE, Mary, p. 39. McIntosh, 'Sovereign Princesses', p. 132.
[46] TNA SP 1/446, f. 14 (*LP* Addenda, I, ii., 1878).
[47] Haynes, p. 509. Whitelock, *Bedfellows*.
[48] Thomas Newton, *An Epitaphe upon the Worthy and Honorable Lady, the Lady Knowles* (London, 1569).
[49] *LR*, I, p. xxx.
[50] Whitelock, *Bedfellows*, p. 270.
[51] C. A. Bradford, *Blanche Parry, Queen Elizabeth's Gentlewoman* (London, 1935).
[52] TNA SP 1/49, f. 7 (*LP* IV 4442 [1]).
[53] TNA SP 1/49, f. 31 (*LP* IV 4442 [4]). Bernard, 'Compton', p. 772.
[54] TNA PROB 11/75/180. BL Lansdowne MS, 62, f. 116.
[55] TEC, 1590, pp. 5-6.
[56] TEC, 1590, pp. 5-6.
[57] TNA PROB 11/34/222.
[58] TEC, 1600, p. 62.
[59] TNA PROB 11/78/139.
[60] TNA PROB 11/32/560. TNA PROB 11/69/142.
[61] TNA PROB 11/42A/105.
[62] TNA PROB 11/42A/105.
[63] Edward Arber (ed.), *Tottel's Miscellany* (London, 1870), p. 170.
[64] TNA PROB 11/36/22.
[65] TNA PROB 11/32/527.
[66] TNA PROB 11/72/704.
[67] HMC Rutland, IV, pp. 268-349.
[68] HMC Rutland, IV, pp. 340-344.

Printed in Great Britain
by Amazon

44512050R00119